To Be the Change You Wish to See

To Be the Change You Wish to See:
A History of the Assembly, Executive, Judicial Administration, & Senate Fellowship Programs

By Elizabeth Barham Austin

Berkeley Public Policy Press
Institute of Governmental Studies
University of California, Berkeley
2007

Library of Congress Cataloging-in-Publication Data

Austin, Elizabeth Barham.
  To be the change you wish to see : a history of the Assembly, Executive, Judicial Administration & Senate Fellowship Programs / by Elizabeth Barham Austin.
    p. cm.
Includes bibliographical references.
ISBN 978-0-87772-424-7
  1. Political participation—Study and teaching (Internship)—United States—California. 2. Civil service—Study and teaching (Internship)—United States—California. 3. California State University, Sacramento. Capital Fellows Programs. I. Title.

JK1764.A97 2007
320.9794071'55—dc22

2006101305

"You must be the change you wish to see in the world."
—Mahatma Gandhi

Contents

List of Photographs

Introduction and Acknowledgements

The Center for California Studies of California State University, Sacramento, administers the Capital Fellows Programs which include the Jesse M. Unruh Assembly Fellowship Program, the California Senate Fellows Program, the Executive Fellowship Program, and the Judicial Administration Fellowship Program. The Assembly program began in 1957 followed by the Senate program in 1973. The Executive and Judicial programs were added in 1986 and 1997 respectively. Today, these four fellowship programs annually offer sixty-four college graduates the opportunity to become directly involved in the work of state government. An academic program at Sacramento State complements the work experience.

Tim Hodson, executive director of the Center for California Studies, commissioned a history of the Capital Fellows Programs in January 2002 to discover and record the history of the fellowship programs, to place the fellowship programs in the context of the development of the California Legislature, and to celebrate the 50th and 35th anniversaries of the Assembly and Senate fellowship programs and the 22nd and 10th anniversaries of the Executive and Judicial Administration programs in 2007. I researched and wrote the history for my Master's thesis in history at California State University, Sacramento (CSUS).

I would like to acknowledge and thank Sandy Harrison for his great editing skills and help in transforming a graduate thesis into this book.

The sources for the history of the Capital Fellows Programs were housed primarily in archives and in the minds of the participants. Unearthing these sources was an intriguing undertaking. A treasure trove of information about the Assembly and Senate Fellowship Programs was located at the California State Archives. The files at the Archives from the Assembly and Senate Rules Committees were especially valuable for the history of these programs during the period following Ford Foundation sponsorship and before Sacramento State became involved. A review of these files yielded over one thousand pages of relevant documentation. The Sacramento State Archives also provided a wealth of information about the fellowship programs during the first years of the University's involvement. The holdings of the Institute of Governmental Studies at the University of California, Berkeley (UC Berkeley), and the files of the Center for California Studies were also valuable sources of information. Memoranda, correspondence, contracts, handwritten notes, press releases, and meeting minutes were among the items included in these files.

Published oral histories offered another fruitful avenue of exploration. With one exception, these oral histories were published through the California State Archives State Government Oral History Program. The exception was an oral history of Joseph P. Harris, one of the UC Berkeley professors who spearheaded the effort to create the California Legislative Internship program in the 1950s. Housed at the Bancroft Library and part of the UC Berkeley University History Series, the Harris oral history provided useful insights into the origins of the first Assembly program. The oral histories yielded a number of references to the participation of interns in both the Senate and Assembly programs.

My oral history interviews with over thirty individuals were a key source of information about the Capital Fellows Programs. Listed in the bibliography, the interviewees included administrators, faculty advisors, interns, and fellows. The majority of the interviews were taped and transcribed. These tapes and transcripts have been deposited at the Sacramento State Special Collections and University Archives.

I also solicited input from interns and fellows through questionnaires distributed to all of the alumni of the fellowship programs for whom addresses were available. Many alumni responded thoughtfully to the questionnaires and their responses offered a valuable perspective on the fellowship programs. Questionnaire respondents are listed in Appendix 9.

I attended several of the orientation sessions conducted for the 2002–2003 class of Assembly, Senate, Executive, and Judicial Administration fellows. Among the sessions that I attended were:

- Meeting with Assemblymember Darrell Steinberg
- Meeting with Ray LeBov, director of the Judicial Council Office of Governmental Affairs
- Meeting with State Librarian Kevin Starr
- California Campaigns (A. G. Block, editor, *California Journal*)
- Executive Fellowship Program Guidelines and Expectations (Sandra Perez, Executive Fellowship Program director and Tim Hodson)
- The Senate Fellow Experience: Former Fellows
- Sacramento State Welcome by Robert Jones and Overview of the Center for California Studies by Tim Hodson
- Committee v. Personal Office Placement

- Former Fellows Perspective of the [Assembly Fellows] Program
- California Budget Update by Elizabeth Hill, Legislative Analyst

Attendance at these sessions gave me a further insight into the fellowship experience.

The end product of my research follows. It is a narrative history that traces the development of the fellowship programs from their beginnings in the 1950s to their status at the close of the twentieth century. The history draws extensively on the interviews with those who were directly involved in the fellowship programs. I provided the background and context for the stories of the fellowship programs that are very effectively told by the participants themselves.

My thanks to Tim Hodson, executive director of the Center for California Studies, who envisioned the history of the Capital Fellows Programs and to Chris Castaneda, director of the California State University, Sacramento, Public History Program, who suggested that I consider researching and writing it. Their support and advice throughout my work on the history have been invaluable. I would also like to thank Sandy Harrison for reviewing the history and offering editorial suggestions.

I am greatly indebted to all of the administrators, faculty advisors, interns, and fellows who have participated in the internship and fellowship programs. I imagine many of them never expected that their memoranda, correspondence, and other files would one day make essential contributions to a history of the fellowship programs. Many of them did, however, make conscious decisions to share their memories and observations about the fellowship programs through oral history interviews and questionnaire responses. I thank all of them for taking the time to tell their stories. I would especially like to thank Alan Rosin, a 1965–1966 Assembly intern, who wrote an early history of the internship program that included significant information and original research that would otherwise not have been available. Our recent interview made a further contribution to the history.

To the archivists who preserved the files of the fellowship programs and made them available to me—thank you! The records at the California State Archives and the California State University, Sacramento, Special Collections and Archives answered many questions about the history of the Capital Fellows Programs. Documents pertinent to the fellowship programs held by the Institute of Governmental Studies at the University of California, Berkeley, were also crucial to my research. The files and in-house publications of the Center for California Studies yielded additional key facts and figures.

Elizabeth Austin
Sacramento, California, April 2005

Preface

Timothy A. Hodson[1]

In 1997, the Center for California Studies devoted its annual Envisioning California Conference to an assessment of three decades of a full-time legislature. The opening session featured legislative veterans whose careers bridged the transition to a full-time legislature. Some decried the change and lamented the loss of a time when legislators could "fight on the floor in the afternoon" but "get drunk together at night" and "didn't need staff to tell them what to do." The last legislative veteran to speak was Jerry Waldie, who authored the constitutional amendment creating a full-time legislature. Waldie gently rebuked his colleagues for allowing "nostalgia for our youth" to cloud their judgment. He then recalled the many occasions when he felt overpowered and outmaneuvered by governors and others whose staffs could produce reports and data that he had no means of analyzing. Waldie concluded that he would have been a better legislator had he had a staff to "tell him what to do."

In fact, by the time Jerry Waldie left Sacramento to become a member of the United States Congress, the Assembly was developing exactly those staff resources. The great legislative renaissance of the 1960s and 1970s transformed most of the nation's state legislatures into modern, effective, and professionalized institutions. A critical part of that transition was Waldie's insight that inadequate staff resources left legislators, individually and collectively, vulnerable to the ex-

---

[1] Executive Director, Center for California Studies, California State University, Sacramento.

ecutive branch and lobbyists. As Alan Rosenthal, the dean of American scholars of state legislatures, concluded, "Probably more than any other single factor, the expansion of professional staffing is responsible for the increase in legislative capacity. . . . The modern system of professional staffing developed first in California, and within a decade it was being adopted across the nation."[2]

The development of professional staff was not easy. The tradition and ethos of a part-time citizen legislature argued against professionalization as did the age-old reluctance of taxpayers to support increases in legislative budgets. Some legislators feared expanding the ranks of legislative staff beyond a few clerical assistants would create ranks of future challengers. Opposition also came from those vested in the status quo. A Sacramento lobbyist in the late 1950s explained his hostility to expanding staff (and inadvertently underscored the need for more and better staff), by saying he wanted to keep legislators "dependent on us, the way God intended."[3]

A critically important first step in overcoming the inertia of the status quo and the antagonism of many was the development of what is now known as the Jesse M. Unruh Assembly Fellowship Program. Administered since1985 by the Center for California Studies of California State University, Sacramento, the Assembly Fellows Program's origins have been traced by Elizabeth Austin in this remarkably interesting and well-researched book. Launched in 1957, the Assembly Intern Program had the explicit goal of, among other things, providing "additional research service . . . for state legislative leaders, selected standing and interim committees, and staff agencies of the legislature.[4]

The implicit goal, however, was to develop a cadre of men and women who could become the nucleus of a professional legislative staff. The success of this effort became manifest in 1971 when the California state Legislature was heralded as the finest in the nation. The Ford Foundation study that ranked California first cited the "amount and quality as well as the extensiveness of coverage availability of professional staff services" as the "outstanding feature of the California Legislature."[5]

Today the importance and value of legislative staff is often clouded by the same factors that undermine the importance of the legislative branch to a democratic society. Trendy, callow cynicism by teachers and academics, news media disdain of political coverage not focused on scandals or electoral horse races, and the many self-inflicted wounds of legislators have all combined to present the professionalized legislature as a dysfunctional collection of professional politicians with cadres of campaign staff and personal retainers. The reality, of course, is more complicated. A professionalized legislature is simply a legislature with the

---

[2] Alan Rosenthal, *Governors and Legislatures: Contending Powers.* CQ Press: 1990, 46.

[3] Lou Cannon. *Ronnie & Jesse: a Political Odyssey.* Doubleday: 1969, 116.

[4] see Chapter One, below.

[5] Citizens Conference on State Legislatures. *The Sometimes Governments: A Critical Study of the 50 American Legislatures.* Bantam Books: 1971, 181.

resources necessary to full its constitutional duties as a separate and equal branch of government. In 17th century England those necessary resources included freedom of members of Parliament from arbitrary arrest. In 18th and 19th century America a critical resource was the ability of a legislature to control the time and length of its own sessions. In 21st century California, the state legislature must have the resources needed to address everything from a $100 billion state budget to keeping pace with technological developments that render traditional laws obsolete or irrelevant. Essential to the ability of the legislature to serve the people and maintain constitutional check and balances is a professional legislative staff.

The creation of this critical resource in California is inextricably the story of the Assembly Internship Program. From 1957, when Assembly interns became the catalysts of the professional staff that liberated the Capitol from its information dependence on lobbyists and governors, to the 1980s and 1990s when the Jesse M. Unruh Assembly Fellowship Program, the Executive Fellowship, Judicial Administration Fellowship and Senate Fellows Programs helped the offices of all three branches of state government reflect the true diversity of California, to 2007 when the Capital Fellows Programs celebrate their landmark anniversaries, fellows have enriched democratic governance in the Golden State.

As the executive director of the Center for California Studies I had long dreamt of chronicling the role of Capital Fellows in modern California government. Fortunately, the history department of California State University, Sacramento, has one of the finest public history masters program in the country and, as such, a reservoir of talented graduate students. In early 2002, Professor Christopher Castaneda, the chair of the history department, suggested to one of his top graduate students that the creation and development of the Capital Fellows would be an interesting thesis topic. Elizabeth Austin accepted the suggestion and the ultimate result is this history. I should note that, consistent with the policy and reputation of her department and her personal integrity, Ms. Austin stated early and clearly that her thesis would be just that: a solid, academic research effort and not a promotional piece or vanity history. I was happy to agree with this stipulation, in large part because I wanted a legitimate history that would stand the test of time and critics.

As the possibility emerged of having Ms. Austin's thesis published, I enlisted the help of Mr. Sandy Harrison. I had known Harrison as a journalist, press aide, and a colleague in the state Senate. Utilizing his considerable skills as a writer and editor, Harrison was able to preserve Austin's research, conceptual framework, and language while largely eliminating those elements so beloved of academic thesis advisors and so frustrating to the general reader.

It is, of course, quite fitting that this history be published by the Public Policy Press of the Institute for Governmental Studies. As Austin has documented, the origin of the Assembly fellows is a conference sponsored by IGS in 1955.

Beginnings: 1955–1957

Beginnings, early to mid 1950s, I was a believer in active participation in government by political scientists, because this would give them a background which they can't get from books.

—Joseph Harris, 1980

The California State Assembly, while it still hasn't acquired a band or a football team, took on two or three aspects of a college campus this fall with the initiation of an experiment in education.

—Luther H. "Abe" Lincoln, 1958

Participant-Observers

The history of the Capital Fellows Programs begins with the work of a political science professor at the University of California, Berkeley (UC Berkeley) named Joseph P. Harris. Motivated by his strong belief in combining academic studies with practical experience, Professor Harris wanted to offer graduate students the opportunity to be participant-observers in the California legislative process. At the same time, members of the California Legislature began to recognize a pressing need for trained legislative staff. Harris developed a proposal for a legislative internship program in the mid-1950s to solve both problems. Newly elected Assembly Speaker Luther H. "Abe" Lincoln later called the proposed internship program the natural answer to the need for students to work in

1

the real world of politics and the need for the legislators to have competent staff.[1]

Harris had joined the UC Berkeley faculty in 1941. As a young United States Air Force recruit in 1918, he had failed at his first attempt to fly solo because the instructor did not permit his students to experience what it was like to fly on their own with an instructor present. That failure taught him "one of the essential facts of life, which I have been aware of and followed since, and that is: people learn not when they are told by others, and they don't learn by reading; they only learn when they *do*." Harris applied this hard-earned knowledge to the education of university students. He "always told them the same thing, that they would learn very little if they relied upon books or upon lectures by the teacher, that they had to get interested in it and had to do the learning for themselves."[2]

Harris' idea of student participation in government as part of an education in political science was not entirely new. In the early 1950s, students from the political science department at UC Berkeley worked as local government interns with the city of Oakland and Contra Costa County. The interns worked half-time and were paid by the city or county. Faced with the difficulty of finding appropriate placements and a decline in student interest in local government, the program had limited success. In 1953, the American Political Science Association began an internship program at the national level that permitted political science or journalism graduates to work for nine months in the offices of members of Congress. The interns received a $4,000 stipend funded in part by the Ford Foundation.[3] After an intensive one-month orientation, each intern served as a staff assistant for four months in the office of a member of the House of Representatives and four months in the office of a senator. These interns in the national program often had little to do because the Congress was fully staffed. Nevertheless, the congressional program was very popular and served as a model for the state legislative internship program developed by Harris.[4]

---

[1] Joseph P. Harris, *Oral History Interview*, conducted in 1980 by Harriet Nathan, Regional Oral History Office, University of California at Berkeley, 124-126; Alan G. Rosin, ["California Legislative Internship Program Report, Draft"], TMs [photocopy], August 1966, Assembly Rules Committee Papers, California State Archives, Sacramento (hereafter cited as ARCP), Section I, 1-3; Luther H. Lincoln, "California's Legislative Internship Program," *State Government* (1958): 12. Lincoln served as speaker of the Assembly from 1955 until 1958. He was a member of the Assembly from 1949 until 1958.

[2] Harris, 2.

[3] Created in 1936 with gifts and bequests from Henry and Edsel Ford, the Ford Foundation is a philanthropic organization that provides grants and loans to fulfill its goals of: strengthening democratic values; reducing poverty and injustice; promoting international cooperation; and advancing human achievement. It operated exclusively in the state of Michigan until 1950 when its scope broadened to the national and international level. The Foundation is entirely separate from the Ford Motor Company.

[4] Rosin, Section I, 1-2; Eugene C. Lee, "The California Legislative Intern Program," *American Bar Association Journal* (1958): 461; Harris, 126. One of Professor Harris'

The Conference on Streamlining State Legislatures

With the backing of UC Berkeley Political Science Department Chair Peter Odegard, who secured departmental funding for the project, Joseph Harris organized a conference to generate support for the idea of employing interns in the California Legislature.[5] When asked by Mary Ellen Leary of the *San Francisco News* what he hoped the conference would accomplish, Harris replied, "Well, frankly, what we are driving at is to create a staff for the committees of the legislature, a staff drawn from the university graduate students in political science and also law and history and economics, to serve for a year as a professional staff."[6] Sponsored by the UC Berkeley Department of Political Science, School of Law, and Bureau of Public Administration, the conference was held on the Berkeley campus in October 1955.[7]

During the two-day Conference on Streamlining State Legislatures, participants representing the Legislature, state agencies, universities, and other interested groups discussed the challenges facing state legislatures. Assembly Speaker "Abe" Lincoln and his assistant Harold E. Bachtold were among those who attended the conference along with Assemblymembers Glenn Coolidge, Walter Dahl, Francis Lindsay, Thomas Maloney, Allen Miller, William Rumford, and Caspar Weinberger. Three members of the Senate, James Cobey, Fred Farr and George Miller, were also present as was the secretary of the Senate, Joseph Beek. Academic representatives included political science professors from UC Berkeley, the University of California at Los Angeles (UCLA), the University of Washington, Stanford University, and Pomona College. Together, the conference attendees considered ways to increase the effectiveness of legislatures by improving legislative organization, procedures, and staffing.[8]

Although no proposals were made or resolutions passed, problems were enumerated and solutions were suggested. The conferees recognized the tremendous

---

students was actually able to write his doctoral dissertation while he was a congressional intern.

[5] Dr. Odegard had recently served on a seven member committee appointed by Henry Ford II to help the expanding Ford Foundation create spending priorities. One of the spending priorities involved strengthening the institutions of democratic government in the United States. One of the goals in hosting the conference was to help create support from the Ford Foundation for the idea of a legislative internship program. Rosin, Section I, 2-3.

[6] Harris, 125.

[7] Members of the committee in charge of the conference were Professors Frank Newman, School of Law; Peter H. Odegard, and Joseph P. Harris, Department of Political Science; and Dean Milton Chernin, Acting Director of the Bureau of Public Administration. Joseph Harris was the director of the conference.

[8] Stanley Scott, *Streamlining State Legislatures; Report of a Conference Held at the University of California, Berkeley, October 27-29, 1955* (Berkeley, 1956), 82-83. A complete list of conference attendees is included in Appendix I.

pressures on California legislators who, faced with the demands of a rapidly growing state, had responded with proposals to address complex needs ranging from
education to transportation. Over six thousand bills were introduced during the
1954–1955 legislative session resulting in the enactment of 1,966 statutes in 1955
whereas only 480 laws were passed in 1925. The legislators needed help to man-
age their massive workload effectively. The Conference on Streamlining State
Legislatures looked for solutions to this management problem by asking the question, "What changes are necessary if legislators are to maintain and improve their
standards of performance?"[9]

In searching for an answer to this question, conference participants considered
the effect of constitutional limitations on California legislative performance. These
limitations included restrictions on the length of legislative sessions: no more than
120 days for regular sessions and thirty days for budget sessions.[10] Additionally,
the California constitution affected the ability of the legislators to respond to the
ever-changing requirements of a growing state by regulating much of the budget.
In 1955, the constitution dictated 35% of the budget and existing statutes dictated
35% leaving the legislators with only 30% of the budget to be used at their discretion. Conference participants also discussed the impact of legislative procedures
and organization on legislators' effectiveness. Beyond constitutional and organiza-
tional limitations, many attending the conference recognized that the ability of the
Legislature to respond to the challenges facing the state was significantly ham-
pered by inadequate legislative staffing.[11]

Legislative Staff and Information Resources in the Early 1950s

The Senate and Assembly did have staff directly assigned to them, although it
was largely clerical. In the Senate, a business manager and one assistant provided fiscal and administrative support to the president pro tempore and the
Rules Committee. The secretary of the Senate had a staff of three or more. The
sergeant-at-arms had a staff of at least eight. Individual senators were assisted
by twenty-one full-time and twenty-five half-time secretaries. The Senate's professional staff totaled twenty-three and the clerical staff totaled sixty-seven. Of
this staff, only clerical employees were assigned directly to individual senators.
In the Assembly, the Rules Committee staff of over twenty-six included the
chief clerk, the sergeant-at-arms, and the chief stenographer. The Assembly's
professional staff totaled twenty and its clerical staff numbered 144. Individual
members of the Assembly were usually assisted by half-time secretaries all year
and full-time secretaries during the legislative session. As Assemblyman How-

---

[9] Scott, 12.
[10] The California legislature began meeting annually in 1947. Regular sessions alter-
nated annually with budget sessions.
[11] Scott, 12-13.

ard Thelin commented, "When I got there [to the Assembly in 1956] all we had was the services of a secretary, and that was it when we were in session. You didn't have any staff really. Out of session, of course, you didn't even have your secretaries. The girls went home after the session was over."[12]

Existing support services for the Legislature included the Legislative Counsel, which had been established in 1913 to act as the legal advisor to both houses of the legislature by offering legal opinions and drafting proposed legislation. The Legislative Auditor's office was created in 1941 to review the state budget and to review appropriations bills. By 1955, the auditor's office was also providing general research service to legislators. Since 1955, the Auditor General had audited state agencies to ensure that spending conformed to statutory requirements. Interim committees were established as early as 1851 to investigate and research complex policy problems between legislative sessions, and in 1955, the California Legislature had 102 interim committees. Clearly, there was a tremendous need for legislative research to address the problems facing a growing California.[13]

Outside the Legislature, there were other resources available to assist legislators. The Law and Legislative Reference Section of the State Library provided information services. Experts in the departments of the executive branch frequently assisted in the preparation of legislative proposals. The resources of California universities were available to legislators. Both the Bureau of Public Administration at UC Berkeley and the Bureau of Government Research at UCLA were actively involved in legislative research. Lobbyists were a recognized source of information and "often they possess[ed] the most readily available fund of factual data for the legislators."[14] With no research staff assigned to individual members, it was common for an assemblyman to say, "Well, I don't have time to research something, so I've got to find out from somebody from the Third House what it's all about."[15] The Third House was a significant presence that served an important role as information broker to the Legislature.

The Legislative Counsel, the Legislative Auditor, the Auditor General and the other outside resources were available to busy legislators and their committees, but they were inadequate. Their efforts were not effectively coordinated, and they were often not used because a legislator or a committee did not know that they

---

[12] Ibid., 27-31; Howard J. Thelin, *Oral History Interview*, conducted in 1987 by Lawrence B. de Graaf, Oral History Program, History Department, California State University, Fullerton, for the California State Archives State Government Oral History Program, 103.

[13] The Legislative Auditor's Office became known as the Legislative Analyst's Office in 1957.

For a detailed history of California legislative services prior to 1955, see Edward F. Staniford, *Legislative Assistance*, Legislative Problems No. 2 (Berkeley: Bureau of Public Administration, 1957), 29-47.

[14] Scott, 34. Lobbyists, also known as the Third House, are legislative advocates for special interests.

[15] Thelin, 103.

offered information services. Information essential to the development of effective legislation was usually provided to legislators by lobbyists and staff from the executive branch. Instead of being forced to rely on legislative agencies and other outside information resources, legislators needed their own assistants.

Recognition of the pressing need for legislative assistance was widespread. In a study prepared at the request of California legislators, Edward Staniford of the Bureau of Governmental Research at UCLA concluded:

> Given administrative assistants, legislators would be better briefed on bills, perform their committee assignments more competently and conserve their energy for policy deliberations which they dissipate in detail matters. . . . The increasing size of most constituencies, plus the increasing complexity of matters under consideration by the Legislature, make it ever more important that the individual legislator have assistance in gathering information to aid him in his legislative work and in serving his constituents.

According to the report from the Conference on Streamlining Legislatures:

> There is a critical need to lighten the heavy workload of the legislators by providing them with expert staff services. Such staff assistance would probably go far toward solving many of the basic problems of overwork, legislative log-jams, inadequate consideration of bills, and length of sessions. To some extent, of course, the existing legislative agencies now provide this kind of help. But each legislator needs to be able to sit down and deal directly with the staff man serving him, and the existing agencies simply do not have sufficient facilities to provide every legislator with personalized service. It has been suggested that each legislator who desires such aid should be given two staff assistants—one a technically trained administrative analyst and the other a leg man.[16]

A background paper for the Conference on California State Government, held September 13–16, 1956, at Stanford University, noted that "a hard-working legislator has great need of such an [administrative] assistant. Given one, he could keep far better briefed on bills coming before standing committees of which he is a member, could do better individual investigation on interim committees, and could conserve for deliberative sessions the energy he now dissipates in petty detail. Some Sacramento observers assert that the need for each legislator is the greatest single need for improved lawmaking in California."[17]

---

[16] Scott, 35, 37; Staniford, 50.

[17] Mary Ellen Leary, "The Legislature," in *California State Government: Its Tasks and Organization; Background Papers Prepared for the Use of Participants in the California Conference on State Government, Stanford University, September 13-16, 1956* (Stanford, Calif.: California Assembly, [1956]), 27. The conference was sponsored by Stanford University in co-operation with the American Assembly. Participants included Assembly Member Thomas W. Caldecott, Legislative Counsel Ralph N. Kleps, UC Berkeley Professor Albert Lepawsky, UCLA Professor Dean McHenry, State Senator

When U.S. Senator and former Oregon state Senator Richard L. Neuberger addressed the Conference on Streamlining Legislatures, he discussed the differences between serving in the U.S. Senate and a typical state senate and remarked, "If there is any one dividing characteristic, it is in the vastly superior information and assistance which are available to a United States Senator. State senators are on their own."[18] Even lobbyists agreed that the Legislature needed to have more effective research and staff assistance.[19]

Legislative Staffing and the Internship Program

The staffing issue created the opportunity for Joseph Harris to implement his idea for a legislative internship program. The Legislature needed staff to help deal with increasingly complex issues that required increasingly complex solutions, but legislators at the conference complained that it was difficult to hire competent staff. Conversely, graduate students in political science, law, and journalism needed first-hand experience in government. Both short- and long-term staffing requirements would be addressed by recruiting graduate students who had academic training in political science, law, or journalism and who could step in immediately to assist legislators and gain legislative experience. The graduate students could also serve as a source for regular staff once they had completed their internships.

As Harris hoped, the Conference on Streamlining Legislatures served its purpose of fostering support for the concept of legislative internships. The conference concluded:

> The creation of legislative internships has been urged as a way to meet a portion of the need for staff assistance. The American Political Science Association, for example, regularly confers internships on mature and highly qualified persons, who are assigned to individual Congressmen, or to Congressional committees and staff. . . . The internships have two purposes: (1) service for the legislators, and (2) education and training for the interns. The interns could be assigned to individual legislators, or they could work with the committees. Although legislative interns would be able to give valuable assistance, many of them would, at the end of the internship period enter other fields, such as teaching, For this reason the interns should not be thought of as an adequate substitute for permanent legislative

---

George Miller, Jr., Legislative Auditor A. Alan Post, Pomona Professor John A. Vieg and Assemblymember Caspar W. Weinberger.

[18] Scott, 68; Staniford, 23-24. The Legislative Reorganization Act of 1946 included provisions for congressional staff assistance. Members of the House usually had a secretary and two clerks. Members of the Senate would also have administrative assistants. Congressional committees had both clerical personnel and four administrative assistants.

[19] Rosin, Section I, 4.

staff, although they would provide an excellent source from which to recruit permanent personnel.[20]

One week after the end of the conference, Harris and Odegard met with two leaders of the California Assembly, Speaker Lincoln and Ways and Means Committee Chairman Thomas Caldecott to discuss plans for a legislative internship program.[21] Harris recalled, "In a long luncheon, we talked this over and they laid down what they would approve and go for. So we took what they agreed to and proceeded to take the steps necessary to have it adopted by the Legislature and to get the cooperation of the leading universities in the state that had the largest number of graduate students."[22]

Agreement on how to fund the internship program was reached at the lunch. The representatives of the Assembly offered to pay for half of the $4,000 annual stipends that would be paid to the interns. Participating academic institutions would fund the other half or secure foundation support.[23]

Support for the Internship Program

Shortly after the conference and the meeting with Assembly leaders, Harris was assigned to the University of Bologna for a year to direct a project in public administration. In his absence, Odegard began the task of organizing support among academics in several universities, the administration of the University of California, and the Legislature, and informed the Ford Foundation about the efforts to create an internship program in the California Legislature.

In his December 1955 correspondence to five academic institutions offering graduate programs in law, political science, and journalism, Odegard explained the idea for the internship program that he hoped to begin in the fall of 1956 and asked if these institutions would be able to help fund the program either themselves or through supporting a request for a Ford Foundation grant.

While the institutions that Odegard contacted all expressed interest in the internship program, few were optimistic about providing financial support, suggesting instead a foundation grant. By March 1956, all five academic institutions had signed on to a proposal to the Ford Foundation through the president of the University of California acting on behalf of the University regents and agreed to send individual letters of support for the program to the Ford Foundation.[24]

---

[20] Scott, 37.

[21] Rosin, Section I, 5. Like Speaker Lincoln, Thomas Caldecott was a Republican from Alameda County.

[22] Harris, 125.

[23] Rosin, Section I, 6.

[24] Dr. Odegard wrote to the chairs of the political science and journalism departments and the deans of the law schools at the University of California (Berkeley and Los

The University regents, however, did not wholeheartedly support the internship proposal presented by President Robert G. Sproul. They had received a letter from Senator Howard Williams, chair of the Senate Finance Committee, suggesting that the Legislature should have an opportunity to act on the proposal before a decision was made either by the regents or the Ford Foundation.[25] The regents withheld their endorsement of the internship program pending study of the proposal by their Committee on Educational Policy. At this point, Odegard decided to postpone the program until the fall of 1957. Tentative approval of the internship program as an "educational experiment" was finally given in June 1956 and a grant proposal to fund the program was submitted to the Ford Foundation.[26]

The Ford Foundation agreed to provide partial funding for an interuniversity internship program in December 1956—if the California Legislature agreed to provide the balance of the funding necessary for the program. The foundation made a total grant of $200,000 to UC Berkeley, which would be disbursed in equal amounts over five years. The grant offered $30,000 each year to fund stipends for fifteen interns and $10,000 each year for administrative costs. The $30,000 for stipends would have to be matched by the Legislature to provide full funding for the interns.[27]

The Legislature Responds to the Internship Program Proposal

President Sproul took the first step to gain legislative approval in January 1957 by writing to Allen Miller, chair of the Assembly Rules Committee and to Hugh Burns, chair of the Senate Rules Committee, to request their support. In his letter, he detailed the structure of the program, which would involve up to fifteen graduate students who would serve in the Legislature for ten months. The students would be selected from the five participating institutions: UC Berkeley, UCLA, the University of Southern California (USC), Stanford University, and the Claremont Graduate School. They would work for a member, officer, committee, or staff agency of the Legislature. Sproul clearly stated the program's combined academic and legislative staffing goals:

> The purpose of such a program would be to provide training not only in the legislative process, but also in the general field of state government and public policy, for a small number of advanced students in political science, law, and journalism. Such training, we believe, would be valuable for students planning careers in teaching, law, journalism, and public service. Another aspect of the program

---

Angeles campuses), Stanford University, University of Southern California and the provost of Claremont Graduate School. Rosin, Section I, 5-7.

[25] Senator J. Howard Williams (R-Tulare County; 1947-1962).

[26] Rosin, Section I, 7-8.

[27] Ford Foundation, *Annual Report; October 1, 1956 to September 30, 1957* (New York, 1957), 22; Robert G. Sproul, letter to Allen Miller, 15 January 1957.

would be to provide additional research service, through the interns, for state legislative leaders, selected standing and interim committees, and staff agencies of
the Legislature.

Soliciting financial and administrative support from the Legislature, Sproul
urged the Legislature to act as quickly as possible so that the first class of interns
would be able to begin in the fall of 1957.[28]

Harris, who had just returned from Bologna and had been surprised to discover that the internship program had not begun, "had the task, which [he] pleasantly, happily assumed, of getting the legislative internship on the way." Representatives from the five participating universities were encouraged to write and
visit the Legislature to encourage approval of the program. In February 1957, Harris made a presentation to the Joint Legislative Committee on Legislative Procedure chaired by Allen Miller. After some committee members expressed objec-
tions to the internship program, Miller appointed a Subcommittee on Legislative
Internships chaired by Senator John McCarthy to explore the question further.
Miller also asked the Citizens Legislative Advisory Commission to become involved in the discussion.[29]

The Citizens Legislative Advisory Commission had been established in 1956
by Assembly Concurrent Resolution 23 to address the issue of legislative staffing.
The advisory commission clearly recognized that lack of staff support was an issue. The resolution establishing the commission went so far as to suggest that the
death of five members of the Legislature during and immediately after the 1955
regular session could be attributed to the "pressures of work [that] have placed an
undue burden upon the individual members."[30]

The advisory commission consulted members of Congress who had experience with congressional interns. The response from Senator John F. Kennedy indicated that "an internship program providing high-caliber personnel could be of
assistance in any legislative body since they were in need of all the expert help
they could get."

But in its May 1957 report to the Legislature, the advisory commission concluded that the internship proposal should be referred back to the Committee on
Legislative Procedures: "(1) since some participation and responsibility devolves
upon members of the legislature, this would involve a determination being made
by the members of the legislature, and (2) the program appeared primarily educa-

---

[28] As stipulated by the Ford Foundation, the Legislature was asked to make an annual commitment of no more than $30,000. The amount would be less if fewer than fif-
teen interns were chosen. Sproul, 15 January 1957.

[29] Harris, 126; Rosin, Section I, 9-10; Allen Miller had attended the Conference on
Streamlining Legislatures and was a supporter of the internship program. Senator John F.
McCarthy was a Republican elected to represent Marin County in 1950. He served until
1971. His district expanded to include Solano and Napa Counties in 1967.

[30] *Assembly Concurrent Resolution No. 23, Statutes of California* 53 (1956 Extraordinary Session).

tional rather than as an aid to the legislative program with which the Commission was concerned." The commission did not think that the interns would fill the need for staff.[31]

The Assembly Takes a Whirl

By mid-1957, interest in the internship program lagged, as Senate and Assembly leaders disagreed on its merits. The Subcommittee on Legislative Internships met once and took no action. The Joint Committee on Legislative Procedure took no action.

The leadership of the Assembly, however, continued to express enthusiasm for the internship program. Allen Miller thought the program was "a tremendous idea. It would be wonderful for the training of these people and they can contribute something in the intellectual, scholarly field, to us, too." But the Senate, which was already better staffed than the Assembly, was skeptical.

According to Larry Margolis, Chief Assistant to Assembly Speaker Jesse Unruh from 1961 to 1965, "The Senate was still too patrician and rural dominated to be able to see that that [the internship program] was a good thing to do." Some senators worried about the discretion and personal loyalty of the interns. One senator expressed a fear that an intern would be in a position to unseat him.

When Assemblyman Allen Miller discussed the internship program with Senator George Miller, Senator Miller exclaimed, "Allen, oh, your naïveté just astounds me. You buy that? You know what? These kids will be coming up here, will be running against you just as soon as they learn where all the dead bodies are buried. They'll learn about this. You're just asking for some candidate kid to run against you, that's smart. I don't want any part of it!"

Miller responded, "Oh, that's a narrow way to look at it. My god, if you can't stand a young, naïve person out of school, with all of your practical experience how to campaign and how to run your office, and you're afraid of them, I mean, that astounds me that you're so chicken that you won't even take a whirl at it." Assemblyman Miller concluded that:

> They [the Senate] started having experts. But they wanted the patronage of assistants, that they had control of or wouldn't be going out loyal to their college, or loyal to some other interest. This was their theory [of] patronage they had over there, with these research assistants and these other type of people. They didn't get any patronage concept with training kids, it wasn't part of that concept. . . . They wanted their own hired help.

---

[31] Rosin, Section I, 10-11.

The Assembly decided to take a whirl at the internship program. The Senate refused.[32]

---

[32] Allen Miller, *Oral History Interview*, conducted in 1987 by Carlos Vasquez, Oral History Program, University of California, Los Angeles, for the California State Archives State Government Oral History Program, 113-116; Larry Margolis, *Oral History Interview*, conducted in 1989 by Carole Hicke, Regional Oral History Office, University of California, Berkeley, for the California State Archives State Government Oral History Program, 81.

The Ford Foundation Years, 1957–1965

After eight years of operation, the California Legislative Internship Program has been judged by all concerned as an unqualified success.
— Eighth Annual Report of the California Legislative Internship Program, 1965

Certainly, I fully believe, we are a better Legislature because the interns have passed our way.

— Jesse Unruh, 1965

The First Year

Ruth Ross was a graduate student in political science at the University of Southern California with an undergraduate degree in journalism. Facing limited job opportunities for women, Ross had been "trying to figure out what direction [she] wanted to go in." In the 1950s, journalism for women usually meant the society page. She had taken the Foreign Service test and had just missed passing. She decided not to take the test again even though she probably would have passed it the second time because "it was the same kind of dead end then for women. I just would have been handing out visas."

Then one of her political science professors, J. Totton Anderson, asked if she would be interested in applying for the California Legislative Internship Program, and Ross said, "Yes."[1] She was accepted and joined another woman and six men

---

[1] Ruth Ross, "History of the Capital Fellows Programs," *Oral History Interview,* conducted in 2002 by Elizabeth Austin, California State University, Sacramento, Special Collections and University Archives (hereafter cited as SCUA), 3-4.

in the first internship program that officially began in Sacramento on September 3, 1957.

Totton Anderson was a member of the executive committee for the California Legislative Internship Program, which included Allen Miller, chair of the Assembly Rules Committee, and one representative from each of the five sponsoring academic institutions: Stanford University, Claremont Graduate School, the University of California at Berkeley and Los Angeles, and the University of Southern California.[2] The executive committee's first task was to recruit the 1957–1958 class of interns. Applicants had to be advanced graduate students in law, political science, or journalism, or former students who had experience comparable to a graduate education. The executive committee asked the political science, law, and journalism departments at each of the sponsoring institutions to solicit applications from their most qualified students. They then chose twelve candidates who were interviewed by the executive committee and several members of the Assembly Rules Committee in Berkeley on June 16, 1957.[3]

Four of the eight candidates selected by the executive committee for the initial year of the California Legislative Internship Program had completed graduate work in political science, two had master's degrees in journalism, one had recently received a law degree, while another had a degree in business administration and qualified for the program because of his experience as a full-time journalist. One member of this group had been employed as an accounting clerk, a second as secretary to the Chief of Staff of the Allied Military Government in the Free Territory of Trieste, and a third as assistant manager of a gas station.[4] These first interns arrived in Sacramento prepared to apply their academic and job skills to the task of assisting members of the California Assembly.

Designed to include both academic and on-the-job training, the inaugural year of the internship program was directed by Professor Eugene C. Lee from the UC Berkeley Department of Political Science with assistance from a department graduate student, Jay Doubleday. Lee and Doubleday planned to be in Sacramento one day each week and to work closely with H. E. Bachtold, assistant to the Assembly speaker, who supervised the interns' activities in the Assembly and served

---

[2] The academic members of the 1957-1958 Executive Committee were: John McDonough (Stanford University Law School), John A. Vieg (Claremont Graduate Schools), J. Totton Anderson (University of Southern California), Dean E. McHenry (University of California, Los Angeles), and Joseph P. Harris (University of California, Berkeley).

[3] University of California, Berkeley. Department of Political Science, *First Annual Report, California Legislative Intern Program for 1957-1958* (Berkeley, Calif.: The Department, 1958), 2; Lincoln, 2; Rosin, Section III, 1. After the initial footnote for an annual report issued by the UC Berkeley Department of Political Science, subsequent citations to the annual report will be shortened to a brief title and page reference.

[4] *First Annual Report*, Appendix 4.

as liaison with the Assembly committees that participated in the internship program.

Prior to the interns' arrival in Sacramento, the Rules Committee in consultation with Lee assigned seven of them to the following Assembly committees: Conservation, Education, Fish and Game, Judiciary, Manufacturing, Oil and Mining, Revenue and Taxation, and Rules. The committee appointed the eighth intern to the speaker's office. In a letter to each of the committee chairs announcing the individual internship assignments, Rules Committee Chair Allen Miller explained the mechanics of the internship program. In addition to detailing intern compensation, the letter noted that interns would be released from committee work each week to attend a two- or three-hour seminar and would participate in occasional field trips that would take them away from committee work. Interns were not allowed to participate in a legislator's personal affairs or in political campaigning, but research, drafting correspondence, handling constituent inquiries, preparing speeches, and arranging committee hearings were appropriate activities. Miller emphasized the importance of the educational aspects of the program, which he called the "pioneer experiment of its sort in the nation."[5]

The interns were introduced to the California Assembly during a four-day orientation. On their first day, they were welcomed by Speaker Lincoln who presided over a lunch attended by the committee chairs who were designated to employ them as committee staff. Based on the program developed for new legislative personnel, the orientation included visits to the offices of the Legislative Counsel, the Legislative Analyst, and the Auditor General. The interns toured the Capitol and were introduced to the Legislative Bill Room, the State Archives, and the State Library.

With this brief introduction, the interns began their work as interim committee staff members in September 1957 when the Assembly was between sessions. Since 1949, the Legislature had convened for 120-day general sessions in odd-numbered years and for thirty-day budget sessions in even-numbered years. The general sessions commenced at noon on the first Monday after the first day of January and continued for a maximum of thirty calendar days followed by a recess of thirty days. After the recess, the Legislature reconvened to consider bills introduced during the first thirty days. The budget sessions convened at noon on the first Monday in March.[6] Between sessions, interim committees continued the work of the Legislature by acting as fact-finding agencies. Assembly standing committees served as interim committees between sessions, holding hearings and conducting research that led to reports and recommendations for legislative action.[7]

Having interns was a new experience for the members of the Assembly who were not always sure how to utilize them. Ruth Ross, assigned to the Revenue and

---

[5] *First Annual Report*, Appendix 6 (Allen Miller to the Honorable Francis C. Lindsay, Sacramento, 23 August 1957).

[6] Beginning in 1958, the budget session commenced on the first Monday in February.

[7] In 1957, the Assembly had twenty-five interim committees.

Taxation Committee chaired by Glenn Coolidge and later Walter Dahl, was "free to pick and choose what I wanted to work on. . . . I had a tremendous amount of latitude." The committee consultant encouraged Ross to research her committee's and other relevant legislation, but he did not give her a specific assignment. She concluded, "I'm not sure that they really knew what to do with interns. We were all left to do whatever. We had pretty creative minds."

Before the Revenue and Taxation Committee hired a consultant, Ross organized two committee hearings. Recalling those hearings, she said, "When we finally did hire a consultant, after those two hearings, he said, 'Why did you invite these people to the hearing? And I said, "I just wanted to be fair. I just wanted to have opposing sides, both sides of the legislation.' And I guess I was being more objective than usual, more than the consultant would have liked." Nevertheless, Ross and the consultant worked well together.[8]

Another intern with a background in journalism drafted speeches for Speaker Lincoln that "were given to professional, governmental, fraternal, and political groups. Most of these talks concerned California's pressing water problem and necessitated research and constant contact with the changing water development picture. . . ." This intern reported, "I have prepared most of the major press releases the speaker has issued concerning appointments, speeches, and reports on meetings. . . . Keeping up with the water picture required attending all of the meetings of the speaker's Joint Water Resources Development Problems Committee and its subcommittees concerned with water."

The intern with legal training worked for the Judiciary Committee. He "prepared research reports on problems of interest to various subcommittees. These reports covered such subjects as treatment of sex offenders, punishment of narcotics violators, establishment of minimum standards for the selection and training of peace officers, tidelands, escheat, payment of jurors' fees, and constitutional rights."

Unlike the other interns, one participant devoted almost all of his time to a single research project. As proposed by House Resolution 124 of the 1957 Regular Session, he compiled a comprehensive bibliography of fifty-five economically important California species of fish and game.[9]

In addition to their committee assignments, several interns participated in the budget session and the subsequent special sessions called by the governor when no budget agreement was reached because of a dispute over California water development. Assembly floor sessions were less orderly and more relaxed in the 1950s than they became after the professionalization of the Legislature in the 1960s. Members used their floor desks for office work and meetings.

Working on the Assembly floor as assistant minute clerk to the Assembly chief clerk Arthur Ohnimus, Ross remembered:

---

[8] Ross, 7-9.

[9] *First Annual Report*, 4.

Again, just to show you how casual things were, during the legislative session, Vince Thomas [D-Los Angeles] came in with tunies . . . and was distributing tunies throughout the chamber. . . . And we had artichokes [from a lobbyist] distributed in the chamber. Then, anytime there was a birthday during that legislative session, we had a birthday cake.

The informality did not, however, mean that no work was accomplished.

On the serious side, it was an extremely controversial year. There were an awful lot of things going on. We had nine concurrent special sessions. Once we did the budget session, a colored flag would go up declaring which session we were in. And the legislation for that session would be printed in that color. Blue one time, red another time, orange another time, green another time. You could only deal with the budget in [that session] so anything extraordinary had to be dealt with that way. . . . We had an awful lot of late night sessions and food was brought in.

Issues covered in the special sessions ranged from the adoption of Korean War orphans to water resources. Ross said:

The voting process in the Assembly was also very interesting. They had and probably still have an electronic vote tally board. Because so much was going on, and all the special sessions were going on, the Assembly chamber was often empty. So when they were on the third reading file and ready for the final vote, those [members of the Assembly] who were there would run around and flip switches for the absentees. They would vote for everybody. . . . Then if the member came in or found out how the vote was, they would come back and amend their vote on that final reading. They could come back and check. Everybody voted. There were no non-votes.[10]

An intern assigned to assist the chief clerk of the Assembly described his experience on the floor during the session:

Opportunity was afforded to work at or with most of the positions at "the desk," and so to become acquainted with the actual running of the legislative session. My principal duty, however, was to act as chief amending clerk. This involved the official preparation of each amended bill for re-printing by the State Printing Office. . . . This desk work required that one be on the floor at all times while the Assembly was in session, and provided the opportunity to witness the legislative process much more closely than would normally be possible for anyone not a member of the legislature.[11]

After the Legislature adjourned, the interns returned to their original committee assignments.

---

[10] Ross, 9–12, 15–18, 20.
[11] *First Annual Report*, 4.

Academically, the internship program included group meetings with the two faculty supervisors an average of twice a month. Among the topics discussed by the faculty and the interns were work assignments, legislative process, and developments in California politics and government.

Although the original plan had called for intensive and formal graduate seminars with readings, written reports, and oral assignments, the faculty supervisors soon realized that regular academic seminars would not be feasible because of the interns' frequent absences from Sacramento on committee business. They also realized that "the varied background of the interns in terms of their previous work in government, politics, and the legislative process diminished the effectiveness of general group discussion," and that "the interest of the interns waned as they became engrossed in work assignments and increasingly assumed the role of legislative employee rather than that of student, of participant rather than observer."

Instead, the faculty arranged for guest speakers to meet with the interns. The speakers included legislative leaders, journalists, and lobbyists who shared their insights about the Legislature as well as faculty from the participating universities and administrators of state agencies. To avoid discussions that wandered or were strictly anecdotal, the interns prepared questions in advance for the speakers that were reviewed and revised as necessary by the faculty supervisor.[12]

In evaluating the internship program, the first annual report of the California Legislative Internship Program concluded that "at the end of the first year of an experimental program, it is unquestionably too early to attempt a full appraisal of its value as an educational tool in the training of lawyers, teachers, and journalists and, correspondingly, as an aid to the Legislature."

It was clear, however, that the interns had made a valuable contribution to the work of the Assembly committees and had substantially increased their knowledge of the legislative process. As the first group of interns, it was also important that they had been able to "obtain acceptance and win respect among the permanent professional staff of the Assembly, a not insignificant fact in the close-knit environment of the state capitol." Interns grappled with questions involving the conflicts between academic theory and legislative practice and became increasingly sophisticated in their analyses and efforts to resolve these conflicts.[13]

Still in its formative stages, the internship program faced important academic and on-the-job issues that had yet to be resolved. Although the group meetings with guest speakers had been productive, they did not provide the desired academic training. The Executive Committee suggested remedying this deficiency by adding a one-month orientation program of intensive academic instruction either

---

[12] *First Annual Report*, 5-6, Appendix 9; University of California, Berkeley. Department of Political Science, *Second Annual Report, California Legislative Intern Program for 1958-1959* (Berkeley, Calif.: The Department, 1959), 9.

[13] *First Annual Report*, 7.

in Sacramento or at one of the participating universities that would be completed before legislative duties began.

The importance of the academic component of the internship program needed to be stressed because of the tendency throughout the program's history for the interns to become too focused on their jobs. In the first year the Executive Committee recognized that "a continuing effort must be made to prevent the interns from becoming too job-centered, to remind them of their uniqueness and of the true purpose of their presence in Sacramento, and to stimulate them to assume personal leadership in making the program as rich an experience as possible" which "requires reminding the interns themselves to get out of their individual offices sufficiently to, in the words of one 1957–1958 intern, 'get the big picture.'"[14]

The assignments received by the interns varied in number, scope, and quality. Legislative personnel did not always use the interns effectively. The availability of committee staff was new to the California Assembly and "there was not always a clear definition of intern responsibility or a sufficiently precise description of an assignment. As in the congressional program, interns frequently had to make their own job and prove their value."

The short budget session affected intern assignments. Ross recalled, "After the session ended, I must have been doing research, a lot of research, but I had an awful lot of [free] time." To fill that free time, she explored the Capitol by getting special permission to climb the dome and by going through a trapdoor behind the speaker's podium to gain access to tunnels under Capitol Park. The internship program administrators hoped that "the existence of the regular 120-day session which will occur in 1959 [will] make the internship even more rich and rewarding to participants than in the 'off' years."[15]

The Assembly was sufficiently pleased with the interns' performance that it voted sixty-seven to six on February 3, 1958, to continue the program in 1958–1959. In the short debate preceding the vote, some members criticized the program for failing to provide members with adequate information about the program and for limiting the availability of interns to a small group of assemblymembers. By a unanimous vote on March 29, 1958, the Assembly passed House Resolution 34 which stated "that the members express their satisfaction with the excellent results already achieved from the program, and commend the interns for their fine work and co-operative spirit."

The interns had equally positive reactions to their experiences in the Assembly. They commented: "In reflecting upon the last ten months, the thing which impresses me the most is the enormous personal growth I can see in myself and in the rest of the interns." "From the point of view of a graduate student in political science who plans to do university teaching, I feel that the internship has been invaluable." "My faith in the democratic system has been increased." "The intern

---

[14] Ibid., 9.

[15] Ibid., 8; Ross, 19.

program has lived up to my fondest expectations. I view the program as an exceedingly worthwhile educational and personal experience."

At the conclusion of the first ten-month internship program, five of the eight interns accepted permanent or short-term staff positions in the Legislature. Four of these interns intended to remain in public service either as legislative or administrative staff. Overall, the California Legislative Internship Program achieved its goals in the first year.[16]

The Next Seven Years

The Assembly and the five sponsoring institutions continued to support the California Legislative Internship Program with the financial assistance of the Ford Foundation for the next seven years.[17] In 1961, the Ford Foundation indicated its strong approval of the program by extending the original five-year grant by two years until June 30, 1964.

The extension included new funding for two legislative research fellowships that would be awarded annually beginning in 1962–1963 to younger faculty members who would serve the Assembly as research assistants. It was expected that "the research fellows will acquire knowledge and experience which will not only strengthen their teaching and research activities, but will also prepare them for subsequent short-term service to the legislature."[18]

Citing the success of the California Legislative Internship Program, the Ford Foundation expanded its support for legislative internships to nine other states: Alaska, Hawaii, Illinois, Indiana, Kansas, Michigan, New York, Oklahoma, and Washington.[19]

The executive committee continued to administer the internship program. According to a 1959 memorandum:

> The Executive Committee, in charge, consisting of one member from each of the
> five universities and the Chairman of the Assembly Rules Committee, exercises

---

[16] H.R. 24, California Assembly, 1958 First Extraordinary Session, *Journal of the Assembly* (29 March 1958): 317-318; *First Annual Report*, 6-7, 9, Appendix 11.

[17] The Ford Foundation and the Assembly each financed half of the stipends paid to the interns. The stipend was $400 per month from 1957 to 1961, $450 per month from 1961 to 1963 and $500 per month from 1963 to 1965.

[18] University of California, Berkeley. Department of Political Science, *Fourth Annual Report, California Legislative Intern Program for 1960-1961* (Berkeley, Calif.: The Department, 1961), iii.

[19] Ford Foundation, *Annual Report; October 1, 1960 to September 30, 1961* (New York, 1961), 39.

general direction over the program, acts as a board of selection, and each year reviews the operation of the program.

Almost all of the academic committee members were political scientists. By the eighth year of the program, the chair of the Assembly Rules Committee no longer participated in the executive committee, which became an exclusively academic body.

The committee gradually reduced both the number of its meetings and its involvement in program oversight. By 1965, its activities were limited to intern selection and the "administration of the program [was] a joint responsibility of the University of California and the office of the chief consultant to the Assembly." The chair of the committee, always the member from UC Berkeley, was solely responsible for the academic component.[20]

Recruitment and Selection

With more time to recruit internship candidates for the second year of the internship program, the executive committee developed different approaches for attracting desirable applicants.

In 1958, the applicant pool was broadened beyond those attending the sponsoring institutions to include students who had completed one year of graduate work at any California institution that offered graduate programs in law, journalism, political science, or related fields. Departments in these three fields at the sponsoring institutions nominated some of their best graduate students while candidates from other departments and institutions applied directly to the program.

Over the next six years, efforts to increase the number of applicants and institutions represented continued. Richard Hanna, chair of the Rules Committee, and Jay Doubleday, the faculty supervisor, promoted the program when they visited several universities in 1959. In response to the concerns of some Assembly staff who wanted to include students from different academic backgrounds, applicants were not limited to the fields of political science, journalism, and law after the first year. Posters and brochures describing the program were developed and distrib-

---

[20] Rosin, Section V, 1-2; University of California, Berkeley. Department of Political Science, *Eighth Annual Report, California Legislative Intern Program for 1964-1965* (Berkeley, Calif.: The Department, 1965), ii. The members of the Executive Committee listed in the annual reports for the first two years of the program were: Allen Miller, Chairman, Assembly Rules Committee; John M. McDonough, Stanford University Law School; John A. Vieg, Claremont Graduate School; J. Totton Anderson, University of Southern California; Dean E. McHenry, University of California, Los Angeles; Joseph P. Harris, UC Berkeley (committee chairman). Subsequent annual reports only listed the chairs of the Executive Committee. They were Joseph P. Harris (1957-1960, 1961-1964) and Victor Jones (1960-1961, 1964-1965) both from UC Berkeley.

uted to college and university campuses throughout California. Interns occasionally visited campuses to talk to students about the internship program.[21]

Written applications were screened by an ad hoc committee appointed by the chair of the executive committee. This committee selected qualified candidates who advanced to an oral interview. Members of the interviewing committee always included the executive committee and Assembly staff from the offices of the Assembly speaker and the Rules Committee. Although members of the Assembly, especially members of the Rules Committee, were invited to interview potential interns, few participated and those who did were often not present for every interview. If assemblymembers voiced a strong positive or negative reaction to a candidate, their opinion would be taken into consideration even if they were not present during the final selection process.

Each candidate was individually interviewed before the committee that usually included twelve to seventeen people. Questions were not predetermined and there was no limit on the number or type of questions asked. Rating sheets were used to help evaluate the candidates. Some interviewers found them to be "quite helpful" but others considered them "a waste of time."[22]

In evaluating the internship applicants, academicians and Assembly staff emphasized different qualifications. Academicians looked for: evidence of academic ability indicated by grade point averages and the writing sample; the ability to respond to questions effectively and articulately; and motivation demonstrated by an interest in California politics. Assembly staff focused on selecting interns whose personality would permit them to work successfully in a political environment. One staff member said, "One intern acting like [a congressional staff member who publicized information from a member's files] and we could lose our whole intern program."[23]

Both academicians and Assembly staff looked for candor and honesty along with good communications skills. According to one staff member, "In a legislative staff situation, we must count on candor when we are asking for information or an opinion. We need a direct and honest answer. Someone evasive could be disastrous."[24]

Although the applicant pool had been expanded to include students from all California institutions in any academic field of study, the successful candidates during the Ford Foundation years were primarily drawn from the five sponsoring

---

[21] University of California, Berkeley. Department of Political Science, *Third Annual Report, California Legislative Intern Program for 1959-1960* (Berkeley, Calif.: The Department, 1960), 12; Rosin, Section II, 2-5.

[22] Rosin, Section III, 6-7.

[23] Victor Jones to the Honorable Jesse Unruh, Speaker of the Assembly; members of the Assembly Rules Committee; and members of the Executive Committee of the California Legislative Internship Program, "Review of California Assembly Internship Program," memorandum, 27 February 1967, ARCP, 7-8.

[24] Rosin, Section III, 10.

universities and from the fields of law, political science, and journalism. By the end of the Ford Foundation's involvement, eighty-eight students had participated in the program. All but four of them were from the five original sponsoring institutions and half of the students were from UC Berkeley. Only six were drawn from fields outside of law, political science, and journalism; eight were women. Although the internship program was authorized to have up to fifteen interns, the number selected varied from eight in the first year to fifteen in the fifth year. The variations may be attributed both to the fluctuations in Assembly demands for legislative assistance and to changes in the interns' plans after being accepted by the program.[25]

Orientation and Placements

Orientation sessions during the remaining Ford Foundation years followed the pattern of speakers and tours established during the first year. The orientation in the second year was lengthened from one week to two weeks to "avoid the excessive fatigue which interns had experienced in 1957." Apparently, the interns in subsequent years were less fatigued because the orientation returned to its original one-week format until the final two years of Ford Foundation support when it was reduced to three days "and the shorter period was entirely adequate."[26]

The interns continued to work primarily for the interim and standing committees of the Assembly and for the office of the speaker. After the first year, placements were made in consultation with the interns who usually received their first or second choice. Initially, the leadership of the Assembly handled placement responsibilities by contacting committee chairs to convince them of the value of having interns and by intervening when problems arose. Successful placements depended on the determination that the committee wanted an intern and would be able to offer the intern substantive work. Later, the Assembly leadership shifted the responsibility for placing interns to the assistant to the speaker and then to the chief consultant to the Assembly Rules Committee.[27]

Intern assignments varied according to whether the Legislature was convened for a budget session or a general session. For 1958–1959, the second year of the program and the first year that interns were present during a general session, they began their work with interim committees in September and switched to standing

---

[25] Participants in the California Legislative Internship Program are listed in Appendix 2.2. The number and gender of students appointed each year along with their institutions, fields of study, degrees and age range are detailed in Appendix 2.3.

[26] *Second Annual Report*, 2; University of California, Berkeley. Department of Political Science, *Seventh Annual Report, California Legislative Intern Program for 1963-1964* (Berkeley, Calif.: The Department, 1964), 3.

[27] The Chief Consultant's Office was created by the Assembly Rules Committee in August 1964.

committees for the general legislative session which began in January. For some in 1958–1959, the change was from the interim committee to its corresponding standing committee; for others, it was to an unrelated standing committee.

In subsequent years, interns tended to be assigned to the corresponding standing committee. In 1960–1961, only four interns changed to a different standing committee. By 1962–1963, all interns remained with their interim committee's corresponding standing committee. Placing interns with standing committees was considered especially important in the beginning because it "tends to establish a precedent for staffing standing committees—a practice that in general had not been followed by the Assembly prior to the 1959 session. The interns demonstrated that they are capable of rendering significant service to the standing committees; their ability to contribute effectively to the interim committee process had already been established in the previous year."[28]

As staff for interim committees when the Legislature was not in session, some interns left Sacramento to work in Berkeley, Oakland, or Los Angeles. When the Legislature was in either the budget or general session, one or two interns would often serve at the Assembly desk either in addition to or instead of their committee duties.

Occasionally, there would be a mid-year change from a committee to the Assembly desk, to the office of the speaker, or to another committee. In 1962–1963, several new assignments were made in "a period of considerable flux and uncertainty" because new committee chairmen were appointed. One or two interns were accused of trying to convince the new committee chairs to select them for their committees. In 1963–1964, an intern shifted from his initial assignment because he didn't have enough work. In 1964–1965, two interns exchanged committee positions because they "believed that the exchange would permit a broader opportunity to work with varying problems, a practical consideration since these two interns had expressed an interest in post-session work with the Assembly."[29] Another change in 1964–1965 was the result of Assembly politics. Intern and future State Senator Barry Keene recalled:

> I was assigned to the Assembly Criminal Justice Committee, which in those days was called the Criminal Procedure Committee. . . . Gordon Winton, an assemblyman from Merced, who was a lawyer, who also had an extensive interest in education and was one of the best legislators from a policy standpoint, was the chair of the committee. . . . He made the unfortunate political decision to run against Jesse Unruh for the speakership, after which he was reapportioned out by Jesse. He lost his legislative spot, lost the committee obviously, and I was cut loose in the middle of my internship. . . . [I] was sent to Assemblyman [Edwin L.] Z'berg's committee, the Assembly natural resources committee [Committee on

---

[28] *Second Annual Report*, 7.
[29] *Sixth Annual Report*, 3; *Seventh Annual Report*, 3; *Eighth Annual Report*, 3.

Natural Resources and Conservation], which was really kind of a break, because environmentalism was just coming into vogue. [30]

Interns in the early years of the program had many different on-the-job experiences that varied according to the requirements of committee chairs and staff and whether it was an interim or standing committee. While working for interim committees, interns did research and wrote reports. Their duties included: arranging hearings, securing witnesses, developing agendas, drafting reports, and handling press relations. Standing committee assignments usually involved legislation. Interns analyzed bills, tracked the progress of legislation, and attended committee meetings. Both interim and standing committee assignments entailed working with state agencies, lobbyists, and constituents. All interns had at least some clerical tasks. Occasionally, interns were not given enough work of any kind.

A survey of interns conducted in 1966 indicated that the general nature of their committee assignments did not change during the Ford Foundation years.[31] A 1959–1960 intern reported that his responsibilities were:

- Planning for committee hearings;
- Selecting and inviting committee witnesses;
- Writing hearing notices and compiling mailing lists;
- Researching and preparing background materials;
- Writing press releases;
- Preparing comments and questions to be used by members at hearings;
- Preparing summaries and reports of meetings;
- Writing an interim committee report on fire protection;
- Assisting in the organization of an advisory committee on fire protection and residential safety;
- Writing speeches for members of the committee; and
- Acting as the committee secretary when necessary.[32]

In his work for the Criminal Procedure Committee, Barry Keene was "cut loose to work on child abuse legislation." According to Keene:

It was a good piece of legislation, and because nobody was really interested in it at the time, I was cut loose to craft it. It was a great experience for me. I didn't know it at the time, but I was learning how to craft legislation, how to put diverse elements together, how to deal with special interests ... negotiating, bargaining, and modifying.

---

[30] Barry Keene, *Oral History Interview*, conducted in 1994 by Carole Hicke, Regional Oral History Office, University of California, Berkeley, for the California State Archives State Government Oral History Program; 13–14.

[31] Jones, 13. The survey was conducted by Alan Rosin. Questionnaires were sent to 101 current and former interns in the spring of 1966. Fifty-five replies were received.

[32] *Third Annual Report*, 3.

Keene said the chair of the committee, Gordon Winton, would ordinarily have carried the bill, but was too busy. As a result, Keene said, he recruited a southern California Assemblyman named Don Allen to carry the bill. The legislation passed and public attention became focused on the issue. A television program of the time called "Slattery's People" even did an episode about a young intern who was developing a bill on child abuse, Keene recalled. "It started snowballing into a public issue of some consequence. I feel that it was an area where I made a contribution even before my legislative career," Keene said.[33] Keene's efforts led to the passage of significant legislation.

There were several exceptions to the general practice of assigning interns to committees. During the legislative session, one or more interns worked at the Assembly desk. Extolling the value of this experience, an intern wrote:

> To some, the clerical work on the Assembly desk would be too routine, too monotonous or too menial. I did *not* find it so. On the contrary, experience in the physical handling of legislation provides an intern with a first-hand appreciation of: (a) the complex route legislation follows; (b) the problems of legislative "bookkeeping;" (c) the use of legislative documents; (d) the use of rules of procedure and the value of a thorough knowledge thereof. Furthermore, . . . one gets an entirely different picture of legislative politics, as practiced on the Assembly floor, while working at the Assembly desk than from sitting in the rear of the chamber or in the gallery. As an assistant clerk, the intern daily observes from a far more intimate position than elsewhere floor tactics, the effectiveness of individuals in floor debate, the pattern of treatment given certain legislation during a given session, etc. Nowhere else can this experience be obtained, least of all in a committee dealing with a specific subject matter.[34]

Interns regularly worked in the speaker's office. In the fourth year of the program, three interns were the entire staff of the newly created Assembly Research Center. Operating under the general supervision of the Rules Committee and the speaker's office, the services of the center included bill analysis, research related to proposed legislation, and preparation of background materials for speeches. Rather than focusing on one committee and developing a relationship with one or two members, the interns at the Research Center were able to complete ninety-two assignments for thirty-four members of the Assembly making the benefits of staff more widely available. Although the center did not continue in the fifth year of the program primarily because of reduced demand for its services during a budget session, it was reincarnated in the sixth year as the Legislative Reference Service. Three interns worked for the Legislative Reference Service until they were moved to committees once the general session began. In the seventh and eighth years of

---

[33] Keene, *Oral History Interview* (Hicke), 15-18. The bill was A.B. 277, 1965 Reg. Sess., Cal. Stat., ch. 1171 (1965).

[34] *Second Annual Report*, 7-8.

the California Legislative Internship Program, interns also worked with the Constitutional Revision Commission.[35]

Faculty research fellows, added when the Ford Foundation extended its funding commitment in 1961, were engaged in work that was very similar to the work of the interns. Faculty fellows were included in the California Legislative Internship Program for three years from 1962 until 1965.

The first faculty fellow, Professor William Young from Fresno State College, was very active with the Ways and Means Committee. During the interim, he completed two significant reports that considered institutional costs and state purchasing. During the general session, he participated in planning the process for budget review. He also represented the chairman of the Ways and Means Committee, Assemblyman Robert Crown, at high level policy meetings.

The second faculty fellow, Professor Cheryl Petersen from Sonoma State College, was involved with the Committee on Finance and Insurance.[36]

The third and final faculty fellow, Professor Gerald McDaniel from Sacramento State College, was also assigned to the Committee on Finance and Insurance. "They didn't really know what to do with me. They weren't sure where I fit," McDaniel recalled. He was assigned to the Finance and Insurance Committee headed by Democratic Assemblyman George Zenovich of Fresno because workers compensation was becoming an increasingly important issue. But that didn't work out, McDaniel said.

"In due course, I found that workmen's compensation is the absolute dullest subject that anybody could ever possibly want to get involved with," he said. So instead, McDaniel remembers, he helped write a report on aircraft insurance. "We had a hearing on small airplanes and the dangers that they incurred in airports," he said. McDaniel said he did much of the reading and research, and then the committee's consultant used that material to produce the final report.

One of McDaniel's assignments involved ghostwriting an article for Assembly Speaker Jesse Unruh. Unruh had received a request from the Council of State Governments to write a follow-up to Assembly Speaker Luther Lincoln's 1958 article on the California Legislative Internship Program that had appeared in the Council's journal, *State Government.* After he wrote a draft of the article, McDaniel noted, "I think they pretty much took it whole and sent it in. For busy people like Jesse Unruh, they farmed stuff out all the time."[37]

Gerald McDaniel also had an opportunity to work on a project that related directly to his academic interests. McDaniel remembered an aide to Governor Pat Brown approached him and asked if he'd be interested in crafting legislation deal-

---

[35] *Fourth Annual Report,* 1, 4; University of California, Berkeley. Department of Political Science.

[36] *Sixth Annual Report,* 3-4; *Seventh Annual Report,* 3.

[37] Gerald McDaniel, "History of the Capital Fellows Programs," *Oral History Interview,* conducted in 2002 by Elizabeth Austin, SCUA, 5-6, 19; Jesse M. Unruh, "California's Legislative Internship Program; an Appraisal after Eight Years," *State Government* 38 (1965): 154-159.

ing with an ombudsman, an originally Scandinavian idea of a government official who responds to citizens' complaints against government agencies. McDaniel was interested, but wondered whether he should be helping the governor when he actually worked for Speaker Unruh.

McDaniel asked his staff supervisor, Lee Nichols, what he should do. "Very shortly after that, he came back and said, 'Let's put something together. Let's let Unruh be the point man. It'll be his bill.' I was excited," McDaniel said.

Working with Stanley Anderson, a professor of political science at the University of California, Santa Barbara, who had been an intern during the first year of the program and who was an expert on the ombudsman program in Scandinavia, McDaniel put together a bill for a state ombudsman and submitted it to the Legislative Counsel for finalization.

Unruh "jammed it through the Assembly," McDaniel remembered, despite some opposition in both parties. "It wasn't a hundred percent by any means but we got it through," he said.

In the Senate the bill went to the Governmental Organization Committee, sarcastically known to reformers as the "Death Committee" for its antireform reputation. "It was one of the most interesting and devastating things. I've cited this many times to classes. They sat up on a high dais. It was an evening meeting. They'd been out and they'd had a five-martini dinner," McDaniel said.

At the hearing, proponents testified why the bill was necessary. Then, McDaniel recalls, "There was this pause and the committee chair said, "I really don't think we need this.' That was the end of the ombudsman.

"What I came to understand, and this was the real impact of it, Jesse Unruh didn't really care whether it passed or not. That was not his point. He could jam it through the Assembly. What he wanted, and what he got, was a lot of publicity because this was the first time I think anywhere in the country where an ombudsman had been proposed for a state. The name itself became known and became a part of the public vocabulary," McDaniel said. [38]

After concluding his fellowship, Gerald McDaniel returned to Sacramento State College where his students received the benefit of his experience. He said to them:

> We can tell you about the structure and the process but at least from my one year experience there, I can tell you that it works that way in a general sense. When you actually get into the legislative process, there's a lot of twists and turns based on party ideology or personal ideology or the particular quirks of a chair and who's close to whom and who's friends with whom and so on. Who's close to the speaker. Who owes whom something. These kinds of trading go on. You can un-

---

[38] McDaniel, *Oral History Interview*, 20-25.

derstand that this is part of the grease that moves things along but it doesn't move it necessarily in any logical way.[39]

He continued his involvement with the internship program as a faculty advisor and member of the executive committee.

Academics

Over time the academic component of the program had declined. During the second year, the sponsoring institutions still considered the internship "an integral part of their instructional programs." Unless an intern had already earned the LL.B. or Ph.D. degree, he or she was required to register as a regular student at one of the five participating institutions. Interns were required to attend a weekly seminar unless "pressing legislative business makes it impossible." The faculty supervisor tried to increase intern participation in the seminars by involving them in the planning process.

The interns' initial enthusiasm for this approach soon evaporated because of distractions created by the legislative session, the difficulty in securing speakers for the seminars, and the growing belief among the interns that the role of observer was played more effectively by attending hearings and sessions rather than academic discussions.[40]

Concern about the need for an academic component persisted both among the sponsoring institutions and some of the interns themselves. The second annual report for the California Legislative Internship Program concluded:

> While it is absolutely essential that the interns participate effectively as employees of the legislature, it is also true that the justification for university participation is diminished to the extent that the role of the serious student becomes submerged. The value of the practical experience is very much decreased unless the participants apply that experience to such basic problems of democratic government as the nature and role of public opinion, the place of interest groups in the legislative process, the effect of institutional arrangements upon the legislative product, the relation of representative to constituent, the interplay of expert and amateur in policy development, the meaning of "the public interest," and many others.

Recognizing the limitations of being just a participant rather than a participant-observer, one intern wrote, "A facile and superficial knowledge of the legislative process is easy to acquire. . . . The Legislature is the inside dopester's para-

---

[39] Ibid., 8.

[40] *Second Annual Report*, 8-9. Throughout the Ford Foundation years, interns often did not register or receive academic credit for their participation in the California Legislative Internship Program. Rosin, Section V, 3-4.

dise, but my own experience has been that a little gossip, prediction and innuendo can go a wearyingly long way."

Suggestions to improve the academic experience included emphasizing the equal importance of study and service to the Legislature, having the faculty advisor take a less permissive approach to the seminar, and organizing one or more intern conferences away from Sacramento.[41]

The difficulty of balancing the academic and work experiences persisted throughout the years of Ford Foundation sponsorship. The executive committee was compelled to adopt a policy statement in 1962 "indicating its firm purpose that the internship program be a serious academic enterprise as well as a meaningful work experiment." The statement was distributed to all interns and members of the Assembly Rules Committee. The executive committee emphasized that attendance at the seminar was expected and absences were only permissible under unusual circumstances.

Although the seminar was the primary component of the academic program, it "presented a continuing problem" because the interns had widely different educational and occupational backgrounds, had different expectations for the program, and quickly became absorbed in their legislative assignments. The faculty supervisor experimented almost annually with different approaches to the seminar. Weekly or biweekly seminars were held for the entire internship year until 1962–1963 when they began to be limited to the first semester. By the eighth year, the seminars were held "periodically" before the session began and then discontinued.[42]

The content and format of the seminar changed from year to year. For the first four years, Eugene Lee and Jay Doubleday organized the seminar around conversations with legislators, lobbyists, administrative officials, and academicians. Although "many of these discussions were of excellent quality, . . . they tended to be fact-oriented and overly concerned with 'inside dope,' while there was a minimum of conceptualization, generalization, and theorizing about legislative and policy processes."[43]

After the first year, the interns prepared and presented reports on different aspects of the Legislature. In 1961, faculty supervisor James Heaphey imposed a more academic structure on the seminar. In the fall, the interns read extensively on a single topic: the relationship between the Legislature and the administration. In

---

[41] *Second Annual Report*, 10-11.

[42] University of California, Berkeley. Department of Political Science, *Fifth Annual Report, California Legislative Internship Program for 1961-1962* (Berkeley, Calif.: The Department, 1962), 6; *Seventh Annual Report*, 3; *Eighth Annual Report*, 3. The faculty supervisors were the following University of California professors of political science: Eugene Lee (1957-1958), Jay Doubleday (1958-1961), James Heaphey (1961-1963), Dwaine Marvick (1963-1964) and Victor Jones (1964-1965).

[43] *Second Annual Report*, 9.

the spring, they developed case studies on this topic that were usually based on their committee assignments.

In the following year, the readings, reports, and discussions focused on seven different approaches to the study of legislatures from psycho-cultural to structural-functional.

From 1960 until 1962, the interns participated in a spring conference and presented papers and led discussions on the legislative process and legislative-administrative relationships. Attended by faculty members from the sponsoring institutions and by members of the Assembly, the conference offered an opportunity "for an informal exchange of ideas and information among legislators, interns, and academicians. Much of its value stemmed from the instructive contributions of the legislators who attended."[44]

During the seventh year, under the leadership of Dwaine Marvick, the seminar returned to its original pattern of weekly discussions with guest speakers. Individual interns were permitted to undertake coursework for credit in areas of interest to them.

By the eighth and final year of Ford Foundation support, the university sponsors conceded the priority of legislative work. Informal meetings and discussions with guest speakers comprised the academic offering. According to the last annual report for the California Legislative Internship Program, "The conflict of past years between the intern's work and the holding of the seminar was largely resolved in favor of the work in the Assembly, especially after the session got under way."[45]

The frequent adjustments to the academic program reflected the interns' dissatisfaction with the seminar. Although some valued the seminar because it offered a chance to apply political science theory to the reality of the legislative process, many felt that it was a waste of time.

John Smart, an intern in the second year of the program, recalled that the seminars "were not terribly productive. . . . [B]y the time we were there a month or so, we figured we knew more about what was going on than [the faculty supervisor] did. He didn't have any experience in the Legislature as far as I know. So [the seminar] was just really a kind of get together."[46]

In a survey of the first five internship classes conducted by a former intern, one participant offered this criticism of the seminar:

> My view is that the greatest benefit from the internship comes from immersion in one's assignment—the best view of the legislative process is from the "inside." However, if the academic features serve to improve perspective and provide an

---

[44] *Fourth Annual Report*, 5.

[45] *Eighth Annual Report*, 3.

[46] John Smart, "History of the Capital Fellows Programs," *Oral History Interview*, conducted in 2002 by Elizabeth Austin, SCUA, 8; Morley Segal, "Evaluation of the California Legislative Internship Program by Former Interns," 1964 (?) TMs (photocopy), ARCP, 7; Rosin, Section V, 6; *Fourth Annual Report*, 7.

opportunity for critical, thoughtful discussion and exchange of ideas, fine; but, on the basis of my experience and observations of the program, I remain unconvinced it has done that. The problem is: faculty members want to train academicians, and the legislators want to develop a professional staff (which they have obtained in some instances) or expert staff assistance for the period of one year (which they have also gotten). In my opinion, the student—the intern—is better equipped to return to the classroom, to the law office, or to the newspaper city room having gotten *away* from academia for a year.

According to a later survey conducted by another former intern, "interns over the nine-year course of the program have characterized the seminar as 'most inadequate, a total waste of time, uninteresting, irrelevant, pedantic and dull.' They have indicated their·distaste for the seminar by deliberately creating work and other excuses to avoid attendance at seminar sessions. The books 'assigned' for the seminar most often went unread. The intern dissatisfaction has cut across lines of academic background, and included the lawyers, the political scientists and the journalists."

The fourth annual report noted:

> For some interns the seminar continued to be a strain; the workload of some was sufficiently heavy at times to interfere with their ability to participate fully in seminar sessions and preparation. Some experienced a reduction in motivation to engage in serious academic work. After several years as students, they were happy to have a job and preferred to be free of academic obligation.

Academic study was not a priority for most of the interns who preferred to take full advantage of the opportunity to be directly involved in the legislative process.

Intern Evaluations

Most interns concluded that their internships were valuable. One principal benefit was the ability to be immersed in the legislative process. An intern wrote, "In my judgement [sic] the single most valuable feature of the program is the opportunity it affords to become involved in the legislative process, and I emphatically do not include here the mere chance to witness proceedings as a 'silent spectator.'"

Another commented, "I believe that the most valuable features of the program (particularly for those who return to teaching or go into law and do not stay with the program), is the opportunity to get behind the scenes and see some of the background of what goes into making up the political process we read about."

An intern from the second year reported, "I feel that I saw as much of the legislative process as it is possible for a person other than a legislator to see." Two other comments from interns during the Ford Foundation years support these assessments:

> The program is, on the whole, a most unusual opportunity for the student interested in public affairs, political parties, the legislative process, or public administration. It provides the intern with a most rewarding experience of having contributed, in a very concrete and meaningful sense, to the important business of policy making and law writing at the state level.
>
> The chief value of the internship was an intangible kind of understanding of the legislative process which comes from knowing how the routine procedures operate, from learning about the attitudes and role-definitions of the legislative staff, from observing the relations between legislators and constituents, lobbyists, and other legislators, and from being a small part of the whole process.

Richard Patsey, a 1960–1961 intern, recalled:

> What stands out is the close association with people whose minds I respected, whose views I respected. I learned a lot from being with them, talking about government, law, society. And I also was getting an eye-opening view to a part of the legislative process that I had not been exposed to, which was interesting. . . . [That view exposed] the role of the lobbyist or the advocate, the role of the legislator in terms of servicing constituents and clients. That's something I didn't know about in government. And while I thought it was interesting, I decided I didn't want to be a legislator after that [because] I thought much of what legislators had to do in terms of servicing constituents was something that I wouldn't find fulfilling. . . . A waste of time in terms of issue developing. . . . One of the best experiences in my life was being in the Assembly internship program. I thoroughly enjoyed it."

The interns derived both practical and intangible benefits from their direct exposure to the inner workings of the California Legislature.[47]

After the Internship: What Next?

For many interns, the program had a significant impact on career development. When Ruth Ross entered a Ph.D. program in political science at the University of Southern California, she decided, "I knew so much about the state legislature [after my internship in 1957–1958], American politics became my major field

---

[47] Segal, 5; *Second Annual Report.* 13; *Third Annual Report*, 10; Richard Patsey, *Oral History Interview,* conducted in 1988 by Carole Hicke, Regional Oral History Office, University of California, Berkeley, for the California State Archives State Government Oral History Program, 13-14, 19.

and comparative politics my minor field. My first book was *California's Political Process*." She believed "all of that grew out of the internship."[48]

Another 1957–1958 intern, James Driscoll, continued to work for the Assembly as assistant to the Assembly fiscal officer and then as chief assistant clerk of the Assembly. He would later become chief clerk of the Assembly and would serve in that position from 1963 until 1986.

Intern Tom Willoughby remembered, "I'd always perhaps imagined that my future would be in city management or something like that, but at the end of the nine-month internship, in perhaps June or thereabouts of 1961 when the internship ended, I was offered a job with what was then known as the Municipal and County Government Committee of the state assembly. That started my career working with the legislature. ,... That career lasted twenty-two plus years."[49]

By the end of Barry Keene's internship, he recalled that "I decided I wanted to do something in government, that I wanted to shape policy."[50] He spent the first two years after the internship working for the Constitutional Revision Commission and would later serve in the California Legislature as an assemblyman and senator. Of the eighty-eight interns during the Ford Foundation years, thirty-six stayed on as staff for at least a brief period after their internships.

Many of the remaining interns who did not join the legislative staff were directly or indirectly involved in government. Some established academic careers in political science while others practiced law. One intern wrote, "The internship reinforced my intention to teach at the college level. The familiarity with state government gained in Sacramento has helped me greatly in teaching courses in American government and in jurisprudence. Understanding acquired by observation as a participant lends substance which permits instruction to be at once solid and enthusiastic."

Another intern found that his experience as an intern contributed to his success as an attorney. He commented, "As a deputy county counsel, I remained in a fairly political atmosphere being assigned to the branch office which advised the huge Los Angeles school system and its important board of education. In my work I made constant use of the legislative materials with which I had become familiar in Sacramento. . . . My work constantly called for painstaking analysis of statutes

---

[48] Ross, 23. Ruth Ross and Barbara S. Stone, *California's Political Process* (New York: Random House, 1973).

[49] Thomas H. Willoughby, *Oral History Interview*, conducted in 1988 by Ann Lage, Regional Oral History Office, University of California at Berkeley, for the California State Archives State Government Oral History Program, 2. At the conclusion of his internship, Willoughby was hired as a full-time legislative staff member as consultant for the Assembly Committee on Municipal and County Government. He served with this committee until 1977. In 1977, he became a consultant to the Assembly Energy and Natural Resources where he remained until his dismissal in 1983 after Assemblyman Terry Goggin was named chairman of the committee.

[50] Keene, *Oral History Interview* (Hicke), 21.

to determine meaning and legislative intent. An understanding of the whole legislative process made this task easier, more enjoyable." Internship experiences affected both career choices and success.[51]

Assembly Reactions to the Internship Program

Despite some deviations from its original plan for academic coursework, the California Legislative Internship Program had achieved its first goal: to provide training in the legislative process, as well as in state government and public policy, for a small number of advanced students from California institutions of higher learning. Based on the Assembly's reaction to the interns, it also achieved its second goal: to provide legislative assistance to the Legislature to supplement existing staff services.

At the end of the eighth year, according to the annual report, "there [was] unanimous agreement on the part of members of the legislature to whom interns have been assigned that the work of the interns has been superior and has constituted an important contribution to the quality of the product of the legislative process." Assembly Resolution 363, passed in April 1965 at the conclusion of the Ford Foundation years, commended the interns for their valuable assistance, which "has produced an enthusiastic response and many favorable comments." It expressed the members' satisfaction "with the excellent results achieved from the program," and praised the interns "for their fine work and cooperative spirit."[52]

Assemblyman George Winton praised intern (and future chief justice of the California Supreme Court) Rose Bird for her work on a bill to establish standardized statewide educational testing. He remembered that "she did a beautiful job. . . . The job she did on the research on the testing was great." He gave her a copy of the bill that resulted from her work. According to Winton, "I had gotten the governor and the speaker and the president pro tem of the Senate to sign it. I had written on it: 'To the real author of,' whatever the bill number was, 'on testing from the ostensible author,' and signed." Throughout the first eight years of the California Legislative Internship Program, the executive committee of the program acknowledged the outstanding and unfailing "cooperation and support of the officers and the members of the Assembly."[53]

---

[51] *Eighth Annual Report*, 4-5; Segal, 3-4. Appendix 2.4 lists the occupations of former legislative interns as of July 1965.

[52] *Eighth Annual Report*, iii, 6.

[53] H.R. 363 (Winton), California Assembly, 1965 Regular Session, *Journal of the Assembly* (22 April 1965): 2968; *Fourth Annual Report*, iv; George Winton, *Oral History Interview*, conducted in 1986 and 1987 by Enid Hart Douglass, Oral History Program, Claremont Graduate School, for the California State Archives State Government Oral History Program, 192,268. After her internship, Rose Elizabeth Bird attended law school and later served as Chief Justice of the California Supreme Court from March 1977 until January 1987.

The California Legislative Internship Program and the Development of Legislative Staff

In addition to the stated goals of training students in the legislative process and providing legislative assistance, another expectation for the internship program was that it would create a qualified pool of future legislative staff members. The second annual report noted, "The assignment of interns to standing committees is of great importance because it tends to establish a precedent for staffing standing committees—a practice which in general had not been followed by the Assembly prior to the 1959 session."[54]

Of the eight interns in the first year, five accepted offers of full-time employment with the Assembly. In the second year, five of the nine interns were offered positions (two were unable to accept because of military service obligations). The second annual report concluded that "the program has proved valuable to the legislature not only by supplementing other staff assistance available, but also by providing a channel through which the legislature may recruit staff for service beyond the internship."[55]

For a few committees during the first years of the program, the intern was the only staff. One intern recalled:

> After about three months with the committee (during which time I cleared all releases, etc., with the chairman), the chairman made it clear to me that I was thereafter to send out information, requests [and other communications] under my own name as the assistant to the committee. Thereafter, I enjoyed almost unlimited freedom of action. Virtually the only supervision came in the form of the chairman suggesting lines of inquiry for me to pursue and people to contact for information.

Another intern observed:

> What few consultants were on the staff normally worked only during the interim. When the legislature convened, they were fired. The only continuous employees were the secretaries who typed correspondence and minutes of meetings and hearings. But the interns stayed on and provided continuity so the committees could for the first time begin looking at bills and analyzing them in some serious way, a function for which they formerly had to depend on lobbyists.

The interns were proving the vital importance of legislative staff to the operations of the Assembly. According to the fifth annual report, "Members of the legislature to whom interns have been assigned universally agree that the perform-

---

[54] *Second Annual Report*, 7, 13.

[55] *Third Annual Report*, 5.

ance of the interns as legislative aides has been superior and that they have made a marked contribution to the work of the legislature."[56]

The California Legislative Internship Program paved the way for a significant increase in legislative staff between 1957 and 1965. During this period, Assembly staff more than quadrupled from fourteen to sixty-four. Its composition also changed from temporary staff hired during the session to full-time professional staff. When Tom Willoughby, an intern in 1960–1961, arrived at the Assembly,

There wasn't a lot of staff. Staff tended to be people, students and others, who were hired on during the six months that the legislature was in session. In other words, when the legislature went out of session, those people went on to other things. It was really shortly after my internship that Jesse Unruh became speaker and had it in his mind that the legislature should have a permanent, continuing staff that could provide the legislature with basically a means to verify the information that they got from lobbyists and from the state administration. Without a staff of its own, the legislature was perceived to be pretty much at the mercy of whatever information was given to them by either special interests or by the state administration.[57]

Larry Margolis, chief assistant to Assembly Speaker Unruh from 1961 to 1965, said Unruh's ideas about legislative staffing weren't especially mysterious.

"It was apparent to Jesse and to other members of the Legislature that if they were going to contend with the executive branch, they were going to have to have help," Margolis said. Specifically, he said, that meant trustworthy information from reliable sources, "which means information sources that you own," Margolis said.

When bills were before the Legislature, supporters, opponents, and the administration all produced information favorable to their points of view, but "you've got nobody digging into it for the Legislature with an independent view of it," he said.

Even the Legislative Analyst and Legislative Counsel had their own agendas and schedules to contend with, Margolis said, and often couldn't respond quickly enough when legislators needed information. "So the only answer was to provide staffing," he said.

The internship program was a key component in that development of independent legislative staff, he added. "It became apparent that we needed (staff) people on these committees . . . the interns were a source. Having that program gave the committee chairmen the feeling of having somebody they could lean on to do some research work or at least find sources of information."

The interns proved so capable that they were often kept on after their internship ended, Margolis said. "There was a tough selection process, so people of real

---

[56] Robert Seaver, "Internships and Legislative Staffing," *State Legislatures Progress Reporter; Supplement* 2, no. 3 (1966): [1]; *Fifth Annual Report*, 4.

[57] Willoughby, *Oral History Interview*, 3.

ability and intelligence came onto the staff, and then the members didn't want to do without them," he said.

"They were so good at what they were doing and represented such a departure from the previous unstaffed condition that there was a tendency to flood the system," he said. The internship program, Margolis said, opened the eyes of legislators to the fact that they could do more with a good staff.

According to Assemblyman Robert Crown, chairman of the Ways and Means Committee and a close associate of Unruh, "The internships laid the groundwork for expansion of staff. We had to prove to people, both inside the Assembly and outside, that it would work."[58]

At first, many members of the Assembly were not convinced that an increase in staff was necessary. Lee Nichols, chief consultant to the Assembly from 1964 until 1967 and one of the architects of the Assembly staffing system, acknowledged:

> Sure there were problems [with the reactions to staff among members of the Assembly]. There were a number of legislators who treated their offices as if they were KGB headquarters. And anybody who got into their office would suddenly discover secrets that they didn't want anybody to know. . . . And they didn't trust the staff. They didn't trust that the staff, the men and women whom we placed in that position, would keep their mouths shut.[59]

Phillip Schott, Chief Administrative Officer for the Assembly from 1963 to 1965 and Chief of Staff for Speaker Unruh from 1967 to 1969, was encouraged to take a job with the Legislative Analyst's Office to make it easier for him to be hired as Assembly staff. He remembered:

> Because most people don't have a recollection of this, but there was a very, very strong resistance to staffing the legislature. I mean, it was crammed down the membership's throat. . . . The members did not want it. The ones who wanted staff were new or very close to Unruh. . . . [G]enerally speaking, most of the Republicans didn't like it; many, many of the Democrats didn't like it. You could kind of do it on an age line: the older and longer tenured members disliked the notion of staff more. . . . Many members saw staffing as a threat to their own self-importance and autonomy, I thought. . . . Really, what they were saying, I think, in their own minds, was, 'I got elected. I can make my decisions. I don't need a bunch of staff people around me helping. They didn't get elected.' That's the thing that we were fighting most of the time.

---

[58] Margolis, *Oral History Interview*, 79-83; Seaver, [2].

[59] Lee Nicols, *Oral History Interview*, conducted in 1991 by Donald B. Seney, California State University, Sacramento, for the California State Archives State Government Oral History Program, 229.

Schott said he went to the chair of his committee, Assemblyman Joe Kennick, and proposed the idea of writing analyses of bills for the committee. The chairman didn't know what he was talking about, Schott said. "I said, 'We'll take a bill, and instead of just putting the bill in front of the committee members when we meet, we'll attach it to a—one side of a sheet of paper cut down to the same size as the bill, with a real quick statement of what the bill does, who's sponsoring it, who's opposing it, just very salient facts on it.' Kennick thought it was a good idea.'"[60]

But not everybody appreciated that type of help. A very conservative Republican named Carl Britschgi scoffed at the very idea of staff help, Schott said. He recalls Britschi asking about "this piece of paper attached to the bill," and being told that it was an analysis of the measure, prepared by Schott.

Schott recalled Britschgi's reaction. "Well I wasn't born yesterday. I mean, after all, I can read. I can read what's in this bill. I'm smart enough to figure out who's for it and who's against it. They're smart enough to come by and see me and say who's for it and who's against it. What's the idea of having this guy, who isn't even elected to office, write this piece of paper and attach it to the bill?"

To which the chair replied, "Mr. Britschgi, don't read it."

Britschgi notwithstanding, the success of the internship program helped convince assemblymembers that legislative staff was an asset. Gradually, the Assembly added staff to provide legislative assistance. In the late 1950s and early 1960s, interns frequently continued their service to the Assembly as permanent or temporary staff.[61]

In 1965, Unruh said, "At this juncture, the Internship Program has been labeled an unqualified success. In fact, the presence of the interns and the work they have done have proved so invigorating to the legislature that in many ways, they have helped in a major change in the staffing of the Assembly and in the higher expectations of legislature output that exist today."[62]

In a speech to the National Conference on Legislative Intern Programs in 1966, Unruh stated unequivocally, "Internship programs are clearly the principal source of legislative staff in California. . . ."[63] Unruh expressed his support of the internship and legislative staffing so often that he commented, "I have spoken so

---

[60] Phillip H. Schott, Oral History Interview, conducted in 1990 by Carole Hicke, Regional Oral History Office, University of California, Berkeley, for the California State Archives State Government Oral History Program, 35–37, 88–89.

[61] The names and positions of interns employed as legislative staff from 1958 to 1965 are listed in Appendix 2.5. Appendix 2.5 also includes the total number of Assembly staff employed from 1958 through 1965 in the years when the Assembly held general sessions.

[62] Jesse Unruh, "California's Legislative Internship Program: An Appraisal After Eight Years," *State Government* 38 (1965): 154–155. This article was ghost written for Jesse Unruh by Gerald McDaniel, the Faculty Fellow who participated in the California Legislative Internship Program in 1964–1965.

[63] Jesse Unruh, "Interns, Externs and Upturns in the Legislative Process" (speech presented at the National Conference on Legislative Intern Programs, Berkeley, California, 13 May 1966), ARCP, 2.

frequently about the importance of our legislatures improving themselves, especially through more adequately trained staff and research aid, that my praise of the internship program may sound like a stuck record. Given the manpower and brainpower needs of the kind of California Assembly which I have encouraged, the internships have been and will be a valuable recruiting ground."[64]

As Unruh realized his goal of providing the Legislature with professional staff, the number of positions available to interns who had just completed the program decreased. Many of the positions were already filled with interns from earlier years or with other professionals. Of the ten interns who participated in 1964–1965, only one was retained as Assembly staff. Nevertheless, of the sixty-four Assembly staffers in 1965, eighteen, or 28%, were former interns.[65]

The partnership between the Ford Foundation, the five sponsoring universities, and the Assembly had played a significant role in the establishment of a professional staff for the California Assembly. Both the Assembly and the interns had benefited from the California Legislative Internship Program's experiment in education.

---

[64] Unruh, "California's Legislative Internship Program," 158.

[65] Over one-third of the eighty-eight participants in the California Legislative Internship Program were working in government at some level. See Appendix 2.4 for a breakdown by occupation of former legislative interns as of July 1965.

Interns and Fellows: 1965–1984

The program was an excellent introduction to state government. The experience is totally unlike classroom discussion.

—William Leonard, Intern, 1969–1970

It was a great experience. It was priceless.

—Mike Thompson, Fellow, 1983–1984

Interns and the Professionalization of the Legislature

The California Legislative Internship Program marked the beginning of the professionalization of California's Legislature. According to Jesse Unruh, "The Ford Foundation's pioneering program of legislative internships at the state level was an inspired move without which it would have been impossible to contemplate seriously the work of legislative reform."[1]

Legislative reform was ensured by the passage of Proposition 1a in 1966, which added annual general legislative sessions of unlimited duration and adequate funding for legislators' salaries and expenses for the staff that was increasingly available to assist individual members of the Assembly.[2] By 1971, a report

---

[1] Unruh, "Interns, Externs and Upturns in the Legislative Process," 2.

[2] Proposition 1a resulted from the work of the sixty-nine member Constitutional Revision Commission established in 1963 under the legislature's Joint Committee on Legislative Organization. It was initially proposed as Assembly Constitutional Amendment No. 13 which passed the Assembly with only one dissenting vote in April, 1966 (A.C.A. 13, California Assembly, 1966 First Extraordinary Session, *Journal of the Assembly* [14

sponsored by the Citizens Conference on State Legislatures rated California's legislature as the most effective in the United States. The report concluded that "the amount and quality as well as the extensiveness of coverage and availability of professional staff services is probably the outstanding feature of the California Legislature."[3]

The increased staff that was part of the professionalization of the Legislature affected the size of the Assembly's internship program. After Ford Foundation support for the internship program ended with the 1964–1965 class of interns, the Assembly Rules Committee agreed to take full responsibility for funding the stipends of the legislative interns in January 1965. The committee, however, decided to limit the number of interns to ten "because of the costs involved and because of the fact that staff needs are not so great."[4]

The internship program was a victim of its own success. It made a significant contribution to increasing the ranks of qualified, well-trained professional staff in the Assembly, and the increased professional staff reduced the demand for interns.

Life Without the Ford Foundation

Although the ten interns who reported for duty in the fall of 1965 were surprised to learn that the program was no longer sponsored by the Ford Foundation, the shift in funding the stipends to the Rules Committee had little immediate effect on program administration or activities. Unexpended funds from the Ford Foundation grant continued to pay the administrative and academic costs incurred by UC Berkeley in the recruitment and selection of interns and in the conduct of a seminar on legislative process until 1967.

Then, in a memorandum dated February 27, 1967, Victor Jones, chair of the executive committee, noted that the recruitment and selection costs for 1967–1968 interns would be covered by funds transferred to UC Berkeley by the Rules Committee. "Provision must now be made for financing the entire administrative and academic phases of the program, if it is to be continued under the sponsorship of the universities and colleges of the state which offer graduate work," the memo said. Jones invited the executive committee, the speaker of the Assembly, the Assembly Rules Committee and their staffs to a meeting "to evaluate the program before either the Assembly or the colleges and universities decided that it should be continued in its present or modified form." Included with the memorandum was

---

April 1966]: 719-720). The voters approved the proposition by a margin of 3 to 1 in November 1966. As a result of action taken following the passage of Proposition 1a, legislative salaries increased from $500 per month—equal to the stipend granted legislative interns beginning in 1963—to $16,000 per year.

[3] Citizens Conference on State Legislatures, *The Sometime Government* (New York: Bantam, 1971), 181.

[4] Jones, 5.

a report completed by intern Alan Rosin under the direction of Lee Nichols, chief consultant of the Assembly. This report reviewed all aspects of the program from its inception and made suggestions for its future.[5]

The Rules Committee decided to fund all costs of the internship program and to replace the executive committee with an executive board. Executive board membership included three representatives each from the University of California, California State Colleges (later California State Universities) and private colleges or universities; the chief administrative officer and one staff member from the Rules committee; and at least one representative from the speaker's office.[6] Otherwise, the Rules Committee left the internship program unchanged.

The newly formed executive board handled the recruitment and selection process in the same way as the executive committee. According to former Faculty Fellow Gerald McDaniel, who continued his association with the internship program by serving on the executive board from 1965 until 1973, the growing number of applications made the initial paper screening process a big task.

> [The paper screening] was from year to year a very hit-or-miss process. One year, we ran up against a deadline. Normally . . . Victor Jones, Vivian Miksak and I would get together down at Berkeley or [Jones] would bring them up [to Sacramento]. . . . We'd just sit down in a room and pass them around and say, "This one looks good," or "That one doesn't look good."
>
> One year, Jones couldn't make it. Miksak couldn't make it. I did the whole thing by myself. One year's class—I forget which one it was— [I] did the paper screening. I don't how many dozens of them I went [through] but I spent all day down in Berkeley one time going through these doing them as best I could. And I guess we survived. It was kind of individualistic at that point.
>
> For a long time, we even had pictures submitted—which became a no-no later—partly because the problem was always to try and recruit minorities. Women for one thing, which could be divined by the name usually. But minorities if we possibly could. We had very few.[7]

By the early 1970s, the paper screening became a more formal process that involved most of the executive board members. In selecting the candidates that advanced to a personal interview, the board made an effort to choose equal numbers from northern and southern California, to limit the number of law school graduates, to include as many minorities and women as possible and to select can-

---

[5] Ibid. Alan Rosin was an intern in 1965-1966.

[6] Charles Bell to Betty Moulds, memorandum, 13 May 1985, Papers of the President's Office, California State University, Sacramento, Archives (hereafter cited as PPO). Executive board members are listed in Appendix 3.3.

[7] McDaniel, *Oral History Interview*, 12. Victor Jones was chair of the Executive Committee. Vivian Miksak was a member of the Assembly staff who was "kind of the mother hen of the legislative interns" (12) from the 1960s until 1974. The number of applications soared to 500 in the early 1970s. Gerald McDaniel, "The Legislative Internship Program in California: A Rambling Narrative" (paper presented at a meeting in Denmark, [1976?]), 3.

didates who were obviously Republican (applicants from the Democratic Party always far outnumbered applicants from the Republican Party). Applicants over age thirty-five were automatically excluded along with those who had no clear reason for applying, who had very low grades, or who seemed to hold radical political beliefs. After the paper screening reduced the applicant pool to approximately thirty candidates, the executive board interviewed and selected the interns.[8] By the late 1960s, the selection process expanded beyond the paper screening and individual interviews to include group interviews. Lindsay Desrochers, an intern in 1974–1975, remembered the interview process:

> It was intimidating for a young graduate student. It was a panel of people, mostly Sacramento people and professors. . . . They grilled you. It was a process of determining whether you were smart enough and then, more importantly, whether you were smart enough to know how to be discreet and not be a loose cannon in a tough environment. I honestly didn't think I'd get it. The final step of it was you were on a panel with the other competitors and questions were tossed at you. . . . There were others in the group whom I thought were far more qualified than I. I was stunned, actually, when I was accepted in the program.[9]

Both individual and group interviews were before members of the executive board. The group interview was designed to reveal the candidate's ability to communicate and solve problems with others.

The academics and the Assembly staff on the executive board continued to view prospective interns from different perspectives. Gerald McDaniel observed "the tension and sometimes disagreements between the academic members of the recruitment [committee] and the staff of people in the legislature because they often saw candidates in much different terms."

> Academic people would say, "This person is really smart. Look at their record. They're articulate. They seem to know what they're talking about when we ask them questions. This person really impressed me because they had this kind of aggressiveness about them." The staff people would say, their main questions were, "Can I live with this person? Will this person be capable of getting along with me and my legislator and the staff and obey orders?" They liked smart people. It wasn't that. They didn't want people that were so smart that they would be independent. They wanted people whom they could mold into their operation.
> Academics didn't see it that way. They didn't have to deal with them in that way. They saw it as if they were recruiting a bright graduate student to a program. . . . Hence, somebody who came in with, for example—this was the 1960s and radical views were building, student uproar at Berkeley, etc., and the Vietnam War and the civil rights movement and everything—somebody . . . who had a background in activism would be enormously appealing to the academicians but

---

[8] McDaniel, "The Legislative Internship Program in California," 3-4.

[9] Lindsay Desrochers, "History of the Capital Fellows Programs," *Oral History Interview*, conducted in 2003 by Elizabeth Austin, SCUA, 2-3.

the staff people would say, "Whoa, this person is going to create problems for us. This battle went on for some time."

The board would disagree and occasionally have close votes but "they made their compromises. Everybody had to move ahead."[10]

John Burton made a serious effort to influence the intern selection process when he was chair of the Rules Committee in the early 1970s, demanding Rules Committee appointments that were based on patronage rather than on merit. In one instance, he demanded that the executive board choose an unqualified candidate from his district. Although the candidate had a low grade point average, the board agreed to interview him. He performed poorly and was not selected. Burton reacted by refusing to appropriate money for the fellowship program.

Charles Price, a member of the executive board, recalled Burton being so angry that he refused to see Charles Bell, chair of the executive board, about the funding. At Burton's insistence, the Assembly Rules Committee refused to appropriate the money through the month of July.

Worried and frustrated, board members sought a meeting with Speaker Moretti, whose staff warned them to be brief. They scheduled a Saturday afternoon meeting with the Speaker at the Mansion Inn. Moretti and his entourage arrived at 2 p.m. "He didn't say a word to us and sat across the table steely-eyed and asked us to say what we had to say with a three to four minute presentation each. There was no mention of John Burton's protégé not being accepted," Price recalled.

A minute of total silence followed the presentations, he said, after which Moretti got up and said the program would continue the next year as it had in the past. "I was reminded of a Roman emperor—thumbs up or thumbs down," Price recalled.

According to Price, the pressure exerted by Burton was a unique occurrence. The Rules Committee generally did not urge the executive board to choose unqualified candidates.[11]

A short orientation and informal discussions with guest speakers continued to comprise the academic component of the internship program. By 1967, Victor Jones had turned over the organization of the academic seminars and academic supervision of the interns to Gerald McDaniel. In 1970, the chief administrative officer of the Assembly appears to have assumed this task along with the responsibility for arranging placements and supervising the internship program, which had previously been handled by the chief consultant's office. By this time, the seminars were held bimonthly under the direction of Assembly staff. For several years, they were supplemented by an annual three-day meeting of interns and academics with guest lecturers.[12]

---

[10] McDaniel, *Oral History Interview*, 10-11.

[11] Charles Price, telephone interview by Elizabeth Austin, 20 September 2002; Ronald Loveridge, "History of the Capital Fellows Programs," *Oral History Interview*, conducted in 2003 by Elizabeth Austin, SCUA, 2.

[12] Information sheet, "California Assembly Internship Program," [197?], ARCP.

Placements were often chosen by the chief consultant or the chief administrative officer to expose interns to unfamiliar territory. Future Congressman Howard Berman, a 1965–1966 intern, was surprised by his placement with the Agriculture Committee:

> I was the one [of the ten interns that year] who had been most active in Democratic club politics, the Young Democrats and things like that. Most of the others had gone into student body politics but I was the one that was most active in the partisan, Democratic politics.
>
> At that time, there was a great conflict between the Democratic clubs and the CDC [California Democratic Council] which was the more liberal faction on one side and Jesse Unruh, who was then the Speaker of the Assembly, on the other. Jesse Unruh's guy, a guy named Lee Nichols, was the coordinator of the program but he was also, I think, the chief administrative officer of the state Assembly at the time. I remember him telling me, "Okay, you've been all involved with all the liberal activists and all that stuff, we're going to give you a little different experience. We're assigning you to the Assembly Agriculture Committee."
>
> [The Agriculture Committee] was [a] totally different [experience from my previous activities] in the sense of very different kinds of issues and much more conservative. The chairman was a guy named John Williamson from Bakersfield. These were not CDC Democratic Club liberal activist types. It was like, "Okay, your educational experience is going to be working for the kind of people you've never been involved with and you've been fighting all this time."

Although Nichols assigned Berman to the Agriculture Committee to expose him to another side of politics, the assignment took an unexpected turn. About ten days into it, Berman recalled, Cesar Chavez began organizing his historic grape boycott effort and march. "I ended up spending a lot of time on farm labor issues," he said, even attending a hearing in Visalia chaired by Robert F. Kennedy.

"It was a very dramatic hearing where the sheriff of Tulare County had arrested a lot of picketers. Bobby Kennedy held the Constitution in his hand and said, 'Have you ever read this?'"

So Berman found, to his surprise, that his work on the very conservative Agriculture Committee actually enabled him to become far more active on issues he deeply cared about: farm worker organizing, collective bargaining, and legalizing undocumented farm workers. He has continued to work closely with the United Farm Workers throughout his years in the Assembly and in Congress.[13]

Berman remained with the Agriculture Committee throughout his internship under the supervision of the chair of the committee, John Williamson, and former intern, staff member Bill Geyer.

---

[13] Howard Berman, "History of the Capital Fellows Programs," *Oral History Interview*, conducted in 2003 by Elizabeth Austin, SCUA, 2-4. Howard Berman served in the California Assembly from 1973 to 1982. He was elected to the House of Representatives in 1982 and continues to represent the 28th District of California today. Lee Nichols was the Chief Consultant of the Assembly.

Like Berman, Lindsay Desrochers was placed with a committee that was not her first choice. Desrochers had hoped to work with liberal Assemblyman Alan Sieroty of Los Angeles on the Criminal Justice Committee. But to her amazement, she was selected by Republican Frank Lanterman, so she complained to Speaker Leo McCarthy's Chief of Staff, Art Agnos.

"I went to Art and I said, 'I can't work for a conservative Republican.' He looked at me and just said, 'Are you in the program? Are you going to meet the terms of the program?' So they assigned me to Frank."

Desrochers was happily surprised by what followed. "Frank was the best thing that ever happened to me in that Legislature, in that environment. He balanced out my point of view about the world. He really took care of me, taught me a great deal. It was the best assignment I could have gotten," she said, calling Lanterman an excellent legislator and person, and crediting him with sharpening her own views through their spirited debates.

As a self-professed Berkeley radical, Desrochers was able to broaden her outlook and learn "a little bit about something beyond the life of Berkeley."[14]

Dan Friedlander, a participant in the 1970–1971 internship program, was also surprised as well as a little disappointed in his placement. After interviewing with different committees, he was assigned to the Assembly Education Committee.

> I was initially quite disappointed because I didn't get the placement I wanted [with the Democratic Caucus]. . . . I had [interviewed with the Caucus] so obviously I was not their first choice. I got my third choice.
>
> It was a unique situation in 1970. The Republicans controlled the Assembly from 1968 to 1970. It was a forty-one to thirty-nine margin. Unexpectedly in November, the Democrats picked up five seats so it became a forty-three to thirty-seven Democratic majority. All the chairs changed. The committee consultants changed. And the [interns] remained in their current assignments with a couple of exceptions. . . .
>
> I went from a Republican chair, Vic Veysey, who actually was running for Congress so he wasn't going to be around anyway, to a Democratic chair, Leroy Greene, who had been the chairman of the committee prior to when the Republicans took control in 1968. . . . The transition for me between chairs was a little tough. I remember, even though I was very Democratic in terms of my own political leanings, I related more to the first chair that I did to the second chair.[15]

As Friedlander discovered, Assembly politics often had a significant impact on the internship experience. Although interns interviewed with members of the Assembly and submitted their placement preferences to Rules Committee staff, the intern's choices did not always match the staff's determination of the best assignment. The political clout of a committee or its chair influenced placements. According to Gerald McDaniel, "the delays and disagreements over assignment of

---

[14] Desrochers, 4-5.

[15] Dan Friedlander, "History of the Capital Fellows Programs," *Oral History Interview*, conducted in 2002 by Elizabeth Austin, SCUA, 6-12.

interns led to an occasional 'revolt' as the interns banded together to insist that one or more of their group be promptly and properly assigned."[16]

Interns to Fellows

By 1972, the Assembly began to raise questions about the value of continuing the internship program. A memorandum from Fred Taugher, the Assembly's assistant chief administrative officer, suggested that the program needed to be restructured or eliminated.

> The current legislative internship was designed over a dozen years ago to meet a need which no longer exists. Many members, staff, and even interns have questioned the validity of the Assembly continuing to sponsor the internship. Certainly, the Assembly should either get out of the internship business or structure a program which will better suit the needs of the Assembly and its interns. . . .
>
>   Admittedly, our current legislative internship program leaves a lot to be desired. It is hardly an educational experience; it is in reality no more than a cheap labor contract. It does not provide an opportunity for many persons to gain insight into the legislative process; it is limited to ten interns a year, all of whom have impressive academic backgrounds but are often politically immature.

Among Taugher's recommendations were: scheduling the program to run concurrently with the legislative session rather than the academic year; varying the assignments to include time with members, committees, and district offices; offering regular opportunities for discussions among the interns and with guest experts; requiring readings and written reports; and hiring a full-time internship coordinator.[17] The internship program did continue and several of Taugher's recommendations were adopted by the Rules Committee and the executive board two years later.

In 1974, the Rules Committee approved significant changes to the internship program. Under the leadership of Chairman Leon Ralph, a strong supporter of the program, the committee doubled the budget for the program and increased the number of participants from eight to ten.[18] It decided to hire a full-time director for the program, increase stipends to $764 per month, institute regular seminar meetings, and extend the length of the internship from nine to eleven months divided between service for five months on the personal staff of an assembly-

---

[16] McDaniel, "The Legislative Internship Program in California," 5.

[17] Fred Taugher to Lou Angelo, Vic Fazio, John FitzRandolph, Bill Hauck, Jim Lane, Gene Leyval, Vivian Miksak, memorandum, 27 April 1972, ARCP.

[18] Ten positions for interns had been approved by the Rules Committee in 1965 but the number of participants appears to have ranged between six and eight in the early 1970s.

member and service for six months with committee staff.[19] The objective of the new program format was to give participants different perspectives on the legislative process and to enhance their understanding of the problems faced by legislators and their constituents.[20]

The Rules Committee also adopted the suggestion of the new chair of the executive board, Ronald Loveridge, to call program participants "fellows" instead of "interns" since "interns [were] everywhere. Fellows was a step up in terms of status and honor. . . . Fellows had a different standing, a different status."[21]

Loveridge believed that the changes heralded a new era for the Assembly program, and reflected changes in the Assembly itself since the program's inception in 1957, primarily through the addition of extensive staffs. "No longer are interns necessary to provide staff support, and the Assembly, thanks to an increase in staff salaries, legislative issues, and general reputation, can hire from among the 'best and brightest.'"

Loveridge proposed changes for 1975–1976 to introduce and expose fellows more fully to the legislative process. "Whether they remain for several years as regular staff members or return immediately to their communities and a profession, the Assembly Fellows should in the future be more aware of the demands upon the legislator, the problems on the State's political agenda, and the legislative policy process from initiation to implementation," Loveridge said.[22]

After the Rules Committee and the executive board determined the details of the new format and the responsibilities of the new director, they inaugurated the Assembly Fellowship Program in 1975–1976.

Miguel Tirado began as the first full-time director in June 1975. Based on his recommendation after directing the program for one year, the director's position was reduced to part-time. Tirado was succeeded by Charles Price in January 1979.

The director's duties included participation with the executive board in the recruitment and selection of new fellows, the coordination of fellowship seminars and the administration of the Assembly Fellowship Program. In an effort to expand and diversify the pool of program applicants, the director visited major colleges and universities throughout California and actively recruited new fellows by sending program information to statewide organizations such as the California Chamber of Commerce and the League of Women Voters, to lobbyists and to academic institutions. Ethnic studies programs were targeted with special mailings. Members of the Assembly and program alumni were asked to encourage qualified individuals to apply. In contrast to the early years of the internship program when

---

[19] Ronald Loveridge to California Assembly Fellowship Executive Board, "Changes in Assembly Program, 1975-1976, et cetera...," memorandum, 30 October 1974, ARCP. Service on the personal staff of a member often involved work in the member's district office.

[20] Ronald Loveridge to State Assembly Fellow Executive Committee, "January 10/11," memorandum, 23 January 1975, ARCP.

[21] Loveridge, *Oral History Interview*, 4.

[22] Loveridge, "January 10/11."

only graduate students were eligible to apply, the program welcomed applications from both undergraduate and graduate students.[23]

Ronald Loveridge summarized the approach to recruitment in the late 1970s and early 1980s:

> In the latter years [of my participation on the executive board], it became more self-conscious that you wanted some Republicans. You wanted some women. You wanted some ethnic diversity. You wanted people with different academic backgrounds. You didn't want everybody from Stanford or a single university. There needed to be some geographic selection. None of that was written on paper but it was understood that you were looking not for a uniform profile but a diverse profile of fellows.[24]

Available statistics for the applications received from 1975 to 1985 indicate that the recruitment efforts were not successful. The total number of applicants actually declined while the percentage of total applicants who were from minority groups and who had only a bachelor's degree remained about the same.[25]

The selection process followed the established pattern of reviewing all paper applications, interviewing approximately thirty to forty applicants in both southern and northern California and inviting the finalists from these interviews to a group interview in Sacramento.

The executive board did make minor adjustments to the selection process between 1975 and 1985. At the beginning of this period, the paper screening was completed by executive board members who were from southern California. By 1978, all executive board members were asked to participate in the paper screening. In 1976, the first former fellow, Lindsay Desrochers, was invited to join the executive board in the selection process as a nonvoting member to provide the perspective of a program alumna. The next year, Desrochers became a voting member of the board. By 1977, current fellows were involved in the selection process. Two fellows participated in the paper screening and in the northern and southern California interviews. All of the fellows were present at the interviews of finalists in Sacramento but did not have a vote in the final selection.

Although the executive board increased the maximum number of fellowships from ten to fifteen in 1977 at the request of Assembly Rules Committee Chairman Louis Papan, the actual number of fellows stabilized at twelve in 1979. Fewer fellows were selected in some years and some fellows selected for the program declined to participate in other years.[26]

---

[23] Miguel Tirado to Wendy Gelbart, 3 September 1976, ARCP; Judy White to Miguel Tirado, 27 October 1976, ARCP; Ronald Loveridge to Members, Executive Board, California Assembly Fellowship Board, memorandum, 8 October 1976, ARCP.

[24] Loveridge, *Oral History Interview*, 7.

[25] See Appendix 2.6 for the available application statistics.

[26] See Appendix 2.6 for available interview statistics. Ronald Loveridge to Executive Board, California Assembly Fellowship Program, memorandum, "Paper screening,

Occasionally, to the dismay of the executive board, the Rules Committee injected itself into the selection process. The 1975–1976 ten-member fellowship class was augmented by a Rules Committee appointment following what the chair of the executive board, Ronald Loveridge, characterized as an "ad hoc recruitment process for the eleventh Fellow" in his letter to Leon Ralph, chair of the Rules Committee.

He added, "While the Board exists at the pleasure of the Assembly, our reputation both as Board members and as academic representatives has centered on the objective integrity of the selection process." The full executive board echoed Loveridge's concern at their September 1975 meeting. After meeting with Ralph, Loveridge assured the executive board that "at least from the present Chairman of Rules, I do not anticipate any future personal appointments to the Assembly Fellow Program."

In 1977, the executive board agreed to Rules Committee Chair Louis Papan's request to ask all fellowship finalists if they were registered to vote. When Proposition 13 passed in 1978, Papan was very angry and was convinced that it had passed because people did not vote. He demanded to know if the fellows who had been selected for the 1978–1979 class had voted and wanted to fire the two fellows who had not voted. Papan only agreed to retain them after a tense emergency meeting with Executive Board Chair Ronald Loveridge and the fellowship program director Charles Price.[27]

After his appointment as the new program director in 1975, Miguel Tirado tried to find a satisfactory solution to the ongoing problem of integrating an academic component into the fellowship experience.

His plan closely resembled earlier attempts to create an effective academic program to complement the practical legislative experience offered by the fellowship: a one-week orientation followed by two-hour weekly public policy seminars with guest speakers that would stimulate discussions about the legislative process. Seminar topics included health care, collective bargaining for public employees, statewide land-use planning and controls, campaign practices legislation and energy.[28]

The director expected fellows to attend all seminars whether they were working in Sacramento or in a district office. By the early 1980s, the orientation was extended to two weeks and the weekly seminars continued. Fred Clark, a fellow in

---

participation of current Fellows in selection process, and Program Director for 1979-80," 28 December 1978, ARCP; Ronald Loveridge to Lindsay Desrochers, 17 February 1976, ARCP; Ronald Loveridge to the Honorable Louis Papan, 7 April 1977, ARCP.

[27] Ronald Loveridge to the Honorable Leon Ralph, Chairman, California Assembly Rules Committee, 29 July 1975 and 11 September 1975, ARCP; Ronald Loveridge to Executive Board Members, California Assembly Fellow Program, memorandum, 11 September 1975, ARCP; Charles Price, telephone interview by Elizabeth Austin, 20 September 2002; Loveridge, *Oral History Interview*, 6.

[28] Miguel Tirado to Ronald Loveridge, 1 July 1975, ARCP; Tirado to Gelbart, 3 September 1976.

the 1981–1982 session, told the executive board that he considered the seminars "to be a highlight of [his] experience in Sacramento. These seminars offered all of us an opportunity to discuss issues with legislators, staff members, lobbyists, and other persons whom none of us could have met with as individuals."[29]

The seminars did not include papers or other assignments. No academic credit was granted for participation in the fellowship program. The fellows often enjoyed the opportunity offered by the seminars to get together with other fellows and to discuss legislative issues with experts, but the weekly or biweekly meetings did not include academic coursework.

Criteria for assemblymembers' participation in the program evolved through the 1970s. In 1975, the Rules Committee established the following criteria:

- The sponsoring Assemblyman [sic] should be actively involved in the formulation of new legislation during the fall recess either through personal investigation or participation in interim studies in order to assure the fellow a relevant legislative experience.
- The sponsoring Assemblyman must provide a clear outline of the goals and tasks the Assembly fellow is to be assigned in the office. This assignment should include [o]pportunities to familiarize the fellow with the district office and its operation.
- The Rules Committee endorses a policy of allocating Assembly fellows to Democratic and Republican Assemblymen in a ratio equivalent to their respective membership in the Assembly.

After interested members submitted information about placement opportunities to the program director, they interviewed the fellows. Following a new procedure of mutual selection, both members and fellows ranked their placement choices. The director then made the final placement decision.[30] The fellows were generally in favor of the new placement procedure. In a detailed review of the fellowship program, the 1977–1978 fellows stated, "The mutual selection system should be retained. Interviews allow the members and fellows to discuss responsibilities and to insure that personalities are compatible *before* final selections are made."

Additionally, the fellows recommended reducing the number of placement interviews.[31] The number of interviews was effectively reduced in 1980 when Program Director Charles Price and Rules Committee Chair Louis Papan decided to review members' requests for fellows and only make a limited number eligible for

---

[29] Fred Clark, Assembly Fellow 1981–1982 to Executive Board, California Assembly Fellowship Program, "Observations & Suggestions re: the Fellowship Program," 8 April 1982, ARCP.

[30] Miguel D. Tirado to Assembly Members, 11 June 1975, ARCP.

[31] California Assembly Fellowship Program, "Assembly Fellowship Presentation," presented 7 April 1978, ARCP.

a placement. Price and Papan decided to make members who had fellows the previous year ineligible for current year fellows.[32]

The placement process did not always satisfy the Rules Committee goal of allocating fellows to Democrats and Republicans in proportion to their representation in the Assembly. In fact, it was often difficult to get Republicans involved at all.

In spite of the program director's efforts to attract the participation of Republican members in the Assembly Fellowship Program by contacting the Republican leadership and the Minority Caucus, only seven of the twenty-six assemblymembers interested in sponsoring a fellow for 1976–1977 were Republicans. Of these seven, two actually interviewed fellows. Since none of the fellows listed the two Republicans as their first, second or third choice, no Republicans received fellows that year.

The challenge of placing fellows with Republican members continued in later years. After receiving a letter in 1979 from Republican Assemblyman Paul Bannai that expressed concern about the recruitment and placement process for Assembly fellows, Louis Papan, chair of the Assembly Rules Committee, replied that "the Executive Board has made a conscious effort both to attract and select Assembly Fellows with Republican backgrounds. Since it is not permissible to request party affiliation of prospective applicants, the program has relied upon the Republican representatives on the Executive Board to assist in identifying and recruiting Republicans for participation in the program. Our experience to date, however, is that the number of Republicans receiving fellows is not a condition of how many formally declared Republican Assembly Fellows are in the program. Rather, it is a result of our inability to interest more Republican members in applying for the program. Our Fellowship Director has repeatedly brought this to the attention of the Minority Caucus staff in the hopes of increasing the interest in the program among Republican legislators."[33]

One Democratic fellow, Lilly Spitz, offered to give up her placement with Willie Brown so that a Republican member would have a fellow in 1977–1978. "It became apparent pretty quickly that we were a group of Democrats and one Republican," she said. "There was a need to have at least one, hopefully more, fellows assigned to a Republican's office."

When it appeared that wouldn't happen, Spitz said, she volunteered to work for Republican Ken Maddy, who chaired the Criminal Justice Committee. But Brown, then chair of the Assembly Revenue and Taxation Committee, nixed that idea, she said.

---

[32] Charles Price to Executive Board Members, California Assembly Fellowship Program, memorandum, 27 August 1980, ARCP. For the 1980-1981 fellowship year, thirty-one members requested fellows. Only sixteen members were declared eligible to receive fellows. Price noted that the current fellows would have preferred thirty-one options to sixteen.

[33] Miguel Tirado to Fred Taugher, memorandum, 11 August 1976, ARCP; Louis J. Papan to the Honorable Paul Bannai, 2 October 1979, ARCP.

"He was very much looking forward to having a fellow in the office and said, 'No, you're not going to give my fellow to a Republican.' So we didn't have much to say about that," Spitz said.[34]

Although the program director and the executive board implemented a policy and practice of seeking Republican fellows and Republican placements, their efforts were frequently unrewarded.

In her placement with Willie Brown, Spitz quickly learned how the legislative process worked. Spitz recalls being treated much like a regular committee staffer with her own bill load to research. After determining the pros and cons, she would advise Brown how to vote on them. She got good advice, she said, from Elisabeth Kersten, a former fellow who was now Brown's chief of staff. Kersten advised her to seek advice from various other members and staffers, depending on their areas of expertise. Then Brown would cross-examine her on her findings, she said.

"I found one of the key rules in working in the legislature is to get to know people who have expertise because you can't have all that expertise. You need to know people who do and you need to have relationships with them so they'll respond when you make a phone call or go by the office or whatever because things happen really quickly over there," Spitz said. [35]

Following the new format introduced in 1975, many of the placements were split between district offices and Sacramento. Ted Lascher, a 1978–1979 fellow, said he had two very good experiences that year; working with Napa Assemblyman Mike Gage on legislation and constituent issues, and doing committee work on welfare and social service issues. He recalls working with the chair of the committee, Assemblyman Richard Alatorre of Los Angeles, and drafting an op-ed piece that appeared in the *Los Angeles Times* under Alatorre's name.

But interns from that year also had to deal with the shockwaves of tax-slashing Proposition 13, and the new crop of politicians who rode its wave into office as 1979 began.

"Prop. 13 had a big impact because . . . the whole question of what exactly the state should fund in the welfare and social services area—in welfare, in supplemental social security income, in foster care payments, in direct social services—all were up in the air," Lascher said. So it fell to the committee and its staff to educate members about the effects of Proposition 13 on all those programs, he said.

On the political side, Lascher recalled, "there were a whole bunch of new members that came in in January of '79, particularly the Republicans. They were different sorts of Republicans. They were the Prop 13 babies, people like Pat Nolan, Ross Johnson. . . . They had a very conservative, antitax agenda. They had

---

[34] Lilly Spitz, "History of the Capital Fellows Programs," *Oral History Interview*, conducted in 2002 by Elizabeth Austin, SCUA, 5.

[35] Ibid., 8-9.

various ideas for welfare reform that usually involved some fairly substantial cutting. The committee dealt with that." [36]

Although splitting placements between district offices and Sacramento was initially regarded as a success, by 1981 the costs and variability in the quality of assignments led the executive board and the Rules Committee to eliminate the district office component. [37]

The interns and fellows who participated in the program from 1966 to 1985 often remained involved in the Legislature either as members or staff. Howard Berman returned to the Assembly as a member from 1973 to 1982. He was elected to the House of Representatives in 1982 and continues to represent the 28th District of California today. Berman concluded that the internship was "a career decisive move on my part. Would I have ended up there on some other path? Maybe, but this really sharpened my interest in doing it and helped prepare me for it as well." He recognized, "In terms of knowing the [legislative] process, [the internship] was the kind of thing you aren't going to get from textbooks and you're not going to get from just being an activist or a volunteer in political campaigns."

Elisabeth Kersten, a 1971–1972 intern, remained as a staffer for the Assembly Ways and Means Committee. Bob Connelly, a staff member who worked with Kersten on the Ways and Means Committee, remembered that "she took our budget and ran it the first year. . . . [S]he was extraordinary. She was a very bright, very competent woman. She stayed on as a staffer, and she made her career in the legislature." Kersten described her experience as "the opportunity to get 'hands-on' experience in public policy decision-making. My work experience as an Assembly [intern] . . . led me to a full-time position with the Committee." Kersten went on to serve as director of the Senate Office of Research from 1983 to 2003.

After his 1978–1979 fellowship, Dotson Wilson was given a full-time position on the legislative staff when Willie Brown was elected speaker. He was first elected to his current position as Chief Clerk of the Assembly in January 1992. According to Wilson, the fellowship gave him the "opportunity to access the legislature."

Mike Thompson, a 1983–1984 fellow, was hired by Rules Committee Chair Louis Papan before his fellowship ended. He remembered, "[Papan] offered me a job. I accepted the job with the condition that I couldn't come to work for thirty days. That was how much longer I had in my fellowship. . . . I said, 'I still have an obligation to the fellowship for thirty more days.' He looked at me like I was from outer space. He said, 'I'm in charge of the fellowship. You're fired from the fellowship. Report to my office for work on Monday.'" After working for Papan, and later for Assemblymember Jackie Speier, Thompson was elected to the state Senate. In 1998, he was elected to the U.S. House of Representatives. [38]

---

[36] Ted Lascher, "History of the Capital Fellows Programs," *Oral History Interview*, conducted in 2002 by Elizabeth Austin, SCUA, 3-6.

[37] Loveridge, *Oral History Interview*, 8-9.

[38] Berman, 9-10; John Robert Connelly, *Oral History Interview*, conducted in 2001 by Charles Wollenberg, Regional Oral History Office, University of California at Berke-

Other interns and fellows used the foundation provided by their experiences in the Assembly to build careers outside the Legislature. Lindsay Desrochers returned to academia to complete her Ph.D. while maintaining a connection with the Legislature by working on budgetary politics in California and serving on the Assembly Fellowship Board. She believes the internship "directed me to an interest in public policy and budgetary politics as a lifetime pursuit. It was very important. I hadn't had that thought previously." Desrochers is currently the Vice President of Portland State University.

Ted Lascher also returned to academia after his fellowship and five years in positions with the California Department of Social Services and the state Senate. He completed his Ph.D. in political science and became an assistant professor of Public Policy at Harvard's John F. Kennedy School of Government before joining the faculty at California State University, Sacramento. Lascher discovered that "once [he] got back to graduate school, I found I had a much more practical orientation than a lot of my colleagues who talked about things in more theoretical [terms]. I think it was a much richer graduate school experience . . . than I would have had otherwise." Today, Lascher is the chair of the Sacramento State Department of Public Policy and Administration.

After her fellowship, Lilly Spitz worked in Willie Brown's office for four more years before she left to start the Women's Legislative Institute "precisely because I wanted to teach people how to be legislative advocates to help empower particularly women's organizations to be a part of the process and to have their voices heard." She "never left the legislative arena. All the jobs that I've had since then, almost twenty-five years ago, maybe more, have been legislatively, public policy related. All of them. I find the work very worthwhile and very gratifying. [The fellowship] definitely changed my entire direction." Spitz became the first chief legal counsel for the California Planned Parenthood Education Fund in 1999.[39]

Who's in Charge?

In the early 1980s, Charles Price was replaced as director of the Assembly Fellowship Program by a member of the Rules Committee staff. According to Price, "About one year after Willie [Brown] took over [as Assembly Speaker in

---

ley, for the California State Archives State Government Oral History Program, 95; "The California Assembly Fellowship Program [brochure for 1981-1982]," ARCP; Dotson Wilson, telephone interview with Elizabeth Austin, 30 September 2002; Mike Thompson, "History of the Capital Fellows Programs," *Oral History Interview*, conducted in 2003 by Elizabeth Austin, SCUA, 9.

[39] Desrochers, *Oral History* Interview, 10; Lascher, *Oral History* Interview, 8; Spitz, *Oral History* Interview, 12-13. Appendix 3.2 lists the participants in the Assembly internship and fellowship programs.

December 1980], there was a meeting about funding [the Assembly Fellowship Program]. Willie Brown didn't know me. I was getting a stipend of about $1,000 per month [for the part-time position of director]. Willie Brown asked, "Well, who's his uncle?" as if it were a patronage job. So I was replaced that year or the next by a staff member from Willie Brown's office. Willie Brown wanted to have as many of his people with jobs as possible."[40] The executive board continued to select the fellows but the administration of the program became the complete responsibility of the Rules Committee.

By 1985, the Assembly Fellowship Program was well-established. Over three hundred interns and fellows had acquired first-hand experience with the legislative process in California. Many had remained to staff the Legislature and other state government agencies while others had applied their political knowledge in academia, local communities, and the private sector. The program had survived without Ford Foundation support and had proved its continuing usefulness both as a resource for the Legislature and as an educational opportunity for talented young men and women. Although their role was periodically challenged by assemblymembers and staff, academics continued to be involved with the program through the executive board and the program director.

The original academic partnership with the Assembly, however, had altered significantly since its inception in 1957. The struggle to devise an effective academic program never moved beyond meetings with guest speakers. The program director, who had been an academic, was replaced with a Rules Committee staff member. Program costs were no longer shared between the universities through the Ford Foundation grant and the Assembly. Instead, funding—and therefore ultimate control—of the fellowship program had shifted to the Assembly.

---

[40] Price, 20 September 2002. Charles Price was the director of the program at least until 1983-1984.

A Separate Program for the Senate

Resolved by the Senate of the State of California, that the Senate requests the Senate Rules Committee to initiate a Senate intern program as a pilot project, to be financed from the Senate Contingent Fund and to operate on a bipartisan basis.
—Senate Resolution 46, 1972

My office would be delighted to have a Senate Fellow again next year. I look forward to another successful year of the Fellowship Program.
—Senator John Garamendi, 1981

Reapportionment Sets the Stage

After rejecting the legislative internship program embraced by the Assembly in 1957, the California Senate slowly began to recognize the value of interns in the late 1960s. Changes in the composition of the Senate facilitated the introduction of an internship program. Before the influx of new senators following the "one man one vote" reapportionment mandated by the courts in 1965, UC Davis observed that the Senate was slow to follow up on the lessons of the Assembly. "It was a very different body from the Assembly—much more rural emphasis, much more conservative, more an old boys club," Sokolow said.[1]

---

[1] Al Sokolow, "History of the Capital Fellows Program," *Oral History Interview*, conducted in 2002 by Elizabeth Austin, SCUA, 6-7. As approved by California voters in 1926 and included in the state constitution, the apportionment plan for the Senate specified one senator for each county. By 1962, this plan resulted in the representation of half of California's population by only three senators from Los Angeles, San Diego and Ala-

After reapportionment, the balance of power in the Senate shifted from the rural to the urban areas of California. Fourteen of the twenty-two new senators elected in 1966 had previously served in the Assembly. Anthony Beilenson, one of the new senators with Assembly experience, noted that the Senate "worked very much the way . . . it had worked a hundred years or so earlier."

But the hitherto conservative Senate now included Assembly veterans who had served under the leadership of Jesse Unruh, a strong supporter both of interns and a modernized legislature.[2]

Early Internships in the Senate

Caution was the hallmark of the Senate's approach to internships. The initial internship program was limited both in numbers and duration. Three interns participated for twelve months each year in a program that lasted from 1968 to 1971.

Funded by the American Political Science Association (APSA) and the Ford Foundation, the internship program was organized and supervised by Al Sokolow. Sokolow noted that following the reapportionment and the 1966 election, some

---

meda counties while 10.7 per cent of the state's population was represented by twenty-one senators largely from rural counties. The 1962 decision of the United States Supreme Court in *Baker v. Carr* endorsed the one man-one vote principle of apportionment and the 1965 decision of a federal trial court in California (*Silver v. Jordan*) directed the California legislature to reapportion the Senate by 1 July 1965. A reapportionment plan finally emerged after the California Supreme Court ruled in another case that both the Assembly and the Senate must produce a reapportionment plan by 9 December 1965 or a plan developed by the court would be implemented. The Assembly and the Senate finally agreed on a reapportionment plan for the 1966 elections which resulted in twenty-two new members in the Senate. Fourteen senators represented Los Angeles County and a fifteenth senator represented part of Los Angeles County. Winston Crouch, et. al., *California Government and Politics*, 4th ed. (Englewood Cliffs, NJ: Prentice-Hall, 1967), 125-128.

[2] Alfred E. Alquist, *Oral History Interview*, conducted in 1987 by Gabrielle Morris, Regional Oral History Office, University of California, Berkeley, for the California State Archives, State Government Oral History Program, 17-20, 39-40; Anthony C. Beilenson, *Oral History Interview*, conducted in 1997 and 1998 by Susan Douglass Yates, Oral History Program, University of California, Los Angeles, for the California State Archives, State Government Oral History Program, 218-225; Charles G. Bell and Charles M. Price, *California Government Today: Politics of Reform*, 4th ed. (Pacific Grove, Calif.: Brooks/Cole, 1992), 187-188; Crouch, et. al., 125-131; Royce D. Delmatier, Clarence F. McIntosh, and Earl G. Waters, eds., *The Rumble of California Politics, 1848-1970* (New York: John Wiley, 1970), 355-357; Milton Marks, *Oral History Interview*, conducted in 1996 by Donald B. Seney for the California State Archives, State Government Oral History Program, 87-88.

senators remained frustrated that the impact of reapportionment hadn't been felt yet. In fact, some of the holdovers had been quietly progressive in the old Senate and were looking forward to playing greater and more openly liberal roles in the new body.[3]

Among them, Sokolow recalled, was Senator Steve Teale "who was interested in doing some stuff in terms of improving the staff capacity of the Senate." Teale appointed John Williamson, a liberal Democrat from Kern County who had just lost re-election to the Assembly, to be the executive director of the Rules Committee. In a conversation with Williamson, Sokolow remembered, "We started to talk about the concept of an internship or fellowship program because we knew what was happening in the Assembly." With Teale's support and the cooperation of the Senate, Sokolow applied for grants from APSA and the Ford Foundation to fund three graduate students for three years. The new Senate intern program would be run by former state Assemblymember John Williamson.[4]

Both Sokolow and Williamson brought Assembly experience to the new Senate internship program. Sokolow had served on the executive board of the Assembly internship program. Williamson had chaired and served on committees staffed by interns from the time of his arrival as a member of the Assembly in 1959. Howard Berman, a 1965–1966 intern, remembered that he "got a lot of direct time with John Williamson . . . the chairman [of the Agriculture Committee]."[5]

The Senate internship program was one part of Stephen Teale's effort to modernize the Senate during the period of internal upheaval following reapportionment. Teale emphasized the importance of taking a gradual approach to the internship program. Sokolow remembered that "Steve Teale wisely said, 'We've got to take it easy with this program. We've got to implement it gradually and see

---

[3] Each intern received a stipend funded by APSA and Ford Foundation grants. For the first ten months of the one-year internship, the interns were paid $100 to $150 per month. During July and August, they received $550 per month. California. Senate. Rules Committee, "Report to the Senate Rules Committee on Proposal to Establish an Internship Program for the California State Senate" (Sacramento, 1973), Senate Rules Committee Papers, California State Archives, Sacramento (hereafter cited as SRCP), 8.

[4] Sokolow, *Oral History Interview,* 8-9. Senator Stephen P. Teale (D) represented Calaveras, Mariposa and Tuolumne Counties from 1953 to 1966 and Alpine, Amador, Calaveras, El Dorado, Lassen, Modoc, Nevada, Placer, Plumas, Sierra, Stanislaus and Tuolumne Counties from 1967 to 1972. John C. Williamson was the member of the Assembly for Kern County from 1959 to 1966.

[5] Berman, *Oral History Interview,* 5. Following reapportionment, Williamson lost his Assembly seat during Berman's internship year. Williamson was a member of the following Assembly committees that included interns: Water (Stuart Hall, 1958-1959; Ron Robie, 1960-1961; and David Epstein, 1964-1965), Constitutional Amendments (John Gunnell, 1960-1961 and Eugene Leyvall, 1961-1962), Agriculture (William Geyer, 1961-1962; George Robbins, 1964-1965; and Howard Berman, 1965-1966), and Ways and Means (Jerold Perry, 1962-1963; John Spellman, 1963-1964; and Edward Juers, Jr., 1964-1965).

how it's going to work in order to make it attractive enough for a large enough number of members so they will want staff people from the program later."[6]

Sokolow selected the interns from among the graduate students in the political science department at UC Davis who were interested in state politics and legislative careers. The Senate Rules Committee placed the interns. Sokolow observed:

> Initially, there was a great deal of sensitivity on the part of Steve Teale, our mentor in the Senate, about where we would place these students. The impression was that most members of the Senate wouldn't know what to do with an intern. . . . They were not really in the mode of using staff in the productive, policy way. There were just a few people that would understand the process. There was a concern on my part with the educational experience of the interns. A concern on the part of Steve Teale and the Rules Committee [about] putting people in a place where they could do some damage. There was a fear of having young people around who had different agendas and who technically were not staff people.

The interns were carefully placed with Senate committees that were willing to give them substantive work to do. They were largely invisible to the rest of the Senate.[7]

Charlene Wear Simmons participated in the second year of the internship program while she was completing her master's degree in political science at UC Davis. During her 1969–1970 internship, many of the new senators who were elected after reapportionment joined to overthrow the "old guard" Senate leadership that had denied them important committee assignments. According to Simmons, the change in leadership had a significant impact on her internship experience:

> I was assigned to the "leadership" committee, Government Efficiency. The committee consultant, Chuck Baldwin, had worked for Jesse Unruh before going to the Senate. . . . Mid-way through the year, there was a "revolt" and the old guard Senate leadership was overthrown. The reformed committee became Government Organization. . . . It was a fascinating and stressful experience.

Although Simmons enjoyed researching and writing analyses for complex and controversial bills, she was distressed by the level of sexual harassment that she experienced as the only woman working at the level of committee consultant in the Senate. Simmons recently observed, "It's unimaginable now to consider what the work environment was like at that time." The Senate internship changed her career focus because she "loved the intersection between research and poli-

---

[6] Sokolow, *Oral History Interview*, 19.

[7] The interns who participated in the first year of the program were Davis Campbell, Ray Davis and Rayce Davies. Second year participants included Joe Serna, Charlene Wear Simmons and Mike Slaughter. There is no record of the names of the third year participants. Sokolow, *Oral History Interview*, 10-11, 14, 19.

tics." After the Senate internship, Simmons completed a Ph.D. in political science at UC Davis then worked in both houses of Congress and the California Legislature. She later worked as assistant director for General Law and Government at the California Research Bureau in the State Library.[8]

Other Senate internship programs were also developed during this period. Senator Mervyn Dymally spearheaded the Fellowship and Internship Training (FIT) program for minorities in the late 1960s. Participants in FIT were placed in the offices of state senators and other elected and appointed officials. Beginning in May 1970, the Senate permitted individual members to select students to work in their offices. During 1971–1972, the UC Davis Law School placed five students enrolled in their Legislative Externship Program with senators who assumed responsibility for their supervision. These internships were arranged by individual senators and did not involve the Senate as a whole.[9]

Senate Internship Program, 1973–1976

In October 1971, shortly after the conclusion of the internship program funded by APSA and the Ford Foundation, the Senate Rules Committee asked its executive officer, John Williamson, to prepare a proposal for the creation of the California State Senate Internship Program.

Support for the continuation of the internship program under the auspices of the Senate was evident in the April 1972 resolution offered by Senator Mervyn Dymally. Dymally had been elected to the Senate in 1966 after serving three years in the Assembly where he had been a member of at least two committees that sponsored interns. Dymally had worked with APSA/Ford Foundation intern Joe Serna in the Senate and had developed the Fellowship and Internship Training Program for minorities. His resolution recognized the importance of the internship program both to the students and to the Senate. It also reflected the need to respond to the student unrest and activism that had emerged in the 1960s. The resolution stated:

- The California Senate at this time has no recognized or continuing program to encourage students to participate in state government or to learn operations and functions of the Senate;

---

[8] Charlene Simmons, "Capital Fellows Alumni Questionnaire," 2003, Center for California Studies, Files of the Capital Fellows Programs (hereafter cited as FCFP). In 2003, a questionnaire was sent to all alumni of the Capital Fellows Programs for whom addresses were available. The questions and the respondents are listed in Appendix 9.

[9] California. Senate. Rules Committee, "Report to the Senate Rules Committee on Proposal to Establish an Internship Program for the California State Senate," 7-8; Alan Rosin, interview by author, tape recording, Sacramento, Calif., 24 June 2003; *A Proposal for a Fellowship and Internship Training Program,* [196?], personal papers of Daniel Visnich.

- A permanent Senate student intern program can be set up and kept functioning for small cost compared to its potentially great benefits;
- Informal student intern programs now functioning in some Senate offices have shown conclusively that, when well directed, such programs can be of great benefit both to students and to the Senate offices involved; and
- A formal student training program can help increase youth interest in state government and help provide the dedicated staff professionals and elected officials so essential to a functioning democracy.

Dymally's resolution concluded with the request that the Senate Rules Committee initiate a Senate intern program as a pilot project financed by the Senate Contingent Fund.[10]

The Senate Rules Committee adopted a proposal in April 1973 that effectively implemented Dymally's resolution. It established five objectives for the Senate Internship Program:

1. Provide legislative experience for graduate and undergraduate students.
2. Provide research and other staff assistance for Senate members and committees.
3. Train graduate and undergraduate students for full-time legislative staff service.
4. Establish direct lines of communication with students and faculties of colleges and universities.
5. Broaden perspectives of students planning academic, business, social, or governmental careers so that they will carry into their chosen fields an understanding of the legislative way of doing business.

The Rules Committee designed the Senate program to achieve the same goals established by the original Assembly internship program.[11]

Created as a pilot program subject to review after two years, the structure of the Senate internship program deviated from the Assembly program by offering both full-time and part-time internships and by choosing interns from both upper division undergraduate and graduate students. Six full-time internships lasting nine months were scheduled to begin either February 1 or October 1.

---

[10] S.R. 46, California Senate, 1972 Regular Session, *Journal of the Senate* (4 April 1972): 1105. The complete text of S.R. 46 is included in Appendix 6.1. S.R. 46 was reported back to the Assembly by the Rules Committee without further action on 1 December 1972.

[11] California. Senate. Rules Committee, "Report to the Senate Rules Committee on Proposal to Establish an Internship Program for the California State Senate," 1. During the development of the Senate proposal, input was received from several former participants in the California Legislative Internship Program including Gerald McDaniel, Alan Rosin, Dan Visnich and William Geyer. Others who contributed to the development of the proposal were Senators Mervyn Dymally and Albert Rodda, Professor Al Sokolow, Robert Holmes, Jonathan Lewis, Frank Mesple, and Bill Culver.

Paid a stipend of $650 per month, the full-time interns were assigned to standing committees of the Senate according to: committee workload; opportunities to involve the intern in a broad range of legislative activity or in challenging research; willingness and capability of committee staff to supervise an intern; and committee subject areas.

Full-time interns had to be given office space that included a desk and a telephone. If requested by a committee chair and approved by the Senate Rules Committee, they were permitted to travel on committee business at Senate expense.[12]

The ten annual part-time internships lasting three to six months each began on the first of February, May, August, or November. Part-time interns participated on the same basis as full-time interns except they were not permitted to travel at Senate expense, were only required to work at least sixteen hours per week and were available to work in the offices of senators who were not committee chairs. Part-time interns received a stipend of $100 per month. Both full-time and part-time interns were financed by the Senate Contingent Fund, which also paid for a half-time internship program coordinator.[13]

A panel appointed by the Senate Rules Committee selected the interns from California institutions of higher education. The selection panel included: two senators, one from each party; one representative from the Rules Committee who did not have to be a senator; two representatives from Senate staff; one member of the UC Davis faculty; and one member of the California State University, Sacramento, faculty.

The selection criteria followed by the panel stipulated that interns should reflect the population of California with respect to sex and race if qualified applicants were available and should not be limited to specific major fields of study. The selection panel was also responsible for developing the procedures for making internship assignments and for suggesting appropriate activities for interns.[14]

The selected interns arranged interviews with interested senators to determine their placements. Senators who participated in the internship program during this trial period included: Alfred Alquist, Peter Behr, Ralph Dills, John Dunlap, Mervyn Dymally, Nate Holden, John Holmdahl, Nicholas Petris, Robert Presley, Omer Rains, David Roberti, Alan Robbins, and Jerome Smith. After placement, the interns attended two orientation sessions followed by occasional seminars with leaders from the government and the press. Attendance at the orientations and seminars was recommended but not mandatory.[15]

---

[12] Ibid., 2-4.

[13] Ibid., 4-5.

[14] Ibid., 2-6. Participants in the Senate Internship Program are listed in Appendix X.

[15] Senate Internship Program Staff to Part-time Senate interns, memorandum, 21 January 1974,SRCP; "1974-75 Senate Interns," SRCP; Jim McCauley, internship coordinator, to Part-Time Interns, memorandum, 20 January 1976, SRCP; Information sheet, "The 1974-75 Senate Internship Program," [1974], ARCP. Of the participating senators, only two (John Holmdahl and Robert Lagomarsino) had served in the Senate prior to 1967. Half of the first part-time group of ten interns was placed with senators elected

Senate Fellowship Program, 1976–1984

In 1976, the Senate Rules Committee took the final step toward an internship program that was structured much like the Assembly program. Responding to a proposal from the internship selection panel, the Rules Committee replaced the combination part-time and full-time internship program with a full-time fellowship program lasting nine to twelve months each year. Following the Assembly's lead, program participants were called "fellows" instead of "interns." The program continued to be administered by a coordinator who was usually a member of the Senate Rules Committee staff. By 1982, the monthly stipend had increased to $1,250.[16]

Senate fellows were selected by a panel of senators, Senate staff, and academicians from an applicant group recruited through press releases and mailings to colleges and universities.[17] From approximately fifty applicants chosen for short personal interviews after a paper screening by the selection panel, twelve were chosen for the fellowships along with a number of alternates. Point systems were developed to evaluate each candidate's qualifications.

For the first fellowship year, 1976–1977, the initial recruiting had followed the earlier format of seeking six full-time participants. Since the Rules Committee decision to enlarge the full-time group to twelve was not made until July 1976, there was not enough time to select an additional six fellows. Fellowship coordinator, Jim McCauley, asked the previously selected fellows to recommend prospects but to no avail.[18]

Subsequent fellowship classes included the full complement of twelve participants. Occasionally, fellows selected for the Senate program were also selected for the Assembly program. For at least one year, this double selection forced the Senate program to draw on its entire list of alternates.[19]

Following a one week orientation during the first week of October, Senate fellows interviewed with individual senators or committees to determine their placements. Prior to the interviews, fellows were given information about senators and committees that were interested in mentoring a fellow and senators were given

---

immediately following the 1966 reapportionment. The remaining senators who participated were elected in the 1970s.

[16] "Senate Fellowship Program," [198?], SRCP, 1. In 1981-1982, the fellow assigned to the Rules Committee, Anne Seymour, served as the Senate Fellowship Program coordinator. The coordinators from 1976 to 1984 are listed in Appendix 7.2.

[17] By 1978, the panel also included a former fellow. Efforts were made to include both Democrats and Republicans on the panel along with representatives of ethnic minorities. Derek Pogson to John Williamson, memorandum 7 February 1979, SRCP. Selection panel members are listed in Appendix 7.3.

[18] Jim McCauley to Fellows, memorandum, 30 July 1976, SRCP.

[19] Ibid.; Derek Pogson to John C. Williams, memorandum, 10 April 1979, SRCP. Participants in the Senate fellowship program are listed in Appendix 7.1.

information about the fellows. Subject to Rules Committee approval, senators made an offer of a position to the candidate that best suited their needs. One of Senator Omer Rains's staff, Ross Pumfrey, referred to this process as a "nerve-wracking annual ritual." Fellows did have the option of rejecting offers if they believed a more attractive offer was forthcoming.[20]

The assignments given to Senate fellows included researching bill proposals and preparing amendments; scheduling committee hearings; responding to constituent complaints and problems; and writing speeches. Charles Pelton, a 1977–1978 fellow in Senator Omer Rains's office, said he was treated and respected as another full-fledged staff member and was integrated totally into both the day-to-day and long-range goals of the office." Pelton said he worked with other staffers and sometimes directly with Rains on legislation, constituent work, special projects, and the fellowship program.

Pelton's legislative duties included "the actual drafting of the bill with Legislative Counsel; steering the measure through policy and, if necessary, fiscal committees; working with concerned individuals (consultants, special interest groups, lobbyists, the senator, etc.) who would like to see the measure amended; answering correspondence about the measure; writing press releases; and, in short, becoming a general expert and trouble shooter on the measure."

Pelton also said he developed his own projects and served as Rains's representative on a task force that led to Rains carrying legislation that he developed.[21]

Michelle Mercer, a 1981–1982 fellow for Senator Barry Keene, had the following duties: serving as an active liaison with district constituencies, writing speeches and press releases, and being responsible for six bills. Mercer "was impressed by the level of work and responsibility which [she] was given. . . . They [Senator Keene's office] trusted me to present bills for Barry [Keene] in front of policy and finance committees (which was definitely exciting the first time!); they allowed me to give speeches I'd written for Barry for a district appearance [that] he was unable to attend at the last minute; and they've encouraged me to travel throughout the district and cultivate good ties with the particular constituencies for which I have responsibility."[22]

Senator Robert Presley's office suggested that "the types, the variety, and the value of the experience you will get while serving your Senate Fellowship in this office will depend in large part on your initiative, your abilities, and your willingness to work." According to the job description given to the fellows, working in Senator Presley's office offered many different opportunities:

---

[20] In 1982-1983, the commencement of the fellowship program was shifted to November. Ross Pumfrey to Dan Blackburn, Sacramento, 5 October 1979, SRCP; [Senate Rules Committee to Senate Fellows], memorandum, 21 December 1976, SRCP.

[21] Charles Pelton, "The Fellowship Experience in this Office [of Senator Omer L. Rains]," [1978], SRCP.

[22] Michelle Mercer to Janet Reiser, Sacramento, 3 August 1982, SRCP.

You will learn how bills are drafted and move through the Legislature, problems they encounter, how they are amended and often compromised. You may get the chance to guide a bill through yourself, and fellows in the past have come up with their own ideas for bills. You will be encouraged to attend committee and floor sessions.

Nothing is more important to a legislator than dealing with constituents. You will get plenty of chances to help answer their letters and phone calls. . . . This is the essence of government—where the rubber meets the road, so to speak— where you can find out how to work the system, how to help citizens overcome the inertia of bureaucracy and get help with their problems in the maze of government agencies.

You will have the chance to find out about the symbiotic relationship between legislators and the news media, how each depends on the other (somewhat grudgingly), how each uses the other.[23]

In addition to the orientation and assignments in senators' offices, the fellowship experience included attending seminars featuring speakers drawn primarily from state government, the press, and lobbyists. For the first few years of the Senate Fellowship Program, only a few speakers were scheduled each year.

Zane Johnston, a 1980–1981 fellow, recalled, "This was perhaps the most disappointing aspect of the fellowship. We rarely had any type of presentation or discussion group with Capitol insiders or various state officials."

After Anne Seymour served as coordinator of the fellowship program during the 1981–1982 fellowship year, a more organized and extensive slate of speakers was presented. Seymour selected speakers based on the fellows' suggestions and speaker availability.

Because we were such a small group, we tried to survey who [the fellows] wanted to meet and what they wanted to hear. Then my job was to get those speakers to them. If there was a congressional delegation coming in, we would have them meet with Congress members. I always tried to stay on top of what were the really cool things going on involving Senate leadership.

We really had an opportunity. These were not lectures as much as they were almost like salons where people would give little presentations and then we would all have a chance to ask questions and really talk to these people and have a dialog about not just who they were and what they were doing but how it related to what we were—we were all very young—and what our career ambitions were.

Subsequent program coordinators followed Seymour's approach. For example, in 1982–1983, there were at least twenty-eight speakers ranging from Jerry Zanelli, the executive officer of the Senate Rules Committee, and Bion Gregory, Legislative Counsel, to Bob Fairbanks, the editor of the *California Journal*, and

---

[23] "Serving as a Senate Fellow in the Office of Senator Robert Presley," [1981?], SRCP. Placements, when available, are listed in Appendix XIII.

Jim Schultz, the legislative advocate for California Common Cause. The Senate fellows occasionally invited the Assembly fellows to attend these presentations.[24]

Both fellows and senators responded positively to the fellowship experience. Josh Pane, a 1980-1981 fellow, observed, "It was a great experience that I will not ever forget. It taught me that if you work hard and serve the people, you too will succeed!" He has used the experience gained as a fellow in all aspects of his current business.[25]

Anne Seymour concluded:

> It was a really good jump start on my entire career because I was just finishing graduate school. . . . At that point in your life, you really don't know what you want to do. . . . What the fellowship program gave me was a framework for my future. I strongly believe that I've ended up twenty years as a national victim advocate able to apply public administration, public policy development [and] outreach to constituents [because of] the fellowship program. It did give me a sense of direction. It gave me a feeling of real confidence in terms of what I could do, not just working in a legislature but in my life. It was a life-altering experience.[26]

For many participants, the Senate Fellowship Program opened the door to a career in the Legislature. After her fellowship, Seymour worked for the Assembly speaker's Office of Majority Services. Michelle Mercer remained as a staff member in the office of Senator Barry Keene. Other fellows who continued to work in the Legislature include: Jose Hermocillo, 1976–1977 (associate consultant with the Committee on Industrial Relations); Rob Feraru, 1978–1979 (senior consultant to Senator John Garamendi); Ann Gressani, 1978–1979 (assistant consultant for the Senate Energy and Public Utilities Committee) and Karen Lowrey, 1981–1982 (consultant for the Senate Education Committee).

Not all aspects of the Senate fellowship experience were positive. Sexual harassment was a problem for at least one fellow. Another fellow complained that "sometimes for weeks upon end, I was sitting at a desk in a closet of a cramped office and doing nothing but writing the same constituent letter over and over again." A third fellow was the subject of a newspaper column that reflected unfavorably on his senator. For one fellow, the worst aspect of her experience was that it ended![27]

Senators and their staff often praised the fellows who worked in their offices. Omer Rains, chair of the Senate Majority Caucus, "continue[d] to be impressed with the caliber of fellows chosen each year. . . ." John Nejedly, chair of the Committee on Natural Resources and Wildlife, stated, "I have found the services of a

---

[24] Zane Johnston, "Capital Fellows Alumni Questionnaire," 2003, FCFP; Anne Seymour, "History of the Capital Fellows Program," *Oral History Interview*, conducted in 2003 by Elizabeth Austin, SCUA, 4-5; "1982/83 Speakers, Senate Fellowship Program," [1982], SRCP.

[25] Joshua Pane, "Capital Fellows Alumni Questionnaire," 2003, FCFP.

[26] Seymour, *Oral History Interview*, 13-14.

[27] Various responses to "Capital Fellows Alumni Questionnaire," 2003, FCFP.

Senate Fellow to be indispensable." Jack Watson, staff director for Senator Alfred Alquist, noted that a 1981–1982 fellow "has been of exceptional value to the Senate Finance Committee, and provided significant contributions to the budget process. . . [He was] a valuable and effective addition to the Committee."[28]

Some senators and staff did, however, voice complaints about the selection process. Senator Diane Watson noted that "the legislative Black Caucus has been concerned over a period of years with the small number of minority candidates and especially Black candidates for the Senate Fellowship Program. One only has to look in the Senate offices to see that our concern is justified." Watson requested that a member of her staff be added to the fellowship selection panel because she "believe[d] this committee should represent a cross-section of the Senate, thus allowing for a more diverse group of Fellows to be selected." Although Watson later retracted this request, it illustrated the difficulty of attracting and selecting a diverse group of fellows.

Jim Lott, staff director for the Committee on Health and Human Services, resigned from the fellowship selection panel because a candidate was added to the list of semifinalists by the Senate Rules Committee after the initial 200 applications had been reviewed, scored, and ranked. He wrote, "I do not appreciate your wasting my time by having me seriously evaluate a multitude of applications only then to have you abridge this selection process 'at will.'"[29]

Nevertheless, the fellowship program had proved its value to the Senate. Although not as popular as the Assembly Fellowship Program, the Senate program usually attracted about 200 applications a year. Both the selection process and the speaker programs had improved. With the number of senators and committees requesting fellows ranging from sixteen to twenty-one, there were always more requests than fellows. By 1984, the Senate Fellowship Program appeared to have become a permanent fixture in the legislature.

---

[28] Omer Rains to Derek Pogson, Sacramento, 31 May 1979, SRCP; John Nejedly to Derek Pogson, Sacramento, 29 May 1979, SRCP; Jack Watson to Janet Reiser, Sacramento, 29 July 1982, SRCP.

[29] Senator Diane E. Watson to Janet Reiser, Director, Senate Fellowship Program, memorandum, 18 February 1983, SRCP; Jim Lott to Cliff Berg, 12 April 1984, SRCP.

Saved by the University

The relations between "Sac State" and our state government have been strengthened and deepened in recent months by our agreement to house and administer the Senate Fellow Program and the opportunity accorded us to locate the headquarters of the Assembly Fellow Program on campus as well.

—Donald Gerth
President, California State University, Sacramento, 1985

We advance to our future, grateful for the opportunity to serve as policy fellows and cognizant of the contribution which the California State University, Sacramento makes toward the development of state leadership and governmental affairs.

—Assembly Fellows, Class of 1986–1987

Proposition 24

The voters of California passed Proposition 24 on June 5, 1984. Along with other provisions relating to the conduct of legislative business, it required a 30% reduction in the legislative budget.[1] Ten days later, Cliff Berg, the executive

---

[1] Proposition 24, also known as the Legislative Reform Act of 1983 or the Gann Legislative Reform Initiative, was approved by 53.1% of the voters. It reduced the Legislature's support appropriations by 30% and limited future support appropriations. Among other provisions, Proposition 24 regulated the appointments of the Speaker of the Assembly and the president pro tempore of the Senate; and regulated the appointment and powers of the standing, select, joint and interim committees of the legislature. In May 1986, the provisions of Proposition 24 regulating the legislature's internal rules, its selection of officers and employees, and the selection and powers of its committees were declared

officer of the Senate Rules Committee, wrote to the members of the Senate fellow's selection panel, "Due to the budget cuts currently being implemented as a result of Proposition 24, the Rules Committee has terminated the 1984–85 Senate Fellowship Program." He expressed his hope that the program would be restored for 1985–86. Funding for the Assembly Fellowship Program continued but the fellows' monthly stipends were reduced from $1,250 to $950.[2]

California State University, Sacramento, to the Rescue

After the official termination of the Senate Fellowship Program, the 1984–1985 Senate fellows experienced several months of uncertainty as the Senate struggled to find a way to keep the program alive. Lynn Vacca commented, "When you think you have the job [as a fellow], then you don't have it, then you do, then you don't—you begin to feel like a ping pong ball."[3] While the fellows waited to learn their fate, the Senate explored the possibility of funding the program through a partnership with California State University, Sacramento.

In early July 1984, the newly arrived president of Sacramento State, Donald Gerth, received a telephone call from Senator Robert Beverly (R-Los Angeles*).* During his tenure as president of California State University, Dominguez Hills, from 1976 until he began his presidency at Sacramento State, Gerth became well acquainted with Senator Beverly whose district included Dominguez Hills. Gerth described their telephone conversation:

> [Beverly] called me and his question was, "In view of the fact that one of these Jarvis-Gann initiatives had passed"—it was Paul Gann actually—"that cut dramatically the size of the legislative budget, would Sac State be willing, would I be willing to take on the Senate Fellows Program?" He had no money. That's why they were willing to give it away. They had no money to run it. I said to him, "I sure would like to. I need to explore it with the chancellor then I'd get back to him within a day."

Gerth consulted with Chancellor Ann Reynolds about this "fortuitous and wonderful circumstance." After receiving her approval of the project, Gerth

---

unconstitutional. The provisions limiting the legislature's budget were also declared unconstitutional. 181 Cal.App.3d 316.

[2] Cliff Berg to members of the Senate Fellowship Program selection panel, 15 June 1984, SRCP; Claire Cooper, "Impending Gann Layoffs Jolt Senate Workers," *Sacramento Bee*, 24 June 1984, sec. A; Thomas R. Hoeber and Charles M. Price, eds. *California Government and Politics Annual, 85/86* (Sacramento, Calif.: California Journal Press, 1985): 53.

[3] Laura Mecoy, "CSUS Comes to the Rescue of Senate Fellowship Program," *Sacramento Bee*, 17 November 1984, sec. A.

"called Bob Beverly back and said, 'You're on.'" [4] One of Gerth's primary goals as president of Sacramento State was the improvement of the university's connection with state government. The Senate Fellowship Program had the potential to be a significant link in that connection.

Legislative internship programs were not new to Sacramento State. Since 1976, the Government Department had offered an internship program with the Legislature for upper-division undergraduate students from all CSU campuses through the Sacramento Semester Program. Like Professor Joseph Harris and the UC Berkeley Department of Political Science in the 1950s, the faculty members of the Sacramento State Government Department were eager to add the Senate Fellowship Program to its internship offerings. "It has always been our belief that a political science education is greatly enhanced by a practical hands-on component, and it has been our feeling also that the practical experience is made far more meaningful if integrated with seminars and workshops designed to enhance the internship itself. If we offer to take on the Senate Fellow Program, we would do so with the understanding that it would become a comprehensive educational experience."[5]

After several months of negotiations, Sacramento State and the Senate Rules Committee agreed to joint sponsorship of the Senate Fellowship Program. The purpose of their agreement, signed on November 1, 1984, was "to enhance the educational opportunity presently provided by the State Senate Fellowship. It is further understood that the annual stipend awarded to the Fellows is a scholarship designed to enable qualified students, regardless of their economic resources, to participate in a unique educational experience jointly offered by the University and the State Senate."

The university agreed to provide graduate level instruction to the Senate fellows by a qualified faculty member, and to utilize fellows as teaching assistants, resource specialists, or docents as appropriate in the university's instructional or community service programs. The Senate Rules Committee agreed to provide the fellows with appropriate staff assignments and to be responsible for disbursing the fellows' stipends.

---

[4] Donald Gerth, "History of the Capital Fellows Programs," *Oral History Interview*, conducted in 2002 by Elizabeth Austin, SCUA, 5-7. According to Nettie Sabelhaus, a member of President pro Tem David Roberti's staff who was the Senate director of the fellowship program beginning in 1985, Tom Burns had the original idea for transferring the Senate Fellowship Program to Sacramento State. At the time of the transfer, Burns was the deputy executive officer for the Senate Rules Committee and a strong supporter of educational programs. It is probable that Senator Beverly was approached to contact President Gerth because of the relationship they had established at CSU Dominguez Hills. Senator Beverly had also just had a fellow in his office in 1983-1984. Efforts to contact Tom Burns to confirm his role in the transfer were unsuccessful.

[5] Elizabeth F. Moulds and John C. Syer, Department of Government, to Donald R. Gerth, President, memorandum, 28 September 1984, PPO.

The agreement required the fellows to enroll as graduate students at Sacramento State and to complete coursework that included an integrative graduate seminar focused on Senate staff experiences, a graduate internship course, and a special studies seminar tailored to each fellow's staff experience. Sacramento State funded the stipends and the academic program administration costs of $98,560 in 1984–1985.

Although the term of the agreement was one year, Sacramento State and the Senate Rules Committee agreed to a letter of intent to operate the program for an additional two years provided that new funding was included in the Sacramento State budget.[6]

The speed with which Sacramento State reached an agreement with the Rules Committee permitted the Senate Fellowship Program to continue with eight fellows in 1984–1985. It preempted an offer from the University of California in October 1984 to assume administrative and academic responsibility for the fellowship program through a cooperative effort among the UC Davis Extension Program, the systemwide California Policy Seminar, and the Senate Rules Committee. The UC proposal suggested that its involvement was appropriate because the original legislative fellowship program in the Assembly had been administered by UC Berkeley.

As Sacramento State President Gerth noted, however, when he forwarded a copy of this proposal to the CSU Provost and Vice Chancellor William Vandament, "The Program has been settled with California State University, Sacramento administering it."[7]

Meanwhile, the Assembly continued to support its fellowship program. The $300 stipend reduction for Assembly fellows that had been announced after the passage of Proposition 24 was eliminated in January 1985. Nevertheless, the Assembly Rules Committee eventually decided to follow the Senate's example of seeking a partnership with Sacramento State. President Gerth recalled:

> About six or seven months later [after Senator Robert Beverly contacted Gerth on behalf of the Senate Fellowship Program], one of Willie Brown's staff members [Michael Galizio] called and said the Assembly fellows were jealous because the Senate fellows had, as an option, not a requirement, that they could take courses and get graduate university credit for the courses and the Assembly fellows could

---

[6] To take advantage of the unexpected opportunity of sponsoring the Senate Fellowship Program, Sacramento State drew on campus instructional supplies and services reserves to fund the stipends and administrative costs. California. Senate. Rules Committee and California State University, Sacramento, "Interagency Agreement," 1 November 1984; Mernoy Harrison to Cliff Berg, Sacramento, 22 January 1985, PPO; Robert O. Bess to D. Dale Hanner, 18 January 1985, PPO.

[7] William B. Baker, Vice President to David Roberti, President pro tem and Chair, Rules Committee, Berkeley, 4 October 1984, PPO; Donald R. Gerth to William Vandament, Sacramento, 29 October 1984, PPO.

not. Would we be willing to take on the Assembly program? And he offered money. So I said, "Sure."

Instead of a burden, the academic component had apparently become so attractive that it motivated the Assembly to establish its own relationship with Sacramento State. The agreement for the year beginning August 1, 1985 and ending July 31, 1986 that formalized the relationship between Sacramento State and the Assembly Fellowship Program did not, however, include any references to an academic program. It merely specified the fellowship program expenses that would be funded through Sacramento State. Budget constraints may actually have been the most significant consideration in the Assembly Rules Committee's decision to work with Sacramento State.[8]

Sacramento State and the Center for California Studies

At Sacramento State, the Government Department's Center for California Studies took over the administration of the fellowship programs. Established in 1983, the Center was the brain child of Elizabeth Moulds, Government Department chair, and John Syer, a professor in the Government Department. The center had four major objectives: help prepare potential public servants by facilitating student internships in state government, foster civic education, conduct workshops and training sessions for state employees, and encourage the exchange of issue area expertise between policymakers and the faculty of Sacramento State.

With the addition of the fellowship programs, the center moved from "baby steps to big giant steps" in its progress towards achieving the first objective. In recognition of the center's expansion far beyond its origins in a few Government Department filing cabinets, the Sacramento State administration allocated 1.4 faculty positions to the center along with office and clerical support in 1985–1986. Bernard Shanks became the first full-time director of the center in September 1986. The growing importance of the center was evident in its relocation from the Government Department to Academic Affairs under the Dean of Graduate Studies in July 1988.[9]

The fellowship programs posed immediate challenges for the fledgling Center for California Studies. While the Senate and the Assembly were primarily interested in financial support from the university for programs that were important for

---

[8] Gerth, *Oral History Interview*, 7; Charles G. Bell, Chair to Assembly Fellowship Executive Board, memorandum, 9 July 1985, ARCP; California. Assembly. Rules Committee and California State University, Sacramento, "Interagency Agreement," 1 August 1985, ARCP.

[9] Donald R. Gerth to Tom Burns, Sacramento, 4 April 1985, PPO; Elizabeth Moulds, "History of the Capital Fellows Programs," *Oral History Interview*, conducted in 2002 by Elizabeth Austin, SCUA, 1-3; Donald R. Gerth to Bernard Shanks, Director, Center for California Studies, memorandum, 19 April 1988, PPO.

both current and future legislative staffing needs, Sacramento State and the center were focused on establishing a foothold as the "Capital Campus."

A successful academic component was crucial to the university's involvement with the Legislature's fellowship programs. Except for the early UC Davis internships, the Senate Fellowship Program had never been associated with an academic institution. The Assembly Fellowship Program had originally been closely affiliated with the University of California, Berkeley, and four other academic institutions, but its academic connections were now limited to the faculty members serving on the executive board. The new association with Sacramento State and the center resurrected the problem of balancing the fellows' two roles as legislative staff and graduate students.

Although both the Senate and the Assembly signed agreements with Sacramento State for the administration of the fellowship programs, the ground rules for the implementation of each partnership remained to be established. The Legislature and the university had to determine how they would share their responsibilities for program funding, fellow selection and placement, and the establishment of a viable academic component. There was an adjustment period for all of the new partners.

Funding

After Sacramento State provided the funding necessary to keep the Senate program alive in 1984–1985, both the Senate and the Assembly programs were financed through a special line item in the state budget for the Center for California Studies. Unfortunately, the amount included in the state budget was often inadequate and the difference was subsidized by Sacramento State. Bern Shanks noted in the center's 1986–1987 annual report that "the most persistent problem with the Fellows program is budgetary. The three programs [an Executive Fellowship Program was added in 1986, see chapter 6] do not receive an adequate appropriation to match their operating costs. Difficulties concerning the administration of contract details continues [sic] to interfere with the normal function of the Fellows programs."[10]

A 1987 Budget Change Proposal for the center noted that "the budget has not been increased to cover increases in stipends and benefits paid to fellows, the increase in the number of fellows, or the increase in administrative support costs associated with operating the Fellows Programs. As a result the Center has been underfunded since 1986/87. Program costs are increasing again in 1988/89 which will increase the amount of underfunding. The amount of underfunding related to

---

[10] Bern Shanks to Bob Bess, memorandum, 22 July 1987, PPO; Nancy Shulock to Louis V. Messner, 11 September 1987; and Memoy Harrison to Bern Shanks, memorandum, 30 November 1987, PPO; Center for California Studies, *Annual Report, Center for California Studies, September 1986-June 1987* (Sacramento: The Center, 1987), [1-2].

the Fellows Programs in the budget year is projected to be $267,185." The number of fellows had increased to twelve in each program and the stipends had been raised to $1,500 plus benefits and university fees but there had been no corresponding increase in the budget.[11]

During the late 1980s, Sacramento State and the center were often involved in fellowship program budget negotiations with the Senate and the Assembly Rules Committees. For example, Shanks recounted a 1988–1989 budget discussion in a memo to President Gerth:

> Today I initiated the first discussions with Nettie Sablehaus [sic] of the Senate Rules Committee staff on the Senate Fellows contract for the 1988–1989.
>
> As you are aware that portion of the contract used for administration of the Senate and Assembly programs was eliminated from the 1988–89 Governor's budget. . . .
>
> Once again the Senate, through Nettie Sablehaus [sic], is expecting assistance from CSUS in meeting their administrative costs. Once again I told Nettie the extra money was not in the Center's budget. I explained that CSUS had been very generous in assisting the Fellows program but this was a very tight budget year and any additional resources would be very difficult to find. . . .
>
> It is my belief that additional CSUS financial support for the Senate (and Assembly) Fellows, above what is budgeted, will only create still more problems for the Center and these programs.

Cliff Berg, executive officer of the Senate Rules Committee, later suggested that the Senate would be willing to fund $14,000 of the administrative costs by reducing the length of the Senate Fellowship Program from eleven to ten months if Sacramento State would fund the remaining $30,000. Although characterized by the Sacramento State Vice President of University Affairs as a "problem [that] seems to resist our best efforts at finding a solution that meets everyone's expectations," the budget problem was resolved by reducing the Senate program from eleven to ten months and by increasing the Sacramento State contribution by $14,728 beyond what was included in the governor's budget for stipends and benefits.[12]

Assembly concerns with fellowship program funding also emerged during budget discussions for 1988–1989. After talking with Bob Connelly, the Assembly Rules Committee chief administrative officer, Elizabeth Moulds reported, "He said that their frank feeling in looking at the budget was that we were using the Fellows Programs to try to get the California Center on the ground. He [commented that they were considering] whether they ought to bring the program 'back downtown.' . . . He will probably leave the program with us, but he needs a little

---

[11] Shulock to Messner, 11 September 1987, PPO.

[12] Bern Shanks to Don Gerth, memorandum, 19 July 1988, PPO; Cliff Berg to Donald Gerth, 3 August 1988, PPO; Robert G. Jones to Donald R. Gerth, memorandum, 5 August 1988, PPO; Nancy Shulock to Donald Gerth, memorandum, 7 November 1988, PPO.

convincing." Connelly apparently wanted the Sacramento State budget to cover more of the administrative costs incurred by the Assembly Rules Committee for the fellowship program.[13]

By 1990, the center was making progress towards securing adequate funding for the fellowship programs. Shanks reported that a balanced budget for the center and its programs was achieved in fiscal year 1988–1989. Jeff Lustig, who became acting director of the center after Shanks resigned in May 1989, noted in the Center for California Studies' 1989–1990 annual report, "Over the course of the year, the Center developed a comprehensive new financial system (including new budgets and bookkeeping systems), secured the proper level of categorical allocations from the State Department of Finance, and supplemented the Center's categorical funding through CSUS. . . . We spent quite a few months working with the State Dept. of Finance, CSUS Academic Affairs, and the CSU Chancellor's Office to ensure that the proper level of Center funding was included in the Governor's 1990–1991 budget." The budget now supported eighteen Senate and Assembly fellows earning monthly stipends of $1,560.[14]

Selection and Placement

Senate

The initial agreement with the Senate stipulated that fellows would be selected by "a recruitment and screening process jointly established by University and [Rules] Committee staff." The recruitment and selection process was directed by a Senate Rules Committee staff member who was also responsible for placing the fellows with Senate offices and committees. The ten-member Senate selection panel included three representatives from Sacramento State for the first two years. Subsequently, Sacramento State appears to have had only one selection panel member.

Nettie Sabelhaus, the Senate Rules Committee staff member in charge of the fellows program, said she wanted a selection panel that would represent the diversity of the Senate. She wanted to include both Democrats and Republicans, fellowship program veterans and newcomers

"We tried (to have) the panel represent a diversity of situations as well in terms of gender, politics, geography, and ethnicity," she said.

---

[13] Betty [Moulds] to Don [Gerth], Sacramento, [1988?], PPO.

[14] Bernard Shanks, Director to Don Gerth, President and Art Williamson, Dean of Graduate Studies, memorandum, [23 January 1989], PPO; Donald R. Gerth to Capitol Colleagues, memorandum, 31 May 1989, PPO; Center for California Studies, *Annual Report, 1989-1990* (Sacramento: The Center, 1990), 12.

The panel members reviewed all of the applications and selected the candidates that they would interview personally. The interviews were scheduled for two days each in northern and southern California.[15]

Sabelhaus said the panel wanted to select a diverse group. So academic success, advanced degrees, or specialized credentials didn't necessary guarantee acceptance, she said.

"You cannot make a group of 18 of those kinds of people. That's a recipe for disaster," she said. "I was always looking for a few people that I regarded as good, renaissance individuals who might be interested in a variety of topics and therefore willing to work on this or that and not just a specific issue."

A successful candidate had to have excellent writing skills. "One of the real deciders of success was someone who could write well," she said. A compelling story was not compelling enough to get past those (writing) issues. You had, at rock bottom, to be able to write succinctly and accurately. Communication skills were really critical."

Sabelhaus said good grades and a work ethic were helpful. One candidate, she said, had unspectacular grades but had launched a successful credit union on his campus. "We appreciated that he showed in other ways that he had the ability to function as someone who'd also benefit from the educational part (of the fellowship)," she said. People who valued diversity, and who were open to the viewpoints of others, were also considered desirable.[16]

Although the selection panel did strive to increase the number of Republicans in the fellowship program, they had limited success. Another issue affecting selection was the question of whether the fellows were alumni of private or public academic institutions. With the involvement of Sacramento State, the selection panel usually accepted at least one (and usually no more) fellow from the state university system. The need to increase ethnic diversity persisted. In 1986, Senator Nicholas Petris wrote:

> As the application deadline for the 1987 Senate Fellowship Program fast approaches, I again, as I have in the past, urge you to take aggressive steps to increase the number of ethnic minorities in the program.
>
> I'm sure you agree that the fellowship program provides one of the few possibilities for energetic and talented minorities to pursue policy making positions in the State Legislature.
>
> Last year I was dismayed to learn that only three of the twelve Senate Fellows selected to this year's program are ethnic minorities. With the combination of Black, Hispanic and Asian ethnic minority groups fast becoming the majority in California, it's clear that the representation on the current fellowship program is not reflective of the State's population. . . .

---

[15] Nettie Sabelhaus, "History of the Capital Fellows Programs," *Oral History Interview,* conducted in 2002 by Elizabeth Austin, SCUA, 23. Selection panel members are included in Appendix 7.3.

[16] Sabelhaus, *Oral History Interview,* 18-24.

In summary, I am formally requesting this year's selection panel set a goal to select more fellows representing ethnic minority groups.

In response to the criticisms of too few Republicans and minorities, Sabelhaus focused on improving recruitment outreach. Her efforts were rewarded with a 68% increase in applications in 1987.[17]

John Syer, the Sacramento State Government Department professor responsible for the academic component of the fellowship program and the academic representative on the selection panel, described the dynamics of the selection panel as they chose the fellows:

We got to know each other [on the panel]. There was a little turnover. Say we had nine people or so, usually six or seven had worked together before. Some years, we almost had consensus. We would walk out of there after the meeting in Los Angeles or meeting in Sacramento, and we would just look at each other and we knew each other well enough that the [fellowship] class would just be there.

There were other years that were very, very difficult. Very painful, very tense. People were irritable, angry with one another. We felt like we hadn't made the class we wanted to make. No two years were the same.

Oftentimes, somebody really did a great job on the interview. People would just write in the margins on their script, "Keeper," or "Number One." We would look across the table at each other and thumbs up. That was good. Others were marginal and had to be talked about. Others were clearly substandard. In a given class, if it were easy, we had consensus about fifteen or sixteen people [out of eighteen]. There was just consensus. In a hard year, we might only agree about half a dozen and we'd have to argue about twelve of them. That was a much more difficult year.

Ultimately, Syer acknowledged, Sabelhaus had the most influential vote on the selection panel.[18]

Both Syer and Sabelhaus believed that the selection process was merit-based. Syer concluded that politics played a very minor role.

There was one time a person went upstairs [to Senator Nicholas Petris] after interviewing with us downstairs in the Capitol, and we got word from Petris' office that we were picking this person. That was clear political tampering. And it turned out he was a terrible fellow. . . . No senators requested him, not one. And Roberti, pro Tem at the time, took him on as a favor to Nettie [Sabelhaus] because Nettie went in and said, "I have this fellow that nobody wants." That stood

---

[17] Minutes of the Center for California Studies Fall Retreat, 21 October 1988, PPO; John Syer, "History of the Capital Fellows Programs," *Oral History Interview*, conducted in 2002 by Elizabeth Austin, SCUA, 25-27; Nicholas C. Petris to David Roberti, Sacramento, 7 February 1986, SRCP; Nettie Sabelhaus to Cliff Berg, memorandum, 20 April 1987, SRCP.

[18] Syer, *Oral History Interview*, 21-22.

as an example thereafter every time somebody tried to pressure us to take [a fellow]. . . . That's the one exception that proves the rule. It did happen to us but after that, we all said, "Now, wait a minute, we're not taking people that we cannot place."

As Sabelhaus noted, "We tried to be sensitive to recommendations of members but we also believed that we were a merit-based program. You can find legions of people who came into this program with no [connections]. They didn't know anybody." The Senate Fellowship Program offered an avenue of access to the political process that was not predicated on prior political connections.[19]

In contrast to the selection process, the placement process was often intensely political. The fellows interviewed with the offices of ten or twelve senators. Both the fellows and the senators listed their top three placement choices. Sabelhaus assigned placements based on these ranked lists. Sabelhaus said members had to demonstrate that they had room for a fellow. They had to have a desk, terminal, telephone, and mentor for the fellow. "And you had to be able to commit to interviewing anyone who wanted to come your way. You couldn't just say, 'Well, I've looked at the list and here are the two people that I want to interview because they appear to be the most conservative (or) the most liberal.' We didn't allow that."

Sabelhaus said the panel encouraged interviews across party lines and urged selections that may not have conformed to someone's specific desires. The fellows were pleasantly surprised when that happened, she said. "We always said to them, 'This interview process will not be what you think. It won't go the way you thought because there is so much more to learn than you have time to learn in the brief period that you've been here.'"[20]

To determine the final placements, Sabelhaus had to balance the desires of the fellows and the needs of the members of the Senate. It was not always an easy task. Both the senators and the fellows were competitive with each other.

> Members who didn't get a fellow would be very upset. My staff's invested all this time, why didn't I get somebody? That's a hard message to deliver. It was because we had the very strong support of leadership here that we were able to survive in this kind of world. . . . Whenever you have only twelve of them or fifteen of them and twenty-six members who want [fellows], that makes a lot of grumpy people.[21]

One senator cornered Sabelhaus on the Senate floor and demanded, "How dare you not give me a fellow?"[22]

Occasionally, fellows would threaten to leave the program if they were given a particular senator. For one fellow who had been highly rated by many Senate

---

[19] Ibid., 16-18; Sabelhaus, *Oral History Interview*, 24.

[20] Sabelhaus, *Oral History Interview*, 7.

[21] Ibid., 15-16.

[22] Syer, *Oral History Interview*, 21.

offices, politics dictated that she did not receive any of her top three choices. Syer observed that placement was "just political to the nth degree." Sabelhaus "was always having to adjust for [the fellows] and help them know that there is no bad placement. . . ." Once fellows were placed, their assignments rarely had to be changed. The matching process, if difficult, was usually successful.[23]

Donna Hoenig-Couch, a 1989–1990 fellow, was surprised to receive a placement with the Budget and Fiscal Review Committee. Sabelhaus convinced her that she would benefit from the assignment and "as it turned out, it was an incredible, incredible placement." Still, Hoenig-Couch remembered:

It wasn't easy. It was an all-male committee for starters. We had staff meetings once a week which [Senator Alquist, the chair of the committee] would preface with, "Gentlemen." I would have to raise my hand.

The beginning was a little tough because it was a committee where you had to prove yourself first and ask for things. They weren't just going to hand you assignments. No one knew where I would go. I wound up working on the Subcommittee on Health and Human Services which really turned out to be a very good fit for my interests.

I had to seek out any help I ever got. I used to call it the cowboy committee because it was like that. I would say that, in contrast to some of my classmates, it was not a nurturing fellowship but having come in and created my own work, I did gain respect very quickly. They treated me as another staffer which I know now was really a compliment though at the time it was really hard.

Donna Hoenig-Couch remained with the Budget Committee for a year after the end of the fellowship.[24]

The placements described by these four Senate fellows are characteristic of the fellowship program assignments:

I was placed with Senator Art Torres and I was interested in working on education issues. He served on the Senate Education Committee. My work consisted mainly of working on a bill to legalize private educational clinics in the public schools, writing letters of recommendation and writing speeches. I worked mainly with [Torres's] chief legislative aide

Linda Tochterman, 1984–1985

I was placed with Senator Diane Watson who chaired Health and Human Services. I worked on bills she sponsored and bills in her committee. I learned so much about the legislative process, policy, [and] California politics.

Ruth Liberman, 1985–1986

---

[23] Ibid., 18-21; Sabelhaus, *Oral History Interview*, 10-12.

[24] Donna Hoenig-Couch, "History of the Capital Fellows Programs," *Oral History Interview*, conducted in 2002 by Elizabeth Austin, SCUA, 9-12.

I was placed in the Senate Local Government Committee's office to replace one of the consultants who was going on maternity leave. I was able to analyze and write reports on about 150 bills that session. Mr. [Peter] Detwiler was an excellent mentor and friend—the things he taught me about writing concisely were invaluable and remain with me now. [I also worked] on a Brown Act reform bill with Senator Kopp and then-Assemblymember Burton.

Dave Kiff, 1988–1989

I worked for Senator Rebecca Mangan (R-Los Altos Hills). She was a smart, principled lawmaker, and I respected her a great deal. I staffed half a dozen bills and I especially recall working with Senator Mangan and Assemblyman Isenberg on a child custody bill. It was a great hands-on experience. The best part of the year was getting to participate in the legislative process and meeting many great people connected with California state government.

Ken Miller, 1988–1989

Placement experiences in the Senate Fellowship Program appear to have been little changed by the new affiliation with Sacramento State.[25]

Assembly

In the Assembly, the recruitment and selection of fellows remained the responsibility of the executive board and a Rules Committee staff member who coordinated the program. Appointed by the Assembly Rules Committee, the executive board included ten members from the Assembly and ten members from academic institutions. Many of the academic members were from UC and several of them had been associated with the fellowship program since its inception as the California Legislative Internship Program in 1957. A representative from Sacramento State, Joe Serna, joined the board in 1987. The executive board chair was selected from the academic members of the board. The Rules Committee also appointed the program coordinator responsible for the day-to-day tasks of administering the fellowship program.[26]

Recruitment of a diverse group of applicants for the Assembly Fellowship Program was an ongoing issue for the executive board and the program coordinator. Both the board members and the coordinator made a strong effort to increase the number of ethnic minorities, the number of academic institutions represented, and the areas of subject expertise within a fellowship class. Among the steps taken to diversify the applicant pool were alerting ethnic studies programs to the existence of the fellowship program, requesting minority legislators to serve as pro-

---

[25] Linda Tochterman, Ruth Liberman, Dave Kiff and Ken Miller, "Capital Fellows Alumni Questionnaires," 2003, FCFP.

[26] Members of the executive board are listed in Appendix 3.3. The Assembly Rules Committee staff members responsible for directing the fellowship program are included in Appendix 3.4.

gram recruiters, using former fellows as spokespersons, and identifying key individuals at as many colleges and universities as possible to act as liaisons with the fellowship program.

Those efforts showed results: an over twofold increase in the number of minority applications from seventeen to thirty-nine between 1985–1986 and 1987–1988. The total number of applications doubled during this period.[27]

The process of choosing the twelve or eighteen fellows from the growing applicant pool did not change after the fellowship program was transferred to Sacramento State. The executive board screened the initial group of paper applications and selected approximately thirty or forty candidates that were invited for personal interviews.

Cristy Jensen, the first Assembly Fellowship Program faculty advisor from Sacramento State, also participated in the selection process, which she described as "wild and crazy." She remembered feeling that the process was strongly influenced by UC, which continued to host the interviews at the UC Berkeley Faculty Club for several years. For Jensen, the most memorable aspect of selecting the Assembly fellows was the decision making process. "That was my introduction to the real world of heavy duty politics. First, the academics and the legislative staff people that were involved had two different definitions of who were good candidates. We were looking for different traits," she said.

The selection process often featured a tension between the academic and political members of the panels, she said, and that often resulted in selection rules being changed or abandoned along the way. "The academics always got outwitted by the politicals. This is what they do. . . . It's what they do every day. It's just we don't do that," she said.[28]

A memo to Elizabeth Moulds from Charles Bell, a longtime member of the executive board, confirmed Cristy Jensen's impressions of the selection process:

> Unwritten rules govern the Program. Close interpersonal relations between Board members keeps [sic] the program sensitive to the Assembly's needs and academic criteria for selection of Fellows. Most of us have served the program off-and-on

---

[27] Charles Bell to Sam Walton, "1986-1987 Fellowship Recruitment Schedule," memorandum, 13 August 1985, ARCP; "Demographic Survey of 1985-1986 Assembly Fellowship Applications," [1985?], ARCP, [7]; Spitz, *Oral History Interview*, 23-25; Lilly Spitz , Coordinator, Assembly Fellowship to Speaker Willie Lewis Brown, Jr., memorandum, 11 March 1986, ARCP; Lilly Spitz to Assembly Fellowship Board, memorandum, 12 June 1987, ARCP; "Proposed Recruitment Plan for Jesse Marvin Unruh Assembly Fellowship Program 1987-88 (for 1988-1989 Class)," [1988?], PPO; "Applicant's [sic] Profile, 1987-1988, [Assembly Fellowship Program]," [1987], ARCP, [1].

[28] Cristy Jensen, "History of the Capital Fellows Programs," *Oral History Interview*, conducted in 2002 by Elizabeth Austin, SCUA, 25-28.

for years so there is a substantial "institutional memory." Murphy's corollary applies here: "Since it works, don't mess with it."[29]

Lilly Spitz, the Assembly Fellowship Program coordinator in 1986 and 1987, remembered the political nature of the selection process and the different approaches used by Assembly staff and academics:

> The political staff had an agenda that was very political in terms of where people were from, issues of background, academic background, cultural background, diversity, campaign experience, etc., etc. Those were all major elements of their process of selection.
>
> The academics were completely different. Theirs was the evidence of critical thinking, the background, familiarity with the issues of the day, articulateness of course, and other academic kinds of criteria.
>
> Then the process of elimination and how that all worked. A candidate who really scored high for this one person, that person had to advocate for them and say why they would be a really good fellow. There was a lot of vote advocacy.[30]

Once past the paper screening, the selection process reflected the political and academic backgrounds of the board members. With a maximum of only one member on the executive board and longstanding traditions in place, Sacramento State had little impact on the final selection of fellows.

Sacramento State had no involvement with the fellows' placements, which were determined by the Assembly coordinator in consultation with the Rules Committee after the fellows interviewed with members and committees. Like the Senate, the Assembly placement process was often very political. One member, for example, never received a fellow because of problems with Lou Papan, chair of the Assembly Rules Committee. He was "aced out of a Fellow consistently."[31]

When the Gang of Five challenged the speakership of Willie Brown during the 1987–1988 legislative session, controversy erupted over whether any members of the Gang would receive a fellow.[32]

Once the preferences expressed by both the members and the fellows were considered, placement priority was usually given to members who had not previously had a fellow. Although fellows were supposed to change their placements at the midpoint of their fellowships, assemblymembers often requested and were granted permission to retain fellows in their original placements.

---

[29] Charles Bell to Betty Moulds, memorandum, 13 May 1985, ARCP, 3.

[30] Spitz, *Oral History Interview*, 22.

[31] "Assembly Fellows—Placements February 1987," [1987], ARCP, 2; "Assembly Fellows—Assignments," [1987], ARCP.

[32] Jensen, *Oral History Interview*, 12-13. The Gang of Five was a group of moderate and conservative Democrats who opposed the speakership of Willie Brown during the 1987-1988 legislative session. The five members were Rusty Areias, Charles M.Calderon, Gary Condit, Gerald R. Eaves and Steve Peace.

Occasionally, fellows were disgruntled with their placements. As program coordinator, Lilly Spitz intervened when problems arose. She remembered:

> There were some feathers ruffled a few times. Perhaps some of the fellows weren't being treated the way they thought they ought to be treated. They weren't given plum assignments, weren't yet being trusted to do major work for the member. My role was to try to be a liaison between the fellows and the members to try to keep everybody happy.
>
> [The fellows] did not walk in the door as competent staffers. Yet that was their vision of themselves. So they had to prove themselves. A lot of them didn't know what it took to prove themselves to be loyal, competent, really go above and beyond what's required of them to demonstrate that they're worth getting plum assignments from the office. How to work with other people, even those that oppose your boss's position, is something you have to learn to do. Some of the people didn't recognize that was a skill they needed to hone.[33]

Most fellows were placed successfully. Positive experiences included Carrie Cornwell's work for two members of the Assembly, Tom Hannigan and Art Agnos.

> When I started with Mr. Hannigan, he was chair of the Assembly Revenue and Taxation Committee, which was one of the reasons I wanted to be placed in his office. Shortly after [the legislative] session adjourned, I wrote, under [the] direction of Dave Doerr, Chief Consultant to the Committee, the end-of-the-year report on the reform of the state's unitary tax that had been enacted in 1986. It was published as an official Assembly publication, and I was thrilled.
>
> In January of 1987, as was the custom then, I was moved to a second placement, Assemblyman Art Agnos's office, where I worked seven days a week: four on legislation, Fridays in the District Office, and Saturday and Sunday on his campaign to become mayor of San Francisco. It was exciting.[34]

Other Assembly fellows commented:

> To be successful here you have to know how to compromise. I learned the most working on bills that had strong opposition.
>
> Sky Thompson, 1985–1986

> Whether you're a nurse or a political scientist, you're going to be working with people. Being a Fellow taught me how to deal effectively with a variety of individuals.
>
> Bob Giroux, 1985–1986

---

[33] Spitz, *Oral History Interview*, 27-28.

[34] Carrie Cornwell, "Capital Fellows Alumni Questionnaire," 2003, FCFP.

The Fellowship Program is very helpful to people without "connections" to break into the legislative field. The experience was valuable in gaining insight into the process.

Tony Nevarez, 1986–1987

The Fellowship year . . . exciting, intriguing and demanding.

Mary Maguire, 1986–1987

Some say it's not wise to watch sausage being made, but as an Assembly Fellow I not only watched, I had my hand on the meat grinder.

Debra Hale, 1987–1988

I had the chance to interact with some of the most creative minds in California.

Marianna Harris, 1987–1988

The fellows' assignments ranged from working on special projects related to unemployment and disability insurance to drafting legislation and conducting research to develop a resource manual on local agency financing options.[35]

Praise from the members of the Assembly matched the satisfaction expressed by the fellows. Typical remarks included:

Again I was very impressed with this session's Assembly Fellows.

Gray Davis

For the past three years I have had the pleasure of working with three fellows from the Assembly Fellowship Program. I found [them] to be highly competent and worthy additions to my staff.

Johan Klehs

I have had an Assembly Fellow assigned to me for the past five months. In that time, [he] has become an integral part of my office. He is involved in several significant long-term projects and as a life-long resident of my district has proven to be an indispensable staff person.

Richard Katz[36]

The Assembly indicated its high regard for the fellowship program by unanimously passing Speaker Brown's 1987 resolution to rename it in honor of former Speaker Jesse Marvin Unruh. The resolution commended the program for "offer[ing] participants practical, first-hand knowledge of the Legislature through work experience and provid[ing] staff assistance for Members of the Assembly and for legislative committees." It noted that "during the last thirty years, this program has produced excellent career staff for the Legislature as well as many who

---

[35] "Quotes from Former Fellows," [1988], ARCP.

[36] Gray Davis to Chuck Price, 22 August 1985, Sacramento, ARCP; Johan Klehs to Lilly Spitz, 14 July 1986, Sacramento, ARCP; Richard Katz to Tom Bane, 7 December 1987, Sacramento, ARCP.

have gone on to successful careers in law, education, business, community service, and elective office." The Jesse Marvin Unruh Assembly Fellowship Program had a positive impact on both the fellows and the members of the Assembly.[37]

Academics

Senate

As the Sacramento State faculty member for the Senate Fellowship Program, John Syer was responsible for "providing direction to the fellows and those legislators or staff to whom the fellows are assigned for the purpose of making their experiences beneficial to both the fellows and the state." Towards that end, Syer participated in the selection process, contributed to the orientation program that introduced the new fellows to the Legislature, and conducted a weekly seminar for the fellows. The fellows received twelve units of graduate credit for their academic work at Sacramento State.[38]

The three-to-five-week orientation program was organized by John Syer and Nettie Sabelhaus. Sabelhaus remembered:

> John and I were very much partners in creating the orientation. At that point, we had a lengthier and a little more complete orientation than the other [fellowship] programs.
>
> The goal of the orientation was to help [the fellows] learn at the front end not just about the legislative process, the mechanics of it, but about the issues of the day. To help them with knowledge about what they're going to be hearing about the coming year.
>
> We'd take what we thought would be the hot topics for the year and try to summarize them by bringing in speakers and taking them out to different experiences. We were the people who created the trip to a prison. We did one day on water where we toured the Delta, and looked at Folsom Dam and talked about the delivery [of water]. Most people have no idea how water flows from northern California to southern California.
>
> We did a day on budget and taxes. Where does the tax dollar come from? How does the budget get divided up? They had some wonderful experiences with people who gave them their time to explain how it all worked.

---

[37] H.R. 20, California Assembly, 1987-1988 Regular Session, *Journal of the Assembly* (17 August 1987): 3872-3873. The complete text of H.R. 20 is included as Appendix 3.1.

[38] Louis V. Messner, Assistant Vice Chancellor, Budget Planning and Administration, to Marilyn Cundiff-Gee, Budget Analyst, Education Systems Unit, Department of Finance, 10 March 1987, PPO. The credits were divided among the orientation (3 units), the seminar (3 units) and the internship (6 units).

Both Sabelhaus and Syer wanted to create a learning environment where fellows felt comfortable asking questions and expressing their opinions.[39]

Syer led the weekly seminar meetings that involved the occasional preparation of book reports. The fellows also had to do a project that "was very open. Some would write about their work or a particular policy question. Others dealt with historical [issues]. Others dealt with reforms, how we could improve what we were doing in California." The projects were not limited in scope or content. Syer recognized:

> [T]he primary reason people came to the fellows program was to get political access. I tried to get as much academic value added as possible but I recognized that they weren't there necessarily for the school room. They were there for the political access afforded them for their future careers. . . . It wasn't a degree program although people could take the graduate units and apply them towards graduate programs and many people did.

He believed that the seminar offered the opportunity for the fellows to place their legislative experiences in context. Syer remembered:

> I wanted [the fellows] to learn from each other. I hoped that they would grow and that they would have an assessment [of the Legislature]. I didn't want them to go naive completely in the Capitol and accept all of the Capitol mores, old ways and values, without reviewing and considering [them] in a larger context. I'm particularly proud of the ones who were able to see how far the Capitol was from the citizenry as a whole, what a specialized culture it was. I very much wanted them to be able to view the fellowship seminar not to just as reinforcement for what was happening at work but also as an opportunity to ascertain what all this meant about the nature of California policy. They couldn't talk about it at work.[40]

The Senate had never before included an academic component as part of the fellowship program and did not consider the seminar to be a priority. Syer observed, "I always knew that the academic component was subordinated to [the fellows'] support of the Senate committees, the Senate offices they were working for. That was in the minds of the students. It was also in the minds of the Senate Rules Committee—that they didn't really want the academic component."[41] The Senate Rules Committee openly acknowledged that the seminar was less important than the placement. In a 1987 memo to the members of the Senate, the committee stated, "If there is any conflict between a fellow's job responsibilities and the seminar, the job is always to take precedence."[42]

---

[39] Sabelhaus, *Oral History Interview*, 4-5.

[40] Syer, *Oral History Interview*, 5-8.

[41] Ibid., 9-10;

[42] Senate Rules Committee to Members of the Senate, memorandum, 8 October 1987, SRCP, 2.

Sabelhaus, however, was a strong supporter of the academic program. She attended the weekly seminars and "was the enforcer who said, 'Why aren't you at seminar today? That's not okay,' because sometimes [the fellows] would get so involved in the world of work that they'd say, 'I don't need this academic part. It's not as important.'" Sabelhaus "never allowed them to prioritize that way. We always said to them, 'They are of equal importance.'"[43]

For many fellows, the seminar was a welcome addition. A 1984–1985 fellow commented, "The course instruction and work represented one of the best political science seminars that I have participated with in many years. The instruction combined both the considerable expertise of the professor, while increasingly drawing on the capabilities and experiences of participants." A 1986–1987 fellow noted, "The academic component was stimulating, but it was also very therapeutic. The bulk of the sessions were share-time, and only 'lightly' academic in the classical sense. I am not advocating more structure. Leaving the sessions open to discussion is a nice way to end the week." Another 1986–1987 fellow criticized the academic component and suggested that the seminars should be more structured. She "felt as though the academic component was just tacked on to justify the program, instead of being a serious effort to engage us in thought and reflection about government and the future of this state." While the fellows may have found it difficult to pull themselves away from their Senate responsibilities, they generally seemed to have appreciated the seminar.[44]

Assembly

For the first year that Sacramento State sponsored the Assembly Fellowship Program, the previously established format of an orientation followed by informal meetings with guest speakers comprised the academic component. During this period, a formal academic program was developed by Sacramento State faculty member Cristy Jensen. The program was introduced to the fellows in 1986–1987. It included both an orientation and biweekly academic seminars with required readings and papers.[45]

---

[43] Sabelhaus, *Oral History Interview*, 13.

[44] "[Senate Fellows Evaluate the 1984-1985 Senate Fellowship Program]," [1985], SRCP; "[Senate Fellows Evaluate the 1986-1987 Senate Fellowship Program]," [1987], SRCP.

[45] There appears to have been some initial confusion about who would be responsible for the academic component of the Assembly Fellowship Program. Sacramento State clearly expected to provide the academic instruction as part of their agreement with the Assembly Rules Committee to sponsor the fellowship program. Nevertheless, in February 1986, the Rules Committee received a proposal from a UC Davis political science professor, Richard Gable, to implement an academic program for the fellows. After submitting his proposal, Gable "was appalled to learn that Sac State was recruiting a person to coor-

During the orientation, Jensen observed, "[The students] wanted to see the names and the people. They wanted the Speaker to come in. They wanted the Leg Counsel to come in. They wanted the players to come in. We had lots of guest speakers. The major thing I tried to do was integrate between speakers. Raise questions. Yesterday, we heard so-and-so saying this, what kinds of questions might you want to ask so-and-so today? Those kinds of facilitative, integrative things."[46] For the fellows, the orientation was an opportunity to meet both assemblymembers and staff.

The seminar was less popular than the orientation. According to Lilly Spitz, the first year was a real struggle because "now, all of a sudden, [the fellows] have to go to class. [They would say], 'We've got bills we have to work on. We can't come to class.'"[47] Most fellows were there for the work experience not for the academics. Still, the fellows ultimately concluded that the seminar was worthwhile. In a letter of appreciation to President Gerth, the 1986–1987 class of fellows lavished praise on Cristy Jensen. The fellows wrote:

> Her performance as our academic coordinator went beyond the call of duty.... She provided a source of cohesion and continuity throughout the year.... Dr. Jensen was a stabilizing force that each of us could turn to for intellectual guidance, personal support and professional advice.
>
> On another occasion we met to discuss our policy papers. These papers were the major portion of our academic year in the program. With a humble bow to our immodesty, we must say you would have been impressed by the intellectual exchange that occurred. Dr. Jensen advanced our knowledge of California history and gave us a historical perspective of the State and its politics that were invaluable in all our efforts to struggle through the policy questions we took on in our papers.[48]

The responses to a survey of the 1987–1988 fellows reiterated this positive reaction.[49]

Administratively, the academic component of the Assembly Fellowship Program was the same as the Senate Fellowship Program: the fellows earned twelve units of graduate credit as regularly admitted students of Sacramento State. Cristy Jensen observed that many Assembly fellows had little or no interest in being Sacramento State students:

---

dinate the Assembly Fellowship program at the same time as [the Assembly Rules Committee was] reviewing the University of California's proposal to collaborate with the Assembly in the implementation of that program." Richard Gable to Sam Walton, 5 and 12 February 1986, ARCP.

[46] Jensen, *Oral History Interview*, 11-14.

[47] Spitz, *Oral History Interview*, 18.

[48] The Assembly Fellows, Class of 1986-87 to Dr. Donald Gerth, President, California State University, Sacramento, 9 July 1987, PPO.

[49] Lindsay A. Desrochers to Executive Board Members, 28 June 1988, ARCP.

For the longest time, the staff at Sac State filled out the admissions applications for the [fellows] because, particularly on the Assembly side, when you have people who were Harvard and Stanford law students, they weren't going to come out to Sac State and register as students. They didn't want any part of being grad students at Sac State. That was probably, over the three years [that Jensen was the CSUS faculty member for the fellowship program], the major challenge.

Many of the fellows initially resented having to register at Sacramento State for graduate credits that were of no interest to them. For the first time in 1988, however, Jensen noticed that the fellows were eager to be part of the Sacramento State community.[50]

Politics affected the Sacramento State effort to establish a viable academic component for the Assembly Fellowship Program. After the 1986–1987 fellows prepared their policy papers for the seminar, the Rules Committee decided that it would like to see them. But the papers hadn't been written with an audience of politicians in mind. For Cristy Jensen, it was a "pivotal, political crisis." Jensen said that the Assembly Rules Committee's demands to the see the students' papers conflicted with the integrity of the academic process. "If it had been made very clear up front before the students had ever written the papers that this was part of the deal, then I would have worked with the students to sanitize the papers so that there weren't sensitive references and we would have given them," she said.

Since that wasn't the case, Jensen added, "I felt I had to protect the fellows as students." Jensen's refusal led to a meeting between university and Rules Committee officials. The Rules Committee backed off and agreed not to insist on seeing the papers.

"That was a very hard time," Jensen remembered, "because the fellows were unsure whether they wanted me to protect them or not. They couldn't really be out there as victims. I had to be silently protecting them. They couldn't tell the Speaker's office that they didn't want to turn in their papers. I had to do that for them." She concluded, "It was a hard time. But we did it. We established the principle that this is an academic seminar." Jensen later suggested that papers might be available in the future if the Assembly requested them in advance.[51]

In 1989, Jensen left her position as the faculty advisor of the Assembly Fellowship Program to become the chair of the Sacramento State graduate program in Public Policy and Administration. The selection process for her successor again raised the issue of Assembly influence on the traditional prerogatives of academia. The search for Jensen's replacement had been conducted by Sacramento State following its usual procedures. The candidate chosen by the Sacramento State Selection Committee was then vehemently rejected by the Assembly Rules Committee for political reasons. The Rules Committee requested that it be included in

---

[50] Jensen, *Oral History Interview*, 9-10; Spitz, *Oral History Interview*, 18; Minutes of the Center for California Studies Advisory Board Meeting, 13 October 1988, PPO, 2.

[51] Jensen, *Oral History Interview*, 18-20.

"all phases of any new search for an Assembly Academic Advisor, particularly in setting forth the duties, responsibilities and desired qualifications for the position."[52]

With the relationship between the Assembly and Sacramento State at stake, President Gerth demonstrated his strong support of the Sacramento State affiliation with the fellowship programs. He met with the chief administrative officer of the Assembly and offered to become personally involved with the fellowship program. Gerth then asked Ken DeBow, a Sacramento State professor of government who was acceptable to the Rules Committee, to serve as the new faculty advisor for the Assembly Fellowship Program. On this important academic issue, Sacramento State had permitted the Assembly to prevail with the proviso that efforts must be made to "institutionalize a selection process which is appropriately cooperative."[53]

Political and Academic Bedfellows: A Shaky Marriage

The legislative budget cut mandated by Proposition 24 forced both the Senate and the Assembly to seek alternative funding sources for their fellowship programs. Almost simultaneously, Gerth arrived as president of Sacramento State with a strong desire to establish the university as the "Capital Campus." Sacramento State sponsorship of the Senate and Assembly Fellowship Programs solved the financial problem for the Legislature and created the opportunity for Sacramento State to establish close ties with the Legislature.

Although Sacramento State sponsored the fellowship programs, the Senate and the Assembly retained significant control over them. Senate and Assembly staff were largely responsible for selecting, placing and supervising the fellows. Sacramento State involvement was limited to the academic component which received greater support in the Senate than in the Assembly. Its association with the fellowship programs had established Sacramento State as a presence in the capital, but whether it would be able to capitalize on that foothold and become full and equal partners with the Legislature in the administration of the fellowship programs remained to be seen.

---

[52] Bob Connelly, Chief Administrative Officer, Assembly Rules Committee to Dr. Donald R. Gerth, President, California State University, Sacramento, 5 July 1989, PPO.

[53] Selection Committee: Assembly Fellows/Government, William A. Dorman (Journalism), Chair to William J. Sullivan, Jr., Dean, Arts and Sciences, memorandum, 7 June 1989, PPO; John C. Syer to Elizabeth F. Moulds, memorandum, 8 June 1989, PPO; Bob Connelly, Chief Administrative Officer, Assembly Rules Committee to Dr. Donald R. Gerth, President, California State University, Sacramento, 5 July 1989, PPO; Donald R. Gerth to Robert Connelly, Chief Administrative Officer, Assembly Rules Committee, 27 July 1989, Sacramento, PPO.

Branching Out: The Executive Fellowship Program

> The Executive Fellowship Program is now a well-established and well-functioning operation that attracts a comparable number of applicants as the legislative programs.
> —Center for California Studies Annual Report, 1996

> The experience of a Fellow transcends the text studied in school, and brings the world of policy and politics into stark, vibrant relief.
> —Robert Mangano, 1998–1999 Executive Fellow

In early 1985, Governor George Deukmejian telephoned Sacramento State President Donald Gerth to ask if the university would develop a fellowship program for the executive branch similar to the programs in the Senate and Assembly. Although the executive branch had made several previous attempts to establish fellowships like those in the Legislature, none of these executive efforts had lasted beyond a few years.[1] Deukmejian offered $25,000 for the initial develop-

---

[1] Prior to the program developed by Sacramento State, the longest lasting executive fellowship program was created by Lynn Schenk when she was Secretary of the Agency of Business, Transportation and Housing during the Edmund. G. Brown, Jr., administration. Center for California Studies, *State of California Executive Fellowship Program, 2003-2004* [brochure] (Sacramento: Center for California Studies, [2003]), [2].

ment of the program and suggested that it should be modeled on the White House Fellows Program.[2] Gerth readily accepted Deukmejian's offer.[3]

Birth of the Executive Fellowship Program

Funding to plan the Executive Fellowship Program was included in the 1985–1986 budget for the Center for California Studies. The budgeted amount of $41,839 was earmarked for the identification of program placements, the creation of an academic component, program advertising, and the selection of the charter class. William Cunningham, the education advisor in the governor's office, assumed responsibility for the program in the executive branch. Richard Krolak, a professor of political science at Sacramento State, was designated as the faculty member in charge of the fellowship program.[4]

Rich Krolak had recently returned to a full-time faculty appointment after a number of years in campus administration. As the director of the new Executive Fellowship Program, he had to hit the ground running. He likened the start-up of the Executive Fellowship Program in 1986 to an entrepreneurial endeavor:

> I was able to come in and use some of my contacts in the executive branch to try to jump start the program. Obviously, it didn't have the kind of history that the legislative programs had. We literally had to start it from scratch and try to make it a viable program, one that would be attractive to applicants just as quickly as possible.

By the time Krolak became involved with the program, the planning process had been completed. He described the hectic atmosphere of his early days with the fellowship program:

> When I came on the scene, [the program] was having to gear up fairly rapidly. We had to try to: one, get representatives from the executive branch who would help in the selection process; find people who were willing to provide placements, explain to them what that meant—get the commitment of time on their part, make sure [they understood] that running these kinds of intern programs takes a commitment of time on the part of the host as well as the participants. There was a fair amount of effort that had to go into creating the slots, making sure they were ap-

---

[2] A brief history and summary of the goals of the White House Fellows Program may be found at the program's website, http://www.whitehouse.gov/fellows.

[3] Gerth, *Oral History Interview*, 8.

[4] Robert O. Bess, Vice President, Operations and Finance (Sacramento State) to William Cunningham, Education Advisor, Governor's Office, 2 December 1985, PPO; Donald R. Gerth to Tom Burns, Deputy Executive Officer, California Senate Committee on Rules, 4 April 1985, PPO; "Background Statement, California State University, Sacramento, Center for California Studies," Sacramento, [June 1985], PPO.

propriate, getting the buy-in from the various executive offices. . . . The first year was really trying to make it a viable program as quickly as possible and have appropriate slots, visible slots, placements in agencies that would resonate with applicants.

The credibility of the Executive Fellowship Program had to be established with both the executive branch and potential fellows.[5]

The first class of ten executive fellows was selected at the same time as the initial placements were being determined. Occasionally, placements were developed to match the interests of the applicants. According to Krolak:

As the participants showed up, there was some last minute activity in terms of generating the appropriate slots, setting up the interviews, making sure we had the right mix of opportunities so that participants would have some viable choices from their perspective. There was a lot of activity literally up to the very day we opened the door.

Without the benefit of the longstanding traditions and procedures of the Assembly and Senate programs, the first year was "pretty much a bootstrap operation."[6]

During Krolak's two-year tenure as academic director of the Executive Fellowship Program, he had to win the support of the executive branch and establish the executive program on the same footing as the legislative programs. To encourage "executive branch buy-in and participation right from the very beginning," officials from the executive branch were involved in both the selection and placement processes. It was important that "like the legislative programs, the people who were going to be the hosts for [the fellows] had an opportunity to weigh in. Part of the process was a judgment being made by the people from the executive branch, it wasn't just the folks from campus," Krolak said. The selection process followed the same format of paper screening and interviews used by the legislative programs.[7]

The effort to establish parity among the three fellowship programs created a significant problem for the nascent Executive Fellowship Program. Sacramento State had reduced the advertised $1,500 stipend for the 1986–1987 Executive fellows to $1,300 and redirected the difference to the legislative fellows to make all stipends equal. For 1987–1988, the Assembly and Senate proposed to increase their fellows' stipends to $1,500 using funds available through the Rules Committees. The executive program did not have access to external funding and, in fact, had suffered a reduction in available funds because its financial administration had been shifted to the Hornet Foundation, which took a 10% fee for its services. Krolak observed:

---

[5] Richard Krolak, "History of the Capital Fellows Programs," *Oral History Interview*, conducted in 2002 by Elizabeth Austin, SCUA, 2-4.

[6] Ibid., 5-7.

[7] Ibid., 8.

First, it is important to understand that the Executive program does not have a centralized "champion" like the Rules Committees for the legislative programs. The Governor's Office plays a minimal role by providing some assistance with the orientation, but plays virtually no role in the selection or placement process, seminar or administration of the program. No staff from the executive branch are assigned to assist the program on an ongoing basis. The real "anchor[s]" for the program are the individual departments where the Fellows are placed rather than one central advocate.

Krolak concluded that securing additional funding from the governor's office was "unrealistic." Eventually, funding was apparently located from other Sacramento State sources to increase the executive fellows' stipends to $1,500. Full parity with the legislative fellowship programs was achieved when the number of executive fellows was increased from ten to twelve.[8]

In 1987–1988 Peter Mehas was appointed as the governor's office representative for the Executive Fellowship Program. Mehas prepared by requesting a review of the program by the 1986–1987 executive fellows. The fellows evaluated their experiences in the first year of the program with numerical ratings (on a scale of one to five, with five the lowest rating) and narrative assessments. The results were alarming. Only the seminar received the average rating of three. Everything else was a four or five.[9]

Among the narrative comments were:

Placement: Many sponsoring agencies were not adequately informed of the purposes of this Fellowship. As a result, many Fellows found themselves in placements which offered little or no exposure to the policy making process or individuals in executive positions. Several Fellows found themselves working as file clerks. Some were not given work assignments, were ignored, and were made to feel as though they were an imposition.

Seminar: This was the weakest component of the Fellowship. The pre-fellowship reading assignments were never discussed, and the few random handouts were presented almost as an afterthought, with no lead/read time for review by the Fellows. A consistent and challenging program of readings from various sources seems essential. . . . Essentially, the seminar could perhaps best be characterized as suffering from "intellectual anemia" with little challenge and no structure. There was no agenda, no syllabus, and no enthusiasm.

---

[8] Rich Krolak to President Gerth, memorandum, 12 May 1987, PPO; "Contractual Services Shortfall in 1987/88," PPO; Mernoy E. Harrison, Vice President for Finance to Robert O. Bess, Vice President for Operations and Finance, Sacramento State, memorandum, 3 February 1987, PPO.

[9] The seven assessment criteria and their ratings were: selection (5), orientation (4), interview process (4), placement (5), seminar (3), administration (4), and extracurricular activities (4).

Executive Fellowship Administration: It is at this level where the bulk of the fundamental and functional problems exist. The thinly concealed lack of enthusiasm for the Executive Fellows Program by the program administration, and the "lesser light" in which the Executive Fellow Program is viewed by the Fellowship administration (*vis-à-vis* the Senate and Assembly Programs) is disturbing, to say the least.

The misrepresentation of the equality of the three fellowship programs, the reality of being perceived as "interns" rather than fellows, and the essential lack of enthusiasm, structure, direction, and basic commitment by the program administrators left many of the Executive Fellows dissatisfied. To say our expectations were largely unfulfilled and our intellectual energies and talent underutilized is to truly understate the point.

Although the fellows offered some constructive suggestions, they emphasized their serious criticisms of the program's first year.[10]

The evaluation by the fellows sparked an immediate reaction from the university. CSU Chancellor Ann Reynolds expressed her concern about the low numerical ratings and concluded "that the participants had many expectations which were left unfulfilled." She asked President Gerth to "consider how the reflections in the evaluation will be used in modifying the Executive Fellows Program."[11]

Within a month, Gerth reported to Mehas that the evaluations had been reviewed and most of the changes suggested had been implemented. A key change involved ensuring that the fellows' expectations matched the realities of the program by rewriting the program brochure, preparing information about host agencies, and streamlining the interview process. Gerth expressed his absolute support for the program and said he would "do whatever is necessary to make that support real."[12]

After a rocky first year following a "very fast ramp-up," the Executive Fellowship Program was still finding its way within the executive branch and Sacramento State. Krolak said:

At the time, we felt that given the assets we had to work with, we did a reasonable job. The program built from there. That second year, we had agencies contacting us. We were able to get a broader, bigger, higher quality applicant pool. We began to get people from out-of-state. It seemed that first year, we at least had not done any great harm and we seemed to have provided a reasonable base for the program to grow.[13]

---

[10] Peter G. Mehas, Assistant to the Governor for Education to Donald R. Gerth, President, Sacramento State, 11 August 1987, PPO; "1986-1987 Executive Fellows Program Evaluation," [1987], PPO.

[11] W. Ann Reynolds, Chancellor to President Donald R. Gerth, 18 August 1987, PPO.

[12] Donald R. Gerth to Peter Mehas, Advisor to the Governor on Education, 22 September 1987, PPO.

[13] Krolak, *Oral History Interview*, 6, 12.

Although the Executive Fellowship Program still faced obstacles on the road to success, it had survived its first two years and was prepared to move on.

Institutionalization of the Executive Fellowship Program

Unlike the Senate and Assembly programs, a Sacramento State faculty member served as the director during the early years of the Executive Fellowship Program. The director conducted the academic seminar and coordinated recruitment, selection, and placements in consultation with a representative from the executive branch. During the first eight years of the Executive Fellowship Program, there were four directors and four executive liaisons. This turnover "slowed the development of a stable program and contributed to a perception of the Executive Program as having administrative weaknesses."[14]

Beginning in 1993, the director's responsibilities were divided between a staff member from the Center of California Studies and a faculty member in charge of the seminar. The program began to stabilize with the appointment of Donna Hoenig-Couch as the center director for the program, John Syer as the faculty advisor, and John Pimentel as the executive liaison. Hoenig-Couch, assistant director of the Center for California Studies and a former Senate fellow, directed the program until 2000. Syer, previously the faculty member for the Senate Fellowship Program, remained as faculty advisor until 1995. Pimentel, Assistant Secretary in the Business, Transportation, and Housing Agency and a former Assembly fellow, served as executive liaison until 1996. The continuity provided by the longevity of these administrators contributed to the successful institutionalization of the Executive Fellowship Program.[15]

Another significant step forward for the Executive Fellowship Program resulted from Pimentel's efforts to increase program awareness in the governor's office. Hoenig-Couch assessed his role:

> Prior to John Pimentel coming on the scene, I think the Governor's Office was unaware that they had Executive fellows. They were scattered around town in different departments and agencies. John made sure that they were on the radar screen for the governor. They met with the governor. They met with the First Lady. They were in the Governor's Council Room for their meetings. They were invited to every event, to the inaugural events, to the dances, to the Christmas parties, to all those things where they would be considered players in the administra-

---

[14] Center for California Studies, *Annual Report, 1993* (Sacramento: The Center, [1994]), 15.

[15] The directors, faculty advisors and executive liaisons for the Executive Fellowship Program are listed in Appendix XVI.

tion. It was also with John that we began to get placements directly in the governor's "horseshoe."[16]

The Executive Fellowship Program had arrived. Its continued growth and development were evident in the program's selection process, placements and academic component.

Selection

The selection process for the Executive Fellowship Program followed the pattern set by the Legislature. As Miki Vohryzek-Bolden, the program director from 1990 to 1992, recalled:

> Reviewing all the applications was a really key piece of the process because you're trying to identify people based on an academic record and a personal statement. I would read those very carefully to get a feel for the person and to make sure that he or she really understands the richness of the executive branch. You [also] look at grades. There [weren't] set weights for the personal statement or the academic [grades]. Letters of recommendation are another piece. By the time you look at the whole record of the applicant, you begin to get a real good picture.

After reading the applications, Vohryzek-Bolden along with a representative from the executive branch and perhaps another Sacramento State representative would select candidates to be interviewed. Vohryzek-Bolden believed that "the interviews were key because sometimes you would have this incredible applicant based on paper. You'd interview them and you would just know it's not a fit." The selection panel also strived for diversity. They were "looking for some balance, whether it's in gender or ethnicity or background."[17]

As the executive program matured in the 1990s, the selection panel expanded to include the program director, the faculty advisor, one other representative from Sacramento State, three members appointed by the governor and one former executive fellow. The selection panel continued to do the paper screening and interview the candidates. After examining the program applications, the panel ranked the candidates and invited the top sixty or seventy for an interview. During the 1990s, the panel tended to select fellows that "would serve government and contribute their high credentials and their many achievements." Sandra Perez, appointed director of the Executive Fellowship Program in 2000, noted that her ap-

---

[16] Hoenig-Couch, *Oral History Interview*, 24-25. Pimentel also tried unsuccessfully to have the name of the Executive Fellowship Program changed to the Governor's Fellowships.

[17] Miki Vohryzek-Bolden, "History of the Capital Fellows Programs," *Oral History Interview*, conducted in 2002 by Elizabeth Austin, SCUA, 11-15.

proach for selecting fellows added an emphasis on including "people who would not otherwise have the opportunity to work in government." The selection panel continued to focus on choosing fellows who reflected the diversity of California.[18]

Political events affected the selection process. The fellows for the 1998–1999 class that would experience the transition between the administrations of Governor Pete Wilson and Governor Gray Davis were chosen for their ability to weather the change. Donna Hoenig-Couch described the selection panel's approach:

> We consciously went into the selection process asking questions that were clearly pointed at how [the fellow] would weather an administration that may be different from [the fellow's] party, different from [the fellow's] ideologies. We were consciously looking for people who were more moderate and were there for the interest of watching the process more than politically aspiring for one administration over the other. I thought we picked a very good class. They were a class of moderates but that was okay for that year.[19]

Another significant change in the selection process occurred after 1999–2000 when questions about ethics and teamwork were added. This was a result of problems with some members of the 1999–2000 class of executive fellows class who demanded that the Center for California Studies provide personal support services and acquiesce to placement changes. Tim Hodson, executive director of the Center since 1993, remembered:

> We have had discussions within the Center about the "arrogance factor." We had one class that was especially troublesome. For example, one fellow called the Center and rudely insist that we make appointments with her health care provider because she was too busy and it was our job to take care of such things. After that and similar instances, the program directors talked about whether we should incorporate very specific questions in the interviews that would try to flush out that type of attitude.

The next year, Hodson said, the center looked for "people who had a sense of humility, who did not foster a sense of entitlement about what they did, [and] who were able to work with other people." In response to the "inappropriate behavior in the late 1990s, which included misperceptions and, in some instances, disdain for what the Center and its Capital partners consider basic professional conduct," the Center incorporated professional development materials and activities into the orientations and seminars for all of the fellows.[20]

---

[18] Sandra Perez, "History of the Capital Fellows Programs," *Oral History Interview*, conducted in 2002 by Elizabeth Austin, SCUA, 8-13.

[19] Hoenig-Couch, *Oral History Interview*, 35-36.

[20] Timothy A. Hodson, "History of the Capital Fellows Programs," *Oral History Interview*, conducted in 2002 by Elizabeth Austin, SCUA, 65-66; Hoenig-Couch, *Oral*

Placements

For the first year of the Executive Fellowship Program, the program director and the executive liaison had to convince offices to offer placements. By the second year, agencies began to contact the program to secure a fellow. In the 1990s, between forty and sixty offices in the executive branch applied annually for fellows. Generating placements that offered constructive learning experiences for the fellows was an ongoing process because of the size of the executive branch and the perennial problem of staff turnover—especially when there was an administration change.[21]

Fellows were placed throughout the executive branch in agencies, departments, commissions, constitutional offices, and the governor's office. The placements included the Health and Welfare Agency, the governor's Cabinet, California Department of Education, Trade and Commerce Agency, California Research Bureau, Governor's Office of Legal Affairs, Office of the State Treasure, and the California State Library. Positions in the governor's office and the Department of Finance were especially desirable because of their high visibility.[22]

A two-way mutual selection process similar to the one used by the legislative fellowship programs determined the placements. Unlike the legislative programs, an important part of the process was exposing the fellows to the diverse placements available in the executive branch. During the early years of the program, they received written placement descriptions. Later, Donna Hoenig-Couch tried different approaches.

> At the end of each day of orientation, I started having ten minute presentations by the offices of mentors who had applied for fellows. Those were okay but it was tiring for the fellows. Even though they had an opportunity to ask questions and hear about the agency, it was tough at the end of the day to keep everybody's attention.
>
> So then we moved the last year [that I was director, 1999–2000] to a job fair where I'd have all of the mentors and the offices meet for a two-day period of time. Allow fellows to mingle and talk.

The job fair was a success. Sandra Perez noted:

> It has worked very well. The value in the placement fair is that it forces the fellows to explore options they normally wouldn't have considered.
>
> Over a period of two days, anybody who wants a fellow and who has submitted an application can come to the fair. [They] set up a table and have displays. They have all their baits like candy and cupcakes.

History Interview, 36-40; Center for California Studies, *Annual Report, 2000* (Sacramento: The Center, [2001]), 24-25.

[21] Krolak, *Oral History Interview*, 11-12; Vohryzek-Bolden, *Oral History Interview*, 4-5; Hoenig-Couch, *Oral History Interview*, 25-26.

[22] The Executive Fellows and their placements are listed in Appendix 4.1.

The "tables are reversed" as prospective mentors promote their office to the fellows and the fellows, in turn, learn about the wide-ranging functions of the executive branch. It's really wonderful to see.

The fair serves two purposes: (1) it forces the fellows to broaden their knowledge and deepen their appreciation of the executive branch, and (2) it provides a noncommittal setting where prospective mentors have the opportunity to chat informally with individual fellows. Adding this activity to the placement process may be a contributing factor to very successful assignments in the last few years.

Based on the information provided by the representatives from the executive branch, the fellows scheduled interviews with prospective placements. After the interviews, the fellow and the placement indicated their top choices and the program director made the final fellow/placement matches.[23]

Although most of the matches were successful, there was usually at least one placement that had to be changed every year. Hoenig-Couch attributed most of the changes to work issues frequently caused by "large bureaucracies and difficulties in knowing how to navigate and find a home for [the fellows'] work."

When it's not good, it's really bad. You put yourself in an enormous Resources Agency, for example, or Social Services. You're in a cubicle and you don't see anybody all day. It can be very difficult if the mentorship is not strong.

Hoenig-Couch contrasted the executive experience with the legislature where "they're more interpersonal and more political."[24]

Effective and involved mentors were especially important to positive fellowship experiences in executive offices. Perez suggested that mentors may actually have been the cause of placement changes.

I have three expectations of mentors and their offices. I make it very clear: if any of these are violated in any way, I think I have grounds to change somebody.

Number one is that they have to give [the fellows] substantive assignments. Number two, professional environment. I don't mean an unrealistic environment because I want them to be in the real world. By unprofessional, I mean uncomfortable or threatening or somehow intimidating. And the third one is program support.

The program directors did not encourage placement changes. As Perez noted, "It's not a quick and easy decision. We don't like to do it. But things happen."[25]

---

[23] Hoenig-Couch, *Oral History Interview*, 26-29; Perez, *Oral History Interview*, 15-16; Sandra Perez, <perezs@skymail.csus.edu> "Exec Fellow Program Changes," 14 November 2003, personal e-mail (14 November 2003).

[24] Hoenig-Couch, *Oral History Interview*, 29-30.

[25] Perez, *Oral History Interview*, 21-22.

The majority of fellows were placed successfully. Unlike the legislative fellows, who had similar job descriptions working for mentors at the same level of government, the executive fellows' experiences, at many different levels of government, varied widely. Hoenig-Couch commented on the many placement offerings:

> We had people who were assigned to legislative units within the executive office so, in some cases, the Executive fellows get a lot of leg[islative] work but it was analysis from the [perspective] of the agency rather than writing legislation.
>
> Some fellows did budget work and budget preparation. We had fellows in the Department of Finance. We had fellows in the Treasurer's Office.
>
> Some did grass roots projects like working for the medically indigent and developing programs, grassroots programs, community-based programs.
>
> We had fellows who were considered the assistant to the director. They did a wide variety of executive types of work du jour—whatever came up that the executive director would give them. In those cases, they probably did a lot of shadowing, attending meetings.
>
> We had fellows in the California Research Bureau who did pure research reports. What else? It was really a wide range.
>
> We had an attorney one year—she had already passed the bar—[who] actually represented the Department of Social Services before the Supreme Court. They've done incredible things.

The diverse placements offered the potential for significant personal and career growth.[26]

The transition from Governor Wilson to Governor Davis offered Holly Fraumeni a unique opportunity.

> My experience as an Executive Fellow was not one of the typical executive office placements. I took a gamble in requesting to be placed in the transition office in October 1998, four weeks before the gubernatorial election. My placement had very little oversight and I was left alone, patiently awaiting the incoming transition team on November 5. There, I learned the true meaning of "survival of the fittest." I had two months to prove myself, handling all the administrative details of change in the transition office.
>
> There I connected with Gray Davis's Chief of Staff who adopted me as his Fellow and became an ideal mentor. Soon I found myself witnessing the historical "turnover" the night before Governor Davis's inaugural, as members of the Wilson Administration slowly filtered out of the "horseshoe" (the governor's office), and the Davis staff moved in. From that point on, my fellowship opened more doors of opportunity than I could have ever imagined in September.
>
> In January, my mentor was appointed the Director of Administration and Protocol, and I seized the opportunity to continue working for him in the "horseshoe." In a short time, I became a primary figure in the organization of President of Mexico Ernesto Zedillo's trip to California, and I was treated as a permanent

---

[26] Perez, *Oral History Interview*, 23; Hoenig-Couch, *Oral History Interview*, 31.

staff member, working long hours and handling an enormous amount of responsibility.

Fraumeni remained on the governor's staff for several years after the end of her fellowship.[27]

The fellows' experiences reflect the diversity and potential of executive placements:

> My placement was as a budget analyst in the Department of Finance. The Program Budget Manager was my mentor and provided me with guidance and opportunities to manage a regular assignment as well as to develop special reports. I had the opportunity to attend high level meetings within the Department of Finance and with the Governor's Office senior staff as well as Agency level meetings.
>
> The program provided an entrée to state government that would not otherwise have been available to me. It offered the opportunity to learn from an insider's perspective.
>
> Sue Van Velkinburgh Bost, 1987–1988

Bost continued to work in the Department of Finance.

> As an Executive Fellow in the Governor's Office of Planning and Research, I worked on policy issues important to the State of California. As a policy analyst under the supervision of the Governor's Chief Economist, I took part in the economic and fiscal assessment of military base closures, health care reform, illegal immigration, tax reform and other pressing policy issues.
>
> I co-authored several publications and orally briefed organizations such as the California Export Finance Office and a trade delegation from the People's Republic of China. Moreover, my work was distributed to key policy makers in both California and Washington, D.C.
>
> Andrew Chang, 1993–1994

Chang went on to work as a manager at A. T. Kearney, an international management consulting firm.

> Under the mentorship of the director of the California Arts Council, I was involved in a variety of executive-level projects, from preparing an economic analysis of the state's investment in the arts to conducting and reporting a thorough evaluation of the Public Art and Design Program. In my daily activities, I was treated as a member of the executive staff and I was given the additional privilege of virtually unrestricted access to meetings and events throughout the state. As a representative of the Council, I met the new chairman of the National Endowment for the Arts, members of the President's Committee on Arts and

---

[27] Center for California Studies, *Executive Fellowship Program, 2000-2001,* [2000], FCFP, 10; Hoenig-Couch, *Oral History Interview,* 35.

Humanities, the mayor-elect of the city of Oakland and the current governor and first lady of the state of California.

Jill Kaiser, 1997–1998

Kaiser was director of the Arts and Business Council of Sacramento from June 1998 until June 2003 and served simultaneously as the vice president of Community Development for the Sacramento Metropolitan Chamber of Commerce.[28]

Academics

The Executive Fellowship Program included an academic component as an integral part of the fellowship experience from its inception. Using the format established by the legislative fellowship programs, the academic program for the executive fellows included an orientation period followed by regular seminars. The weekly seminars were designed to "provide Fellows with opportunities to broaden their learning beyond work experience." Weekly seminars allowed fellows "to share the lessons of their experiences, analyze and review current scholarship on California state government, and hear guest speakers."[29]

The content of the seminars depended on the faculty advisor.[30] Miki Vohryzek-Bolden emphasized writing and had the fellows do a lot of position papers. To reward and challenge them, she inaugurated the *Executive Fellows Journal,* which showcased their end-of-the year research papers.[31] The fellows also discussed their work experiences. Vohryzek-Bolden "tried to create a safe, comfortable learning environment for them to speak freely about the issues that either they were dealing with and/or that were related to the topic of the day." Required outside reading provided context for the seminar discussions. [32]

A different faculty advisor led the seminar every year or two until Ted Lascher joined the Executive Fellowship Program from 1996 to 2001. As a faculty member in Public Policy and Administration (PPA), program director Hoenig-Couch felt that he brought a "real rigor to the seminar that was very much appreci-

---

[28] Center for California Studies, *Executive Fellowship Program, 1999-2000,* [1999], FCFP, 8-9; Center for California Studies, *Executive Fellowship Program,* [1995], FCFP, [7]; Sue Bost, Andrew Chang and Jill Kaiser, "Capital Fellows Alumni Questionnaires," 2003, FCFP.

[29] Center for California Studies, *Executive Fellowship Program, 2000-2001,* [2000], FCFP, 4.

[30] The faculty advisors for the Executive Fellowship Program are listed in Appendix XVI.

[31] Papers for the first two volumes of the *Executive Fellows Journal* were selected and edited by Vohryzek-Bolden and published in 1991 and 1992-1993. Papers for the third volume of the *Journal* were selected and edited by Ted Lascher and published in 1999-2000.

[32] Vohryzek-Bolden, *Oral History Interview,* 5-9.

ated." Previously, she said, there had been "a lot of falling off on the part of the students" but "when Ted came, he gave a regular PPA seminar which was really complemented by assignments that related to the work that [the fellows] were doing. The seminar evolved from one that was good but undefined to one that was very well formulated."[33] Lascher recalled:

> I tried to make [the seminar] less institution oriented and more policy oriented. [I] also tried to work in some more exercises and group projects.
> The first couple of years they didn't do a big paper. And then over time, partly as a result of the feedback that I got, I decided to have them do one big paper. We actually tried to get going on the *Executive Fellowship Journal* [but] we were only able to do one [because] it's very time intensive.
> One of the things I did was to regularly reserve a topic every few weeks for them to [plan and present]. It gave them a chance to do something that interested them. [The presentations] were uneven. Some of them were really good. One group did water policy. It was very good, very thoughtful.

Lascher observed that the mix of fellows significantly affected the success of the seminar. He noted, "In a group like that in particular, two or three people can make a huge difference because of the way everybody is so interconnected in a way that really doesn't happen in my normal graduate [classes]."[34]

Although the executive fellows frequently praised the seminar (especially after the first year when they had labeled it the weakest component of the fellowship), they occasionally resembled their legislative counterparts in their tendency to neglect it. Rich Krolak recalled:

> There were a couple of occasions where I had to go to the mentors and have conversations about, "There is an academic component here. They're registered with the university. If they stop coming to the class then they won't be a part of the program. If you think they're that good, they'll roll onto your budget and off of my budget." Sometimes [the fellows had] a tendency [to] get caught up in their work environment and clearly begin to see the academic [seminar] as secondary at best in some cases, but we worked through that. It wasn't a major problem.

While Vohryzek-Bolden "didn't ever have difficulty getting them to class because it's also an opportunity for all of them to catch up with each other," Lascher believed that "there's an irreducible lack of real enthusiasm for a seminar" among at least a few of the fellows each year. He found that "in the first semester, people are more willing. They're just happy to be there and make the effort. But as time goes on, a few people get a little impressed by their own importance. That's a

---

[33] Hoenig-Couch, *Oral History Interview*, 33-34.

[34] Ted Lascher, "History of the Capital Fellows Programs," *Oral History Interview*, conducted in 2002 by Elizabeth Austin, SCUA, 11-12, 19-20.

common problem." Attendance at the seminar was required but the pull to stay on the job often conflicted with the mandate to be in class.[35]

Executive Fellowship Program Parity

By the end of the 1990s, the Executive Fellowship Program had achieved parity with the Senate and Assembly Fellowship programs. Its initial image had been transformed from "something of a throwaway and something of a bastard stepchild" to a program with a proven track record that was valued by both the executive branch and Sacramento State.

The executive and legislative programs had many characteristics in common. They all followed similar processes for recruitment, selection, and orientation; encountered many of the same administrative problems; paid the same stipends; required participation in an academic seminar; awarded academic credit for participating in the fellowship program; offered the same number of fellowships; and were joined under the aegis of the Center for California Studies.

The executive program was also unique among the three fellowship programs because its placements offered a diversity and breadth of experience not available in the Legislature. The Executive Fellowship Program added a new dimension to the participant-observer experience in state government and increased the visibility of Sacramento State as the "Capital Campus."[36]

---

[35] Krolak, *Oral History Interview*, 9-10; Vohryzek-Bolden, *Oral History Interview*,8; Lascher, *Oral History Interview*, 13; Perez, *Oral History Interview*, 26-27; "1986-1987 Executive Fellows Program Evaluation," [3].

[36] Krolak, *Oral History Interview*,16; Lascher, *Oral History Interview*, 24; Hodson, *Oral History Interview*, 115; Center for California Studies, *Annual Report, 1996* (Sacramento: The Center, [1997]), 28. Although the number of fellows increased to eighteen in 1989-1990 for the Assembly Fellowship Program and in 1990-1991 for the Senate Fellowship Program, the number of Executive Fellows lagged behind and did not increase from twelve to fifteen until 1994. The number Executive Fellows did not equal the number of Assembly and Senate Fellows until 1996.

Towards a Full and Equal Partnership: The Assembly and Senate Fellowship Programs in the 1990s

> The experience gave me the confidence to serve in public and government service and in intensely political environments. I do not come from a political family, and indeed, I am the first in my family ever to go to law school or to pursue government service as a professional career.
>
> —James C. Ho, 1995–1996 Senate Associate

> I was placed in the office of a newly elected and targeted member of the Assembly. This was a great experience because there were few staff members and the member I worked for treated me as though I was "regular staff."
>
> —Patrick O'Donnell, 1998–1999 Assembly Fellow

Proposition 140

In 1990, voters passed Proposition 140 and turned the California Legislature upside down. Proposition 140 reduced the Legislature's expenditures on in-house operations and limited state senators to two four-year terms and members of the Assembly to three two-year terms. The budget reductions and term limits imposed by Proposition 140 had both immediate and long-term effects on the Legislature and its fellowship programs.[1]

---

[1] Proposition 140, entitled "Limits on Terms of Office, Legislators' Retirement, Legislative Operating Costs," was approved by 52.17% of the voters. Although the provi-

In the year following the passage of Proposition 140, the Legislature cut its spending by about 40%. Much of this cut was realized through staff reductions as 650 of the Legislature's 2,500 staffers accepted "golden handshake offers" to leave their jobs voluntarily. Many who left were the most senior and experienced staff. Turnover among the remaining staff accelerated, and the departures decimated the corps of expert staff that had been a key component of California's professionalized legislature since the 1960s.[2]

By 1999, the term limits established by Proposition 140 had dramatically changed the make-up of the Legislature. The number of experienced legislators in the Assembly and Senate declined sharply. Members of the 1990 Assembly and Senate had either left the legislature completely or had been elected to the other chamber. Twenty of the 1990 assemblymembers had shifted to the Senate; one of the 1990 senators had switched to the Assembly. Only two assemblymembers had more than four years' experience. From 1990 to 1999, the average number of years served in the Assembly declined by almost 80%. In the Senate, the average declined by almost 75%. While the number of experienced legislators declined, the number of women and Latino members grew. The Legislature increasingly reflected the diversity of California's population at the close of the twentieth century.[3]

The budget reductions and turnover among legislators and their staff that resulted from Proposition 140 had significant consequences for the legislative fellowship programs. The Senate and the Assembly both shifted funding for the legislative programs' directors and their assistants to the Sacramento State budget. The fellows became Sacramento State employees. With the decline in experience of legislators and legislative staff, the demand for fellows rose. New assemblymembers and senators insisted more than ever before that the fellows mirror the diversity of the Legislature. Tim Hodson, a longtime Senate staffer, left his position as chief consultant for the Senate Elections and Reapportionment Committee to become the new executive director of the Center for California Studies. Along with other developments in the 1990s, these changes gradually altered the relationship between the Center for California Studies and the Legislature.

---

sions of Proposition 140 were challenged in the courts, the legislative budget reductions and term limits were not overturned.

[2] Vic Pollard, "Legislative Staff: Coping with Term Limits and an Unstable Job Market," *California Journal* 25, no. 6 (1994): 15-16; Ken DeBow and John C. Syer, *Power and Politics in California*, 6th ed. (New York: Addison Wesley Longman, 2000), 148-149.

[3] In 1999, 25% of the California legislators were women (up from 17.5% in 1990) and 19% were Latino (up from 6% in 1990). Mark Katches, "No More Museum Pieces: the California Legislature is a Whole New Place Since Term Limits Swept It Clear," *State Legislatures* 25 (1999): 24-26; A.G. Block, "The Minnies," *California Journal* 31, no. 6 (2000): 8-10; DeBow and Syer, 149-151.

Funding: Staff, Stipends, and Fees

Proposition 140 completed the shift in legislative fellowship program funding to the Center for California Studies that had commenced with the passage of Proposition 24 in 1984. After Proposition 24, fellowship programs in the Senate and Assembly had been financed through a line item in the state budget for the Center for California Studies. The Senate and Assembly, however, continued to pay a half-time staff person to direct the programs and a full-time clerical assistant to the director.

William Pickens, associate vice president for administration at Sacramento State, noted the potential threat to the fellowship programs caused by this arrangement after Proposition 140 was approved:

> Proposition 140 restricts the Legislature's expenditures on its own activities, and the Fellows' current funding pattern could mean a serious disruption for the [fellowship] program—especially in the voluntary assignment of legislative staff to coordinate the program downtown. Our [Sacramento State] campus is quite concerned about protecting these high priority programs in the wake of Proposition 140.

Proposition 140 created uncertainty at Sacramento State about adequate funding to continue the fellowship programs.[4]

The funding concerns ended in 1991when the Senate and Assembly Rules Committees reached an agreement with Sacramento State President Donald Gerth to transfer funds to support 1.5 positions for each legislative program from the Assembly and Senate budget to the Center for California Studies. Hodson described one major consequence of the payroll shift:

> [The transition to the University payroll] has been very important to the development of the [center's] full and equal partnership [with the Legislature] because the program directors were no longer legislative employees. They [were] University employees. Particularly now that we're in the second generation, almost third generation, there's a real feeling that the loyalty is to the University. They understand that they're paid by the University and that we're loyal to the programs, and that means to our partner, but they're partners not bosses.

Although all but one of the program directors were former legislative staffers, they gradually established strong ties with the university.[5]

---

[4] William H. Pickens, Associate Vice President for Administration to Lou Messner, Assistant Vice Chancellor, Budget Planning and Administration, memorandum, 1 March 1991, PPO.

[5] Four legislative staff members transferred to the Center: Cheryl Minnehan and Gloria Cain were the full-time clerical assistants; Monica Neville and Nettie Sabelhaus were the half-time program directors for the Assembly and Senate respectively. The As-

In another adjustment to Proposition 140, the Senate and Assembly Rules Committees requested that the center take over payment of the fellows' stipends and benefits. Previously, funds for the stipends and benefits had been included in the line item and "passed through" to the Legislature via an annual contract. Accommodating this request, which had the benefit of making the fellows "a permanent part of the university's personnel," was complicated because the existing categories suitable for the fellows either did not include health benefits, or required membership in the Public Employees' Retirement System (PERS). The provision of health benefits was essential, but the cost of PERS membership, which included health and retirement benefits, exceeded the amount available for benefits in the fellowship program budget. Special legislation was required to establish a hybrid classification for the fellows.

The passage of Senate Bill 1242 waived the PERS requirement for legislative and executive fellows. Another measure, SB 1174, allowed payment of health and medical benefits to fellows through PERS "only to the extent that funds are made available therefore in the annual Budget Act."

Effective September 1992, the new classification of legislative/executive fellow continued the fellows' status as students and paid them health benefits as official university employees.[6]

---

sembly program directors are listed in Appendix 3.4. The Senate program directors are listed in Appendix 7.2. Pickens to Lou Messner, 1 March 1991; Minutes, Fellows Directors Meeting, 17 September 1991, PPO; Center for California Studies, *Annual Report, 1990-1991* (Sacramento: The Center, [1991]), 5; Hodson, *Oral History Interview*, 4, 39; Friedlander, *Oral History Interview*, 35-36; Robbin Lewis-Coaxum, "History of the Capital Fellows Programs," *Oral History Interview*, conducted in 2003 by Elizabeth Austin, SCUA, 2.

[6] SB 1242 was signed by the governor in October 1991. SB 1174 was approved in September 1992. Since the new employee classification was not available until September 1992, the Sacramento State Hornet Foundation paid the Assembly and Senate fellows' stipends, fees and benefits for the 1991-1992 fellowship year through a contract with the University following the same arrangement that had been used by the Executive Fellowship Program. David L. Wagner, Dean, Faculty and Staff Affairs to William Pickens, Associate Vice President for Finance, memorandum, 7 June 1991, PPO; William H. Pickens, Associate Vice President for Administration to David Wagner, Dean, Faculty and Staff Affairs, memorandum, 24 May 1991, PPO; William H. Pickens to Nettie Sabelhaus, Director of the Senate Fellows Program and Monica Neville, Director of the Assembly Fellows Program, memorandum, 7 June 1991, PPO; William H. Pickens to Wayne Quinn, Acting Director, Hornet Foundation, memorandum, 20 June 1991, PPO; Minutes, Center for California Studies, Statewide Advisory Council, 10 October 1991, PPO; William H. Pickens to Nettie Sabelhaus, memorandum, 28 June 1991, PPO; Susie Milliesdottir, Classification Coordinator, Faculty and Staff Affairs to Kathy Mandel, Director, Compensation, Policy and Personnel Programs, Sacramento State, Chancellor's Office, memorandum, 24 October 1991, PPO; June Cooper, Vice Chancellor, Human Resources and Operations to Presidents, memorandum, 1 September 1992, PPO.

Legislation was also required to resolve the longstanding funding issue of financing tuition for nonresident fellows enrolled as graduate students at Sacramento State. The fellowship program budget had always included funding for resident tuition fees but had not covered nonresident tuition fees.

Since there were often several nonresident fellows, the Center for California Studies frequently faced a budgetary shortfall. In 1991, for example, the $8,700 discrepancy had to be covered by savings realized after the early departures of several 1990-1991 executive fellows.

Enacted in October 1991, Assembly Bill 2055 eliminated this perennial problem by granting resident classification to all students in the legislative or executive fellowship programs during the period of the fellowship.[7]

The monthly stipend paid to the participants in the fellowship programs was another recurring financial challenge. In the early 1990s, annual efforts to increase the stipend failed and the stipend stagnated at $1,560 through 1993-1994. Finally, in 1994-1995, the stipend was raised 5% to $1,638 following recognition that "the disparity between a static stipend level and an increasing cost of living [was beginning] to have adverse affects on both the applicant pool and selected Fellows and Associates." The raise received bipartisan support in the Legislature despite the challenges of a state budget deficit.[8]

The center continued to request annual cost-of-living-adjustments (COLAs) to the stipend with mixed results. Before the next stipend increase to $1,707 was granted in 1997-1998, some fellows were forced to find additional employment during their fellowships to support themselves financially. A 1996-1997 Senate fellow commented:

> The worst [fellowship] experience was trying to juggle the responsibilities of a more-than-full-time job while also trying to research and write a paper of the caliber of the case study. Given the rather Spartan stipend, I had to work a 20-hour part-time job on the weekend to meet my expenses . . . and I don't think I have ever been that exhausted for that long of a stretch of time.

---

[7] The provision for resident classification for all fellows was incorporated into Tom Hayden's bill, AB 2055, which dealt with nonresident tuition fees for community colleges. William H. Pickens, Associate Vice President for Administration to Robert Jones, Vice President for University Affairs and University Liaison to the Legislature, memorandum, 26 March 1991, PPO; Center for California Studies, *Financial Outlook, Fall 1991*, 1991, [1], PPO; Minutes, Center for California Studies, Statewide Advisory Council, 10 October 1991, PPO, [2]; Center for California Studies, *Annual Report, 1991-1992* (Sacramento: The Center, [1992]), 4-5.

[8] Center for California Studies, *Annual Report, 1998* (Sacramento: The Center, [1999]), 28; Center for California Studies, *Annual Report, 1999* (Sacramento: The Center, [2000]), 30; Center for California Studies, *Annual Report, 2000*, 29.

From 1998 to 2000, the stipends were raised annually by 5%. In the face of growing state budgetary problems, no increase was granted for 2000–2001.[9]

Demand for Fellows

Always popular if not always adequately compensated, the Senate and Assembly fellows were in ever greater demand as a result of the term limits and legislative budget reductions imposed by Proposition 140. Inexperienced legislators quickly realized the value of trained fellows.

Hodson observed:

> Members come in and quickly find out that a fellow is a very valuable commodity who has been selected through a rigorous selection process. Fellows have gone through an orientation that has taught them more than some regular staffers in the Legislature. They are prescreened, preselected, pretrained and can come into an office, hit the ground running, and be able to do wonderful things as a professional staffer. Those fellows have become a sought-after commodity as a staff resource.

Sixty assemblymembers and thirty-two senators requested fellows from the 2000–2001 class.[10]

The constant need to acquaint an ever-changing legislative membership with the benefits and responsibilities of participating in the fellowship program created a challenge for the program directors. Robbin Lewis-Coaxum, director of the Assembly Fellowship Program since 1998, commented:

> When [the new assemblymembers] come [to Sacramento], almost everyone wants a fellow. I think the biggest challenge facing the program is just ensuring that people understand what the fellows program is and having the meet-and-greets with members just so they know what the Center offers, what the program offers. That it isn't just free staff. That they have class on Friday.
>
> I think in a nonterm-limited environment, it would be a lot easier to run the program because you wouldn't have to keep going out and saying, "This is what the Center is and this is what we do. This is what the program is. This is the criteria." [There] is constant education and training about the fellows program. From the administrative standpoint, there's a lot more of a challenge just because in-

---

[9] Center for California Studies, *Annual Report, 1997* (Sacramento: The Center, [1998]), 21; Center for California Studies, *Annual Report, 1998*, 28; Center for California Studies, *Annual Report ,1999*, 30; Center for California Studies, *Annual Report ,2000*, 29; Nora Lynn, "Capital Fellows Alumni Questionnaire," 2003, FCFP.

[10] Hodson, *Oral History Interview*, 27-28, 83-84; Center for California Studies, *Annual Report, 2000*, 26, 28.

stead of having to meet with two or three members a year, we have to meet within the next month [February 2003] with thirty-two members.

Lewis-Coaxum noted the benefits of a term-limited environment for the fellows:

> From the fellows' standpoint, the world is opened up to you. You can work for leadership. You can work for a member that is in their last term. You can work for a newly elected member. You can work for a committee but mostly you're working for the chair of the committee. You can work in personal staff. You can have a combo placement with personal staff, committee. You decide that as a fellow when you interview.

Term limits multiplied the effort required to advise members of the Legislature about the fellowship programs and broadened the placement possibilities.[11]

Staff departures and turnover after Proposition 140 increased the workload and employment opportunities for many fellows. John Syer reported in 1992 "that recent cutbacks in Capitol staff had placed heavy demands on fellows in state offices and agencies." As staff left and jobs became available, the number of fellows hired as full-time staffers after their fellowships rose.

Hodson observed:

> The staff turnover creates more job opportunities. The number of fellows who stayed on with their placements or their offices, particularly in the legislative programs in the seventies and eighties, were less because staff was fairly stable. There weren't a lot of vacancies so the member would say, "I'd love to hire you but I don't have payroll [or] space for you. I don't have a vacancy."
>
> These days, there's just an incredible amount of turnover. One-third of the Assembly changes every two years. The leadership is desperate to retain staff and desperate to find experienced staff to help the new members. Many times, the fellows are snatched up, are approached by the leadership who say, "We want you to stay."

Twelve fellows were hired from each of the 2000–2001 Assembly and Senate Fellowship Programs. Lewis-Coaxum noted, "Two of my former fellows last year [2001–2002] are chiefs of staff. I think two are legislative directors. In a term-limited environment, that's what happens." In 2001, slightly more than half of all legislative offices employed former fellows. Hodson concluded, "We are clearly fulfilling our goal of providing leaders for state government."[12]

---

[11] Lewis-Coaxum, *Oral History Interview*, 11-12.

[12] There were ten Assembly Fellows and six Senate Fellows hired from the 1998-1999 class, six Assembly Fellows and eleven Senate Fellows from the 1999-2000 class and twelve Assembly Fellows and twelve Senate Fellows from the 2000-2001 class. Minutes, Center for California Studies, Statewide Advisory Council, 6 February 1992, PPO; Center for California Studies, *Annual Report, 1999*, 29-30; Center for California Studies, *Annual Report, 2000*, 26, 28; Center for California Studies, *Annual Report,*

The impact of new legislators and staff turnover affected the experiences of many participants in the legislative fellowship programs including 1996–1997 Assembly Fellow Mark Stivers who recalled:

> I picked the office of a freshman legislator. After two months, the chief of staff/mentor left the office and there was high staff turnover throughout my two-year stint in the office. I, however, developed a good relationship with the legislator and had many opportunities open to me that I wouldn't have gotten in other offices with more experienced and stable staffs. I carried four of the boss' more major bills in the Fellowship year, staffed Natural Resources and other committees including Judiciary. In some respects, it was baptism by fire, but I had great opportunities.

Stivers continued to work in the Legislature after the end of his fellowship.[13]

Kyri Sparks McClellan, a 1995–1996 Assembly fellow, also enjoyed working for a first-term legislator:

> I worked for first-term Assemblymember Kerry Mazzoni's office. With the assistance and mentoring from Ms. Mazzoni and her Chief of Staff, I drafted and analyzed legislation, researched and wrote speeches and press releases, advised the assemblymember on pending Judiciary Committee issues, met with lobbyists and constituents, generated policy papers on legislative issues, staffed Women's Caucus meetings, events and press conferences, and coordinated the Legislature's 1996 "Woman of the Year" event.
>
> I chose to work for Ms. Mazzoni at the time because she had a small office and after interviewing with the staff, I knew that I would get hands-on experience. She also had earned an early reputation of being effective by working with "both sides of the aisle" [which] appealed to me. To this day, I am still close with Ms. Mazzoni and her former staff members.

McClellan's understanding of the state legislature became an invaluable asset when she went on to work in San Francisco's City Hall.[14]

For 1998–1999 Assembly Fellow Emilee Ford, high staff turnover created a mentoring challenge:

> I was placed with Assemblymember Kevin Shelley. My assignments were similar to other Legislative Aides: staffing legislation, staffing committees, press work, constituent correspondence, preparing talking points, and miscellaneous office work.
>
> Because Assemblymember Shelley's office struggled with high staff turnover, I worked with several supervisors during the fellowship and didn't really

---

2001, (Sacramento: The Center, [2002]), 30, 32; Lewis-Coaxum, *Oral History Interview,* 24; Hodson, *Oral History Interview*, 28, 110-111.

[13] Mark Stivers, "Capital Fellows Alumni Questionnaire," 2003, FCFP.

[14] Kyri Sparks McClellan, "Capital Fellows Alumni Questionnaire," 2003, FCFP.

have one mentor. However, my supervisors were always willing to help me learn the legislative process and I was trusted with high priority projects.

Ford continued to use "the fundamental knowledge of the legislative process and the Capitol environment" gained during the fellowship when she went on to work as the chief of staff for Assemblymember Simon Salinas.[15]

Staff changes prompted by Proposition 140 immediately affected April Manatt's 1990–1991 Senate fellowship:

> I was assigned to Senator [Marian] Bergeson's personal legislative staff for about 75% of my Fellowship, and her Local Government Committee staff for about 25%. As a legislative assistant, I researched and wrote bills, worked with committee staff, executive branch officials, the press, and lobbyists.
>
> I was mentored by Christopher Kahn, Marian's chief of staff, himself a Fellow the prior year. For the Committee, I was mentored by Peter Detwiler, the principal consultant, and wrote and published a local government primer called, "What's So Special about Special Districts."
>
> My fellowship started the year Proposition 140 passed. Because of dramatic staff reductions in Marian's office, I accounted for 50% of her professional staff. Because I was needed so desperately, I was able to work on a very wide variety of issues and take 100% responsibility for many projects. This was the best part of my experience. The downside of all this responsibility was that I was a little over my head occasionally.

After the fellowship, Manatt remained on the senator's staff until 1998.[16]

In addition to the challenges and opportunities offered by working with new legislators and revolving staff, the 1995–1996 class of Assembly fellows endured an especially wild session with three speakership changes. After Democrat Willie Brown's fourteen-year reign as speaker ended in June 1995, he was followed by three Republicans in rapid succession: Doris Allen (June 1995–September 1995), Brian Setencich (September 1995–January 1996) and Curt Pringle (January 1996–November 1996).

For the Assembly fellows, it was a tumultuous year because their "placements were not final until well past the start of [their] fellowship (which was October 30) and work on substantive pieces of legislation was scarce, given the split and the decreased chances of passage." Still, the "class was pretty good-humored about it all and had a lot of fun getting to know each other in the meantime."[17]

---

[15] Emilee Ford, "Capital Fellows Alumni Questionnaire," 2003, FCFP.

[16] April Manatt, "Capital Fellows Alumni Questionnaire," 2003, FCFP.

[17] Jayna Ng, "Capital Fellows Alumni Questionnaire," 2003, FCFP; DeBow, 28-29; Sabelhaus, *Oral History Interview*, 40.

Fellow Diversity

Fellows who participated in the Senate and Assembly programs in the late 1990s increasingly reflected the growing diversity of the state of California and the Legislature. Although not always achieved, diversity had been a goal for the fellowship programs since the 1970s. Once term limits took effect, the influx of new members broadened the diversity of the Legislature and increased demand for a diverse group of fellows.

Controversy over the diversity issue during the selection of the 1998–1999 Assembly Fellowship resulted in the Assembly's threatening to take away the program's funding. Tim Hodson remembered:

> When Antonio Villaraigosa was speaker of the Assembly [beginning in February 1998] and the first big wave of Latino members came in, the selection process selected one Latino out of eighteen. We don't have quotas. We don't have set asides. We never have. [But] we want a fellows program that represents the diversity of the state, geographically, politically, ideologically, demographically.

Hodson told the Assembly Fellowship Program director that she should seek a diverse class of fellows:

> I told [the program director] that one of the things she had to do as program director was to keep an eye on the entire applicant pool, [and use her influence to try to produce a class reflective of all California's diversity]. . . . In particular, I mentioned to her a concern that I had that the Republicans not be short shrifted.

At the first meeting of the selection panel, the program director discussed the selection criteria and informed the panel members that they would abide by Proposition 209. The director said there would be no preferences at all given to race or ethnicity, but then she proceeded to announce that six of the eighteen slots were reserved for Republicans. Not surprisingly, the Democrats on the selection committee were unhappy.

Hodson described the consequences of the announcement:

> I got the calls to explain why we were doing quotas for Republicans but the selection committee members were told they couldn't even consider the ethnicity or race of an applicant. They made it very clear that they were not advocating violating Prop 209 but they also felt that we were [violating] the spirit of 209 because we were doing set asides for Republicans.
>
> The Speaker had asked his staff and Assemblymember Cardenas to look into the situation. I had several meetings with them. They had serious questions about the judgment of the program director and, frankly, I shared those concerns. I didn't consider this kowtowing to politicians. It was a situation where we had just insulted a Capital partner by saying we were going to give special treatment to

one party but not the other on top of having an applicant pool that was anything but reflective of California or even the state Assembly.

Although the program director resigned, Hodson convinced the Assembly staffers and Assemblymember Cardenas that the real problem was not the program director but a steady decline in the number of applications, which had reduced the pool for selecting a diverse fellowship class. The Assembly agreed to give Hodson and the center a year and $20,000 to improve their outreach efforts and create a more diverse applicant pool.[18]

During the next year, the center began a very aggressive outreach program with the help of outside consultants. Applicants were recruited from a wide range of colleges and universities through mailings, advertisements, and on-campus visits. Advertisements were placed in publications directed at Latinos, African Americans, and Asian Americans.

Other improvements in the outreach process included: identifying and personally contacting principal "influentials" and organizations in the Latino, Asian-Pacific, and African-American communities throughout the state; updating the mailing lists for the Assembly and Senate Fellowship Programs; rewriting and redesigning the program brochures; making brochures and applications available on the center's website; providing members of the Assembly and Senate with information packets that included brochures, flyers, and draft press releases; and meetings with Assembly and Senate members and staff to follow-up on the information packets and solicit other outreach assistance.[19]

The intensive outreach efforts were rewarded. Hodson recalled:

Within a year, we had significantly increased the pool and the diversity. I went back to Mr. Cardenas [and said,] "Here's what we did." Mr. Cardenas read the report as we were standing in hallway. Then he stuck his hand out and said, "Congratulations," and he'd tell the Speaker everything was okay.

---

[18] Hodson, *Oral History Interview*, 51-55; Center for California Studies, *Annual Report, 1998*, 24; Timothy A. Hodson,<hodsonta@skymail.csus.edu> "Changes," 10 November 2003, personal e-mail (10 November 2003). Proposition 209, "Prohibition Against Discrimination or Preferential Treatment by State and Other Public Entities," was approved by the voters in 1996. It prohibited state, local governments, districts, public universities, colleges, and schools, and other government instrumentalities from discriminating against or giving preferential treatment to any individual or group in public employment, public education, or public contracting on the basis of race, sex, color, ethnicity, or national origin. It eliminated state and local government affirmative action programs in the areas of public employment, public education, and public contracting to the extent these programs involved "preferential treatment" based on race, sex, color, ethnicity, or national origin.

[19] Hodson, *Oral History Interview*, 54-55; Center for California Studies, *Annual Report, 1998*, 24-27.

Hodson attributed much of the success to the new director of the Assembly Fellowship Program, Robbin Lewis-Coaxum, who was described in the center's 1999 annual report as having "single-handedly restored the Center's credibility with the Assembly."

According to Lewis-Coaxum, diversity was crucial to an effective fellowship program:

> In my mind, diversity is very important given the composition of the house—by gender, by ethnicity, by partisanship, or whatever. That is something that should always be coveted as a positive in terms of the fellows—especially in terms of an academic seminar. You bring in people with opposing views.

She gave these examples of the importance of diversity:

> We were talking to the Committee on Human Services. They were talking about welfare reform and the issue of food stamps came up. I had the nicest Republican fellow sit there and talk about, "When I was in Chico, I would see these women coming in and they'd buy lobster. It's just so awful with the taxpayer's money." Then another fellow said, "Excuse me, I grew up on welfare. We had food stamps. We never up to this day, never had lobster" and proceeded to say how his family grew up. Then another fellow said, "I've never known anyone on welfare before. Can you tell me what welfare is like?"
>
> That's why diversity is so important [because] if you've never experienced something. . . . I had one fellow say to another fellow, "Do you think it's real, this driving while black?" He goes, "Let me tell you my experiences and how many times I've been stopped." If you don't have that diversity of thought, I think you lose a lot. I think it's really important that the fellowship program bring in the best and brightest but also be very conscious to make sure it looks like the composition of the house.

Following the selection of the 1999–2000 fellowship class, the center institutionalized the outreach campaign "which admittedly was undertaken in a crisis mode" by creating a full-time position of Capital Fellows Outreach Coordinator and an Outreach Advisory Task Force along with a new outreach plan that was implemented in the fall of 1999.[20]

---

[20] Hodson, *Oral History Interview*, 55-56; Center for California Studies, *Annual Report, 1999*, 4, 27-29, 61-65; Lewis-Coaxum, *Oral History Interview*, 28-29. Trina Gonzalez, a "standout as an Executive Fellow," joined the Center as its first Capital Fellows Outreach Coordinator in September 1999. Available application statistics from 1993 to 2005 are included in Appendix 8.3.

Other Developments and Activities

Senate Fellows Temporarily Become Senate Associates

Concern that the name "fellows" implied discrimination against women, compounded by the mistaken impression by the leader of the Senate that he'd been deliberately snubbed, led to a controversy that got the program's name changed in 1994. Hodson said a failure to communicate led to the controversy.

Hodson recalled that Senate President pro Tem Bill Lockyer thought "fellows" was a sexist term and recommended something more gender neutral. That resulted in Nettie Sabelhaus and Greg Schmidt, Lockyer's chief aide, researching the origins of the word "fellow." They concluded that while in some cases it is used mainly to refer to men, in academia it is completely gender neutral.

"Then we had a failure to communicate," Hodson said. "To put it simply, Nettie thought Greg had informed Lockyer of this. Greg thought Nettie had informed Lockyer." But neither had.

So when Lockyer was saying goodbye on the Senate floor to that year's Senate class, he said that it would apparently be the last one. Since the university and the center felt they could ignore the inquiries and wishes of the Senate, they could operate independently, without the Senate, he said. [21]

According to Hodson, Lockyer's comment provoked an immediate response from the Center for California Studies. "We immediately realized that it had gone beyond the question of gender-specific, gender-neutral vocabulary and it had been perceived by Senator Lockyer as a deliberate slight," said Hodson. Worsening the perceived snub, Hodson said, was the fact that both he and Sabelhaus had worked with Lockyer in the past.

"We sat down immediately and said, 'What can we do? We never intended to do this.' He said, 'I think you ought to come up with a gender-neutral term.' He didn't want to hear anything else," Hodson said.

After returning to campus, Hodson said, campus officials decided that a name change wouldn't harm the core values of the fellowship program, and it could deter problems caused by the leader of the Senate being angry about a perceived slight. "And so we changed the name," he said.

The Senate Fellows became the Senate Associates until John Burton replaced Bill Lockyer as President pro Tem. Encouraged by his chief of staff, Alison Harvey, a former Assembly fellow, Burton asked the Center for California Studies to return the program to its former name of Senate Fellows in 1999. [22]

---

[21] Hodson, *Oral History Interview*, 42; Sabelhaus, *Oral History Interview*, 33-34. Bill Lockyer served as president pro tem of the Senate from January 1994 until February 1998 when he was succeeded by John Burton.

[22] Hodson, *Oral History Interview*, 42-43.

The Assembly and Senate Fellowship Programs are Published

Both the Assembly and Senate fellows continued to participate in a regular academic seminar usually taught by a Sacramento State faculty member. For the Assembly fellows, the seminar included weekly discussions and periodic papers. By the end of the seminar, each fellow had completed a major policy paper that the faculty advisor, Ken DeBow, "wanted them to write not as a staffer for Assemblyperson such-and-such but as a person seeing from outside the scene, making a cool-headed rational analysis of whatever it was that they were talking about—which was more or less successful depending upon the students."

At the suggestion of Bob Connelly, the Assembly Rules Committee's chief administrative officer, many of these papers began to be published periodically in the early 1990s as the *Assembly Fellowship Program Journal*. Paper topics included youth violence, gun control, class size reduction, and property tax revenue shifts. The *Journal* appeared annually until 1997 when the program director and the faculty advisor decided to publish the papers less frequently.[23]

A new approach to teaching the seminar in the mid-1990s led to the publication of case studies written by the Senate fellows. After former Senator Barry Keene taught the seminar in 1993–1994, he "suggested the idea of a case project utilizing Capital Fellows . . . to CCS [Center for California Studies] Executive Director Tim Hodson."

Based on his experience in the public management program at Harvard's Kennedy School of Government in 1981 that used case studies extensively, Keene believed that "carefully selected, studiously researched, well written, course-relevant cases can be highly successful teaching instruments."

Hodson was intrigued by the idea because the scholarly literature included very few case studies based in California. In June 1995, he invited Howard Husock, director of case studies at the Kennedy School, to explain how to write and teach cases in a one-day workshop. Although all three of the fellowship program faculty advisors were offered the option of incorporating case studies into the seminar instead of term papers, only Ann Bailey decided to try the case study approach with the Senate fellows.[24]

The center contracted with Barry Keene to serve as the case project director for the Senate Fellowship Program. Working together, Keene and Bailey "taught

---

[23] DeBow, *Oral History Interview*, 9; Hodson, *Oral History Interview*, 94-95; Center for California Studies, *Annual Report, 1997*, 22; Ken DeBow to President Gerth, memorandum, [1990], PPO; Bob Connelly to Dr. Donald R. Gerth, 5 July 1989, PPO; Donald R. Gerth to Jeff Lustig, memorandum, 30 October 1989, PPO.

[24] Barry Keene, ed., *California Public Management Casebook* (Berkeley, Calif.: Institute of Governmental Studies Press, 1999), vii, 7; Hodson, *Oral History Interview*, 90-92; Center for California Studies, *Annual Report, 1995*, (Sacramento: The Center, [1996]), 27; Barry Keene, "History of the Capital Fellows Programs," *Oral History Interview*, conducted in 2003 by Elizabeth Austin, SCUA, 30-34.

case teaching and case writing, and then [they] coordinated that with the seminar, so that the students wrote these public policy cases as their major project in the seminar, then taught them to each other." Keene described the development and implementation of the case project:

> We asked the students to come up with ideas about cases. We said, "These will become your projects. If the cases are good, we plan to publish them. Their reactions gave rise to numerous administrative issues. For example, should a fellow be able to veto use of his or her case [as one of the published case studies]? What if it's an excellent case? What if people at CCS and interviewees invested a lot of time in it?
>
> For example, we had two splendid cases. One was done by [a fellow] who worked for a very conservative [legislator]. He produced a brilliant case on the poisoning of Lake Davis. Then, he concluded at some point along the way that if he ever ran for political office, here would be some document that somebody could excerpt something from. In my view, this was extreme paranoia. We said, "Why don't you use a pseudonym?" He replied, "You can track pseudonyms."
>
> Then there was another woman who produced a great case. It had to do with the reconstruction of the Santa Monica freeway which was done in record time [after the Northridge earthquake in 1994] with a public subsidy for rewarding the contractor for time of completion. It was a tremendous case in a lot of ways. The question of whether the public should pay someone extra to get a job done when it gets done earlier than expected. There were a lot of issues in it. She vetoed it.

Although some of the cases "were duds [and] some of them were highly biased," there were usually four or five outstanding cases every year that were ultimately edited and published by UC Berkeley's Institute of Governmental Studies. The first two volumes of case studies published in 1999 and 2000 included discussions of the motorcycle helmet law, the Medfly threat, the California Air Resources Board, the reconstruction of a freeway through West Oakland and redevelopment in Indian Wells.[25]

Community Service

In addition to their responsibilities as staffers and students, the fellows volunteered for community service. Nettie Sabelhaus, director of the Senate Fellowship Program, recalled:

---

[25] The two volumes of cases studies are: Barry Keene, ed., *California Public Management Casebook* (Berkeley, Calif.: Institute of Governmental Studies Press, 1999) and Barry Keene, ed., *Making Government Work: California Cases in Policy, Politics, and Public Management* (Berkeley, Calif.: Institute of Governmental Studies, 2000). Ann Bailey, "History of the Capital Fellows Programs," *Oral History Interview*, conducted in 2002 by Eliabeth Austin, SCUA, 3; Keene, *Oral History Interview* (Austin), 35-39.

We tried to do a little bit of public service each year. We'd go out and talk to some classes. Every year was a little bit different. There were a couple of teachers who'd remember us and invite us back year after year. There was a group of sixth graders out just behind Arden Fair in an area where lots of different languages are spoken. Kids are living in some of those motels back behind Auburn Boulevard. We'd talk to them. The fellows would get up there, looking very different, to say, "I was like you then. You can do this. Stay in school and go to college."

Senate Associate Jose Sigala established the State Senate Pen Pal Program with fifth graders at Sacramento's William Land School in 1993. Each fifth grader exchanged several letters with a state senator. At the end of the school year in May 1994, the class was invited to a Senate floor session where each student was introduced to his or her pen pal.

Senate Associate Julie Wong initiated the Capitol Kids Program at William Land School in 1995. Senate, Assembly, and Executive fellows met with William Land fifth graders at regular lunches to teach them about state government. Fellows also participated in Habitat for Humanity building projects, gave tours of the state Capitol, mentored high school students interested in public service, and served meals to the hungry at Loaves and Fishes.

Erin Peth, a 1998-1999 executive fellow, said, "We realized that we had a chance to combat the general apathy exhibited towards politics by mentoring, educating young people, and encouraging understanding and involvement in government."[26]

Towards a Full and Equal Partnership

When Hodson left his position as a Senate staffer to administer the fellowship programs as the new director of the Center for California Studies in August 1993, he observed that the university's relationship with the Legislature "was not a full and equal partnership. The senior partner [was] the Assembly and the Senate and the junior partner was the university."

Hodson believed that "term limits and some of the partisan changes in the early nineties" gave him the opportunity "to firmly establish that the fellow programs are not the creatures of our partners downtown." With experience in the Legislature as a member of the Senate staff coupled with academic credentials as a

[26] Sabelhaus, *Oral History Interview,* 30; Center for California Studies, *Annual Report, 1994,* (Sacramento: The Center, [1995]), 23-24; "Fellows and the Call to Public Service," *Californiana* 9, no. 2 (1999): [2]; "Capital Kids Program," *Californiana* 5, no. 1 (1995): [1].

Ph.D. in political science with a university teaching record, Hodson was well suited to bridge the two worlds of the fellowship programs.[27]

Under his leadership, the relationship between the center and its Capital partners gradually became more balanced. From Hodson's viewpoint, the status of full and equal partners has been achieved.

> To illustrate why it's a full and equal partnership, the selection committees for each of the four programs [the Judicial Administration Fellowship Program was added in 1997, see chapter 8] have essentially full and equal representation for the university. In the two legislative programs, there is a majority of legislative staff but they're divided between Democrats and Republicans. In the Executive and the Judicial, it's more fifty-fifty.
>
> The selection process is another example of how we have a full and equal partnership. Recently, we received a request from a legislator to accept an application from a constituent three weeks after the deadline. We decided that simply wasn't possible. The leadership told us clearly that they would back us, that we didn't have to worry about the legislator making trouble for us.

Although "some folks down in the Legislature think the seminar is a monumental waste of time, they will, nevertheless, help us enforce the rule that attendance is mandatory. They will not allow a fellow in their office to skip a seminar."[28]

> In the last several years, we have been routinely backed up by the Rules Committees and the governor. I would say we have a very healthy relationship now. We recognize and appreciate the role of our capital partners. We appreciate and accept the fact that their agendas are not necessarily the same as the University's. Our capital partners accept us as full partners and will respect our preferences. They also understand that our needs are not necessarily the same as theirs.

In part, he attributed the transition to a full and equal partnership to the effects of Proposition 140 "because the people, particularly in the Assembly, who regarded the Assembly Fellowship Program as an arm of the speaker's office, are simply no longer around. [With] the new people, you sit down with them, you say, 'This is how it used to run. This is the way it runs now. This is the way we'd like to have it run.' And no one's ever argued." Although the Legislature would always have the ability to cut off funding for the fellowship programs, the Center for California Studies had become an essential partner in their successful administration.

---

[27] Hodson, *Oral History Interview*, 2, 12, 20, 119.
[28] Hodson, *Oral History Interview*, 13-15.

New Directions: The Judicial Administration Fellowship Program

> As both competition for scarce public resources and demands on an already busy court system increase, it is more important than ever to develop a corps of effective court administrators and judicial policy analysts.
> —Center for California Studies, Program Maintenance Proposal, 1997–1998

> The ultimate measure of the strength of the third branch is the quality of its judicial officers and nonjudicial personnel. Every effort must be made to ensure that the best and the brightest are attracted to service in the judicial branch.
> —Commission on the Future of the California Courts, 1993

During his interview for the position of executive director of the Center for California Studies, Tim Hodson had suggested the possibility of establishing a fourth fellowship program that would benefit the courts of California. Hodson's idea for a judicial fellowship program began to take concrete form after he attended the 1995 LINKS conference hosted by the University of Colorado where he learned about a University of Georgia program that focused on court administration. Inspired by the program in Georgia, Hodson returned to California and approached the Judicial Council about becoming involved in a fellowship program that would "educate and train professionals and leaders in the growing complexities of the court system."[1]

---

[1] Sacramento State President Donald Gerth initiated the first LINKS conference which was held at Sacramento State in 1993. The LINKS conferences focused on public service partnerships between universities and state governments. The speaker at the 1995

129

The Judicial Council was a logical choice to join the Center for California Studies in sponsoring a fellowship program in judicial administration. Created by a constitutional amendment in 1926 to serve as the policymaking body of the California courts, its purpose is summarized in its mission statement:

> Under the leadership of the Chief Justice and in accordance with the California Constitution, the Judicial Council is responsible for ensuring the consistent, independent, impartial, and accessible administration of justice.

The administrative role of the Judicial Council made it a good match with the fellowship program Hodson envisioned.[2]

The council reacted positively to Hodson's proposal for a Judicial Administration Fellowship Program. The proposal coincided with a drive to improve the administration of the courts spearheaded by Chief Justice Ronald M. George who had assumed the leadership of the court system in May 1996.

Efforts were already underway to ensure trial court funding stability and to unify the superior and municipal courts in each county. Other reforms then in the making to streamline the administration of the courts included: the creation of specialty courts for drug offenses, domestic violence, the homeless and the mentally ill; the one-day or one-trial rule for jurors; a program to increase the number of court interpreters; and the improved application of technology.

The timing seemed right for a judicial administration fellowship program that had the potential to provide a cadre of trained administrators to serve the largest court system in the United States.[3]

---

conference that motivated Timothy A. Hodson was LaVerne Williamson, Court Futures Consultant and former Legislative Policy Analyst with the Georgia state Senate. Timothy A. Hodson, <hodsonta@skymail.csus.edu> "Judicial Administration Fellowship Program," 1 August 2003, personal e-mail (1 August 2003); Donald R. Gerth, "Opportunity and Responsibility: the Link Between Public Universities and State Capitals," pt. 1 of *Opportunity and Responsibility: the Link Between Public Universities and State Capitals, a National Conference, April 14-16, 1993 at California State University, Sacramento* (Sacramento, Calif.: Center for California Studies, [1993?]; Hodson, *Oral History Interview*, 9-10; Ray LeBov, interview by the author, Sacramento, Calif., 6 December 2002; Center for California Studies, *State of California Judicial Administration Fellowship Program* [brochure] (Sacramento, Calif.: Center for California Studies, [1997]), FCFP, 2.
   [2] Judicial Council of California, *Profile*, [2003], http://www.courtinfo.ca.gov/courtadmin/jc/documents/profilejc.pdf (28 July 2003). The Judicial Council has twenty-seven members: the Chief Justice of California, who serves as the council's chair; fourteen judges appointed by the Chief Justice; four attorneys appointed by the State Bar Board of Governors; one member from each house of the California Legislature; six advisory members, including court executives; and the Administrative Director of the Courts.
   [3] LeBov, interview; Judicial Council, *Profile*; Phil Isenberg, Assemblyman, Ninth District to Donald Gerth, President, Sacramento State, 11 January 1996, FCFP.

Funding

Armed with the enthusiastic support of the Judicial Council and Sacramento State President Donald Gerth, the Center for California Studies requested $189,000 in the 1996–1997 budget to finance five judicial fellows, along with a half-time director and a half-time clerical assistant. This first effort foundered in March 1996 after failing to win the approval of the governor's office. With renewed determination, the center pursued funding for the Judicial Administration Fellowship Program in the 1997–1998 budget. The center's budgetary proposal explained:

> The existing Fellowship Programs have been limited to the Executive and Legislative branches of California government. The third branch of government in California, the Judicial branch, does not currently benefit from the involvement of Fellows nor are Fellows able to learn more about the Judicial branch through the Fellowship Programs. Increasingly, applicants to the three existing programs have law degrees and many express academic and career interests in law and the judiciary.
>
> Court administration is a critically important area of public policy. Recent policy initiatives by the Governor and the Legislature, including trial court funding reform and court consolidation, are based, in part, on the recognition of the need to increase administrative efficiency in the judicial branch. As both competition for scarce public resources and demands on an already busy court system increase, it is more important than ever to develop a corps of effective court administrators and judicial policy analysts.
>
> Judicial Administration Fellows would provide immediate support for California's judicial administration system as well as recruitment and training for future judicial administrators. Judicial Administration Fellows would not be law clerks. Rather than working with individual judges, the Fellows would be placed with the Judicial Council, the Administrative Office of the Courts and, possibly, counties where court consolidations have created centralized court administrations. The Judicial Fellowship will produce individuals uniquely qualified to assist the judicial branch through these structural transformations.
>
> The proposal is to fund five Judicial Fellows in 1997–1998 as well as one half-time director and one half-time clerical position. The Judicial Council would be a co-sponsor of the Program, just as the Governor and the Legislative Rules Committees co-sponsor the existing Executive and Legislative Fellowship/Associate Programs.

The second attempt to secure funding succeeded and in February 1997 Sacramento State announced the new Judicial Administration Fellowship Program.[4]

---

[4] Hodson, *Oral History Interview*, 9–10; Gerth, *Oral History Interview*, 19; Center for California Studies, *Annual Report, 1995*, 26; Center for California Studies, *Program Maintenance Proposal for Fiscal Year 1997–1998*, 1996, FCFP, 9–10; "New Judicial Administration Fellowship Program," *CSUS News* (21 February 1997), FCFP; Timothy A. Hodson to Ray LeBov, Judicial Council; Carrie Cornwell, Judicial Council; Karen Yelverton, CSU; Nettie Sabelhaus, Center for California Studies, memorandum, 27 Au-

Recruitment and Selection

Before funding was approved, planning for the Judicial Administration Fellow-ship Program began. Anthony Williams, the Judicial Council liaison and a 1990–1991 Assembly fellow, remembered:

> We started with simultaneously trying to get funding in the [1997–1998] budget and also developing the structure [of the fellowship program]. On my end, that included identifying placements and putting together an interview selection panel, developing questions, developing the brochure, [and] trying to figure out the mar-keting of it. That all took place in a matter of four or five months.

Williams worked closely with Donna Hoenig-Couch who had added the half-time position of Judicial Administration Fellowship Program director to her half-time responsibilities as the Executive Fellowship Program director.[5]

Following the model established by the other fellowship programs, Hoenig-Couch and Williams quickly developed and mailed 8,000 brochures that described the program and solicited applications. Williams observed:

> We were targeting the same population as the other programs so we got some benefit from that. We also wanted to reach out, probably more so than the other programs, to law schools. While we did that, we also wanted to emphasize that it was not a legal clerkship program. That it was a judicial administration program. There were a lot of law students who [thought], "I'm going to go work for a judge doing research." That's not what the program was about.

The recruitment efforts generated many inquiries and netted thirty-four appli-cations. A selection committee screened the applications, interviewed approxi-mately half of the applicants and selected five fellows and five alternates.[6]

In subsequent years, although the number of applications fluctuated, the re-cruitment and selection process followed the same pattern. June Clark, who suc-ceeded Anthony Williams as the Judicial Council's liaison in 2000, detailed the process:

> The process is done by a committee. The director [at the Center for California Studies] sets up a committee of five. . . . The five of us represent different per-spectives. Donna [Hoenig-Couch] represents the program. I represent the Judicial Council. We have a court executive officer representing the trial court system. We have a former fellow, and we have the academic advisor bringing the aca-

gust 1996, FCFP; William Vickrey, Administrative Director to Honorable Pete Wilson, Governor, State of California, 9 February 1996, FCFP.

[5] Anthony Williams, "History of the Capital Fellows Program," *Oral History Inter-view*, conducted in 2003 by Elizabeth Austin, SCUA, 12.

[6] Williams, *Oral History Interview*, 13.

demic perspective. All five of us review the applications and rank them. The rankings are tallied then Donna and I go through the tallied rankings and make the decision about who will be interviewed.

After the interview, the selection committee engaged in a "lengthy but collaborative and collegial and effective process" of picking the judicial fellows.[7]

Placements

Unlike the other fellowship programs, the selection process included placement decisions. The candidates were informed about possible placements prior to the interview and asked to indicate their top three choices at the interview. The selection committee then chose the five finalists and assigned placements simultaneously. Hoenig-Couch described the unique characteristics of the judicial program placement process:

> [B]ecause we have people statewide, we are selecting the fellows and placing them at the same time. It's the only way we can do it because [otherwise the placements] would be too late. They don't get to interview.
> They have duty statements for the courts. They read the duty statements and they come to the interview with their choices and the reasons for those choices. We use part of the interview as an opportunity to talk to them about their choices and whether they have accurately read [and] understand the nuances of a particular court.

June Clark elaborated on how the fellows are matched with their placements:

> We factor in the candidate's rankings and discussion of the various placements and why they ranked them the way they did: their interests, their background, [their] personality because the placements are so different. When I say personality, I mean a very outgoing, social person might do better in a placement that requires a lot of interaction with other folks but there are placements that are more research oriented, for instance, and less interactive. We factor all those things in.

Clark noted that the assignments did not always match strong experience in an area with placements directly relevant to that experience.

---

[7] June Clark, "History of the Capital Fellows Program," *Oral History Interview,* conducted in 2002 by Elizabeth Austin, SCUA, 2-3. The total number of applications for 1997-1998 was 34; for 1998-1999 was 37; for 1999-2000 was 40; and for 2000-2001 was 54.

One of the things that we think is important about the program is that it be a growth experience. In my view, sometimes what we're doing is pushing the envelope a little bit, pushing the candidate a little bit out of their comfort zone.

Sometimes, we'll give more weight to what we think than what the candidate thinks. It's always proved a really good plan. We've had instances where the fellows have said at the end of the year, "I wasn't sure if this would work but I look back now and I've learned so much and changed so much and [grown] so much." I think that's a positive thing for this kind of a program. It's not a job. It's an opportunity to be exposed to a potential profession.

Placements

For the first year, placements were made with the administrative office of the Alameda County consolidated courts, the administrative office of the Sacramento County consolidated courts, the Judicial Council office in Sacramento and the Administrative Office of the Courts (AOC) in San Francisco. In 1999, placements were developed in Los Angeles in addition to the northern California locations.[8]

More so than any of the other fellowship programs, the Judicial Administration Fellowship Program assignments varied widely. They included policy analysis; planning and development; court project development and implementation; judicial and administrative staff education; development of curriculum-based judicial and administrative staff education programs; legislative analysis and advocacy; human resource management; information systems development; and budget development, management, evaluation, and review.

The placements reflected the six areas targeted by the Judicial Council's strategic plan for improving the California court system: access, fairness, and diversity; independence and accountability; modernization of management and administration; quality of justice and service to the public; education; and technology.[9]

The fellows' descriptions of their placements reveal their diversity:

It has been my privilege to work at the Judicial Council Office of Governmental Affairs and to experience the lobbying process as a representative of one of the three branches of government. My duties ranged from lobbying for legislative approval of the judicial branch budget to giving a presentation to the Task

---

[8] The Administrative Office of the Courts was established in 1961 to staff the Judicial Council and implement its policies. The placements for the fellows in the Judicial Administration Fellowship Program are included in Appendix 5.1. Clark, *Oral History Interview*, 3-4; Center for California Studies, *Annual Report, 1997*, 21; Center for California Studies, *Annual Report, 1999*, 29; Williams, *Oral History Interview*, 15; Hoenig-Couch, *Oral History Interview*, 43.

[9] Revised periodically, the Judicial Council adopted its first strategic plan in 1992. The plan included a mission statement, guiding principles, goals, objectives, and strategies. The latest revision of the strategic plan is entitled *Leading Justice into the Future*. Judicial Council of California, *Leading Justice into the Future*, 2000, <www.courtinfo.ca.gov/reference/documents/stplan2k.pdf> (7 August 2003).

Force on Trial Court Facilities. More importantly, I was responsible for ensuring the passage of legislation sponsored by the Judicial Council.

Taryn Ravazzini, 1997–1998 Judicial Fellow

My placement in the Administrative Office of the Courts' Technology Policy and Planning Division provided me an opportunity to work in the area of technology and law, a field that I have been interested in throughout my time as an undergraduate.

My placement allowed me to explore many of the different issues that are affecting the courts as they attempt to utilize new technologies to make themselves more efficient. For example, I was able to assist in updating the courts' employee computer usage policies. I also researched the legal issues affecting the utilization of video technology by the courts. For example, how does the Sixth Amendment right to confront an accuser affect the use of video by the court? I also had the opportunity to assist the staff in developing the courts' tactical and strategic plan for technology.

Henry Oh, 1998–1999 Judicial Administration Fellow

Between my placements in the Sacramento and Yolo Superior Courts, I worked on an exciting range of innovative projects undertaken by the Courts to improve access, fairness, and service to the public. Each placement provided me with insight into important collaborative efforts that strive to ease public navigation and understanding of the complex and often daunting world that is the California court system.

The first half of my Fellowship was spent working with the Planning and Operational Support Team at the Sacramento Superior Court. While in Sacramento, I assisted with the Court's newly established Self-Help Center, wrote grants, and developed a guide to the Family Relations Court.

The second half of my year was spent at the Yolo Superior Court in Woodland. A rural court located 25 miles outside of Sacramento, Yolo offered many exciting opportunities on projects ranging from web development to the establishment of a program to assist victims of crime with state compensation applications. I also wrote grants to secure funding for a juvenile violence court, developed public information materials, and assisted the Court with budget development for the next fiscal year.

Amy Loeliger, 1999–2000 Judicial Administration Fellow

Although some fellows initially experienced times when they did not have substantive work to do, their placements "always worked out in the end."[10]

Regardless of the placement, the Center for California Studies reported an "overwhelmingly positive response from the Judicial Branch sponsors." Anthony

---

[10] Center for California Studies, *State of California Judicial Administration Fellowship Program, 2000-2001* [brochure] (Sacramento: Center for California Studies, [2000]), FCFP, 4, 11; Center for California Studies, *State of California Judicial Administration Fellowship Program, 1999-2000* [brochure] (Sacramento: Center for California Studies, [1999]), FCFP, 9; Center for California Studies, *State of California Judicial Administration Fellowship Program, 2001-2002* [brochure] (Sacramento: Center for California Studies, [2001]), FCFP, 9; Clark, *Oral History Interview*, 17.

Williams observed that "the support from the judges and the court administrators was tremendous."

June Clark commented that the sponsors had all raved about the program:

> They all rave about it so much that I [often get calls from court people who] say, "When can I get a fellow? I want one. I just met with your group. They're fabulous. I want someone in my office." It's been really nothing but raves.

Ray LeBov, director of the Judicial Council's Office of Governmental Affairs, assessed the fellowship program as "hugely successful."

The praise inspired the Center for California Studies to request a budget augmentation that would double the number of fellows beginning in 2000–2001. The request was successful and the number of fellows in the Judicial Administration Fellowship Program increased to ten.[11]

Academics

Like the other fellowship programs administered by the Center for California Studies, the Judicial Administration Fellowship Program included an academic component that consisted of an orientation followed by regular graduate-level seminars.

The usual challenges of successfully integrating an academic component into the fellowship experience were compounded in the judicial program by its diverse work assignments in geographical locations throughout the state. Hoenig-Couch noted, "it's a real struggle in terms of time and travel and getting everybody in one place" for the seminars, which initially met biweekly and then just monthly. The seminar was especially difficult when there were only five fellows because "it was difficult to form a cohesive dynamic among the group."[12]

The two- to three-week orientation in Sacramento at the beginning of the fellowship year introduced the fellows to each other, to the judicial system, and to Sacramento State before dispersing to their placements. The orientation often included meetings with justices of the Supreme Court. Williams recalled two of those meetings:

> I believe it was the first class that I took to meet with one of the Supreme Court justices, Ming Chen. He gave them well over an hour, sitting and chatting about all sorts of things, getting to know each of the fellows and talking to them about their backgrounds. For each one, he seemed to know somebody who was associated with the fellow. That got us off to a really good start.

---

[11] Center for California Studies, *Annual Report, 1999*, 30; Clark, *Oral History Interview*, 16; LeBov, interview.

[12] Hoenig-Couch, *Oral History Interview*, 48–49.

There was another year when it was Justice Kennard and she did the same thing where she just dazzled them for a good chunk of time.

Chief Justice Ronald George also met with the fellows. Hoenig-Couch said he "really made them feel at home." The orientation was the best chance for the judicial fellows to develop the collegiality that was more easily established in the legislative fellowship programs where the fellows saw each other regularly.[13]

Developing a meaningful academic curriculum was "probably the biggest challenge that the program faced." Williams observed:

> We were trying to do something that hadn't really been done anywhere else: create a judicial administration curriculum tied to a program like [the Judicial Administration Fellowship Program].
>
> We started out by looking at the only model that existed. There was a program in court administration at USC that was helpful but not entirely. There were a couple of classes in court administration but to really understand the management issues that were going on in the courts, what issues they faced and how to develop a curriculum that responded to that was hard because nobody had ever done it in any comprehensive way.

By 1999, the Center for California Studies recognized that "our weak link remains the academic component of the program. In our judgment, we have not fulfilled the promise to provide a graduate-level curriculum that meets the goals and standards we set for ourselves and the ones that the court placements demand."[14]

The program director and faculty advisors experimented with different approaches to the seminar in an effort to find the most workable format and an appropriate curriculum. Instead of meeting every two to three weeks, the fellows began to meet every month or six weeks because of time and travel constraints. Project assignments between meetings kept the fellows in contact. Weekly teleconference meetings supplemented with monthly meetings in person may be the format of the future.[15]

Curriculum development was initially impeded by the rapid turnover in faculty advisors—a different advisor from a different Sacramento State department was in charge of the seminar for each of the first three years. In 1999, an faculty advisor was selected whose public policy and administration background was well suited to the requirements of the Judicial Administration Fellowship Program.

Anthony Williams concluded, "Eventually we got it right but it did take the first few years to work out a lot of the kinks and get the right fit in terms of a faculty person and develop the right kind of curriculum." The curriculum continued

---

[13] Williams, *Oral History Interview*, 20-21, 24-25; Hoenig-Couch, *Oral History Interview*, 56.

[14] Williams, *Oral History Interview*, 19; Donna Hoenig-Couch and Timothy A. Hodson, Center for California Studies to Elizabeth Moulds, Vice President and Chief of Staff, Sacramento State, memorandum, 25 January 1999, FCFP.

[15] Hoenig-Couch, *Oral History Interview*, 48-49.

to evolve in response to the needs of the courts. Hoenig-Couch's ultimate goal is "a really focused curriculum that blends [the] areas of administration and management with legal studies." She acknowledged, "We're not there yet but we're working on it."[16]

The Judicial Administration Fellowship Program: A Preliminary Assessment

The original proposal for the Judicial Administration Fellowship Program promised two significant benefits: immediate support for California's judicial administration system, and recruitment and training for future judicial administrators. Clearly, the fellows have provided meaningful and productive support for the judicial administration system. In addition to participating effectively in the ongoing administration of the courts, they have also exposed the system to new perspectives.

June Clark observed:

All the placements report, and I have seen, that the fellows bring new ideas. They ask questions that old timers have stopped asking. Or that should be asked. They start up new programs. Their excitement about a particular area gets the court excited about that particular area, about community outreach programs or things like that.

The fellows have infused the court system with "enthusiastic, fresh thinking."[17] The Judicial Administration Fellowship Program has been less successful thus far in generating a group of trained judicial administrators who remain in the court system. Although some fellows have secured employment in court administration, they are the exceptions rather than the rule. Clark offered an explanation for this limited success:

As a practical matter, it is more difficult for this program than the other [fellowship programs] to serve as a stepping stone to court administration positions directly following the program. There are several reasons for that. One is [that] a lot of our candidates are considering or planning to go to law school. They're not interested in finding work the month after the fellowship ends.

Another idiosyncrasy with this program is that the work that the fellows do as fellows is work that, as employment candidates off the street, they wouldn't be qualified for. They don't have the requisite experience or education . . . because so many of the court administration positions, that are commensurate with the

---

[16] The Judicial Administration program directors, faculty advisors and Judicial Council liaisons are listed in Appendix 5.2. Williams, *Oral History Interview*, 18-20; Hoenig-Couch, *Oral History Interview*, 50-51.

[17] Clark, *Oral History Interview*, 12.

kind of work the fellows are doing, are higher level. The fellows don't come in and do brand-new-employee work.

Participants in the Judicial Administration Fellowship Program have not had the same opportunity or desire for immediate employment found in the other fellowship programs. Clark has "finally come to realize that the year is a great experience for [the fellows] and the [judicial] branch gains a lot from the program in that [fellowship] year." The possibility remains that the judicial fellows will return to the field of court administration later in their careers.[18]

With its steadily rising popularity among both applicants and placements, the program as a springboard for future court administrators remains a work in progress, and the academic component continues to evolve. The possibility of expanding to eighteen fellows exists but future expansion depends on budgetary considerations.

---

[18] Clark, *Oral History Interview*, 9-11; Hoenig-Couch, *Oral History Interview*, 45-46.

Conclusion: The Capital Fellows Programs

When the first group of graduate students ventured into the Assembly in 1957, they began an experiment in education that laid the foundation for four fellowship programs serving all three branches of state government. After more than forty years, the success of the fellowship programs has validated Joseph Harris' belief in the value of "participant-observers" who gain practical experience in state government while providing much-needed staff services.

The benefits of these programs to the participants, to their placements in state government, and to the development of Sacramento State as the "Capital Campus" are widely recognized. The interns and fellows, who have frequently referred to their participation in the program as a "life-changing experience," have often gone on to long and productive careers in public service. The legislative, executive, and judicial sponsors have strongly endorsed the fellowship programs. The ever-increasing demand for fellows is clear evidence of their support.

Sacramento State President Donald Gerth has stated unequivocally that "the single most important thing that happened to move us toward being the state's Capital University is the Fellows program."[1]

Effective administration has been essential to the success of the internship and fellowship programs. The responsibility for administering the internship and fellowship programs has shifted with the vagaries of funding and politics, from the University of California to the legislative Rules Committees to the Center for California Studies at Sacramento State.

When Tim Hodson arrived at the center in 1993, he discovered that the fellowship programs had been largely "left to govern themselves." They were separate entities with "very little communication, cooperation, [or] collaboration

---

[1] Donald Gerth, *Oral History Interview*, conducted 2002 by Elizabeth Austin, 23.

[among] the three programs. The three programs did not perceive themselves as being linked."

Through the development of common administrative practices and increased interaction among the fellows, directors, and faculty advisors of all four programs, the Center for California Studies successfully encouraged the development of a collective identity for the fellowship programs. A new name, the Capital Fellows Programs, was adopted in 2000 to acknowledge the growing sense of solidarity among the Assembly, Executive, Judicial Administration, and Senate Fellowship Programs.[2]

Although each fellowship program has retained unique qualities based on the characteristics of its sponsor, they have all been united under the leadership of the Center for California Studies. For the center, the successful administration of the programs has depended on its ability to maintain good relations with its legislative, executive, and judicial partners despite budget crises and other political upheavals.

The center's 2001 annual report summarized the impact of the Capital Fellows Programs:

> More than 1,100 men and women have served as Capital Fellows. Building on their Fellow experience, many have gone on to successful public service careers both in and out of government. From Congressmen to assemblymembers; teachers to judges, business and university leaders to filmmakers and e-commerce pioneers, fellow alumni have and continue to make significant contributions to the public life of California.
>
> Combining public service with academia, the fellowship programs have successfully developed public servants educated for leadership.[3]

Final Reflections: In Their Own Words[4]

Administrators

To the university, [the fellowship program] is one of the activities which is central to our mission as a capital university, the state's public university in the state capital. Just as you would expect Fresno State to have a strong program in agriculture, and they do, because they're in the heart of one of the richest agricultural

---

[2] Timothy A. Hodson, *Oral History Interview*, 3, 19; Center for California Studies, *Annual Report, 2000*, 4.

[3] Center for California Studies, *Annual Report, 2001*, 26.

[4] These comments are excerpts from oral history interviews, questionnaire responses, newsletters and brochures. The positions held by the administrators and faculty advisors at the time of their involvement with the fellowship programs are indicated. The fellowship year and, if available, the current positions held by the fellows quoted are also indicated.

1.1. Luther H. "Abe" Lincoln, Assembly Speaker, 1955–1958

1.2. Jesse M. Unruh, Assembly Speaker, 1961–1968

1.3. Mervyn Dymally, State Senator, 1967–1975

2.1. Donald R. Gerth, President of California State University, Sacramento, 1984–2003

2.2. George Deukmejian, Governor, 1983–1991

2.3. David Roberti, Senate president Pro Tempore, 1980–1994

Ronald M. George, Chief Justice, California State Supreme Court, 1996–

3.1. 1965 Assembly Interns Farewell Party (future U.S. Rep. Howard Berman, first on left, front row; Program Director Gerald McDaniel, back row with hat)

3.2. 1970–1971 Assembly Fellows with then Assemblyman John Burton (center)

4.1. 1977–1978 Assembly Fellows

4.2. 1980–1981 Assembly Fellows

5.1. 1987–1988 Assembly Fellows with Assembly Speaker Willie L. Brown, Jr. (far left)

5.2. 1989–1990 Assembly Fellows

6.1. 1997–1998 Assembly Fellows (future Assemblymember Audra Strickland, third from right, first row)

6.2. 1998–1999 Assembly Fellows with Speaker Antonio R. Villaraigosa (center)

7.1. 1999–2000 Assembly Fellows (Program Director Robbin Lewis Coaxum, front row center)

7.2. 2005–2006 Assembly Fellows

8.1. 1987–1988 Executive Fellows with Governor George Deukmejian (Program Director Richard Krolack, second from left)

8.2. 1993–1994 Executive Fellows with Governor Pete Wilson

9.1. 1996–1997 Executive Fellows

9.2. 1997–1998 Executive Fellows

10.1. 2001–2002 Executive Fellows (Faculty Advisor Robert Waste, front row, second from left; Program Director Sandra Perez, front row, third from left)

10.2. 2005–2006 Executive Fellows

11.1. 1997–1998 Judicial Administratioin Fellows

11.2. 1999–2000 Judicial Administration Fellows with Chief Justice Ronald M. George

12.1 2001–2002 Judicial Administration Fellows (Program Director Donna Hoenig-Couch, back row, far left; Program Assistant Claire Bunch, back row, third from right)

12.2. 2003–2004 Judicial Administration Fellows

13.1. 1987–1988 Senate Fellows (future State Senator Dean Flores, top row, third from right)

13.2. 1988–1989 Senate Fellows (Future Board of Equalization Member Betty Yee, front row, third from right; U.S. District Judge Yvonne Campos, front row, third from left)

14.1. 1990–1991 Senate Fellows

14.2. 1992–1993 Senate Fellows (Program Director Nettie Sabelhaus, fourth from right; future Assemblymember Jose Solorio, sixth from right; Faculty Advisor John Syer, eighth from right)

15.1. 1995–1996 Senate Fellows seminar with Senator Ken Maddy

15.2. 1999–2000 Senate Fellows

16.1. 2002–2003 Senate Fellows (Faculty Advisor Roger Dunston, center)

16.2. 2005–2006 Senate Fellows

valleys in the world, you would expect a public university in the capital of the world's fifth nation-state to use Gray Davis's terminology, to be strong in the area of public affairs. The Center for California Studies and these fellows programs, which made the institutionalization of the Center possible, are central to our mission as a Capital University.

Donald Gerth, President, Sacramento State

[The fellowship programs] have absolutely increased awareness of the presence of California State University, Sacramento, in the Capitol to the legislators. I go down with a group from the state universities for its annual lobby day. As we visit legislators' offices, the first thing they say is, "I have a fellow," or "I don't have a fellow this year but I had one last year," or "Let me bring my fellow in." It is the first identification that comes through. . . . We really try hard to be of service to the legislature. Our mission is to be heavily engaged in the preparation of public servants. We have a real commitment to public service. A lot of our students want to move in that direction. I think that they understand that genuinely in the Capitol now. That's a major piece of what we're about. That building is filled with our former undergraduate interns, with our fellows. They are staffers. They are members.

Elizabeth Moulds, Vice President and Chief of Staff, Sacramento State

One of the most important goals of the fellow programs is to develop political, governmental leaders of the future who have public service skills, public service commitment, public service ethic. We explicitly want to develop people who will stay in government service. We like the idea of judicial fellows staying with the courts. We like the idea of legislative fellows staying in the legislature. We like the idea of executive fellows staying in the executive branch. We like the idea of having them go to work for a city government or a county government or a school district or whatever. That doesn't mean we consider it a failure if someone says, "I was a teacher and now I want to go back and be a teacher again." That's fine, too. The phrase I use is, "We don't care whether you become governor of the state or the best PTA president your local school ever had but we want you to become leaders. We want you to become committed to public service."

Tim Hodson, Executive Director, Center for California Studies

I really do credit Don Gerth for his vision and commitment and tenacity in making [the fellowship programs at CSUS] work. . . . Those early days, he just said, "This is the way it's going to be. This is what we're going to have. We're going to have these opportunities and we're going to make these opportunities." Especially in the Assembly Fellows Program where the UC had had such a powerful tradition. . . . Don Gerth made the Capital Campus part of his vision.

Cristy Jensen, Faculty Advisor, Assembly Fellowship Program

Program Directors and Faculty Advisors

It's a great program for the fellows. I think it's a great experience with a great set of opportunities. It's a great learning experience. I like it best when they take [the experience] and then go up to graduate school with it and go back to the community or local government rather than staying [in the Legislature]. It opens up some doors. It opens some experiences that they could never get just out of college.

Ken DeBow, Faculty Advisor, Assembly Fellowship Program

We're all one Center. We're Capital Fellows [but] we're Assembly and we're unique. Just by virtue of it being the lower house, you're going to probably do longer hours. You're going to have to probably get your hands dirtier. When they schedule, they probably will caucus for five hours before the session actually starts. The Senate's just run much more efficiently by virtue of the fact that it's the upper house. Fewer people to have to deal with. You have to understand coming out of the gates that the Assembly is the lower house. It's the people's house. You're going to run into a lot more activity during the floor session. The chaos is going on. Everyone is talking to everyone else. You're thinking, "How are they passing bills?" That's the lower house. You just deal with it.

[The Assembly Fellowship Program] is where [the legislative] staff comes from. This is it. I get calls all the time from lobbyists or whoever, "Any former fellows looking for work, here's my card. Let me know. We really want a fellow." Because they've been trained. They have a year under their belt. They've had five weeks of intensive training and a year under their belt. Low-pay, coveted individuals that are bright. Obviously, to make the cut, they're the best and the brightest.

[The fellowship program] is a value not only to the individuals seeking to become a part of public policy and [to understand] the legislative process. On the legislator's side, they see it as free, quality, professional staff that they get to have. It's also an opportunity for many members to actually be mentors, to train and give back and contribute. I think it's a two-way road. I think it's also the responsibility of government to provide that avenue, that access, to individuals that have studied and trained and worked to be able to be a part of the process and to have that door opened to them. If you close that door, you'll have to know somebody that knows someone else to be able to get in.

Robbin Lewis-Coaxum, Director, Assembly Fellowship Program

We always made the point to [the executive fellows] that this is not a job search process. Don't necessarily expect that you're going to have a position in state service when [the fellowship] is over. Some of them did stay. Some of them were, in fact, recruited and stayed on permanently. But I think all of them walked out with a better understanding of what goes one in the executive branch. To that extent, you've got another group of people who are that much more knowledgeable about what's going on. My sense is that most of them ended up still participating, if not direct participants in the public sector, in peripheral areas, in advocacy or whatever, and therefore had a better understanding about how government works.

Richard Krolak, Director, Executive Fellowship Program

I think that, for the vast majority of [fellows], [the Executive Fellowship Program] is a really good experience. I think people feel like they understand state government. They appreciate it much better. They appreciate the complexities of the process. Just in terms of understanding and appreciation, they very often get a much better sense of what they like. Some people find, "I really like this political stuff." That's really good. Some people find they don't. They like research. It helps people sort that out.

For state government, it's very valuable because [the fellows] are very talented people. It really is one of the only ways that complete outsiders can come in. Later on, you'll need to be both talented and have connections but you really don't here. People can come in complete outsiders. That's really valuable. It's a way of getting talented people from various, different places, a way to come in without any connections.

Ted Lascher, Faculty Advisor, Executive Fellowship Program

[Mentoring] is one of the most rewarding parts of my job. It's very time consuming. It's not free labor like some people have occasionally seen these kinds of programs. You have to put some effort into it to make it rewarding. When you do, the rewards are above and beyond the professional assistance you've gotten from the fellow.

I love watching the evolution of the fellows we've had from the beginning of their year here to the end of their year here. I love watching them get excited about what they're doing. I love watching how they're single-handedly dealing with this negotiation or that lobbying process when six months ago, they didn't know what the words meant. It's just so rewarding.

It takes a while for people to find out what they can give the fellow. I'm not aware of a situation where, at the end of the year, a fellow said, "This was a sheer and utter waste of time." I remember, particularly, one incident where the fellow was very aggressively complaining. There was a lot of back and forth between the Center and this fellow and occasionally, it was between me and this fellow. At the end of the year, I received a note from the fellow saying, "I know I complained a lot during the year but I apologize for that and I have to tell you that I wouldn't have changed anything about it. In looking back, I see that everything I did was important to the system and I learned from it. I wouldn't have done anything differently." I think that's part of the growth experience.

June Clark, Judicial Council Liaison

[The fellows] had the best training you could have for [legislative staff work] so, of course, they would be in demand. That's not a surprise. But some of them would then build on that, say "Well, I never thought I wanted to go to law school but now I really do and this [fellowship] has really helped me figure that out." Or, occasionally, somebody who was just so turned off by politics. I told them that too, "If you spend a year here and find that this is not your calling, you have done yourself a favor in a relatively brief amount of time." I think it's different for everybody. In the end, we never saw it as just [a training program for staffers]. We hoped that it was actually a place where they would take the message of public policy out there to the larger community. Go do something else and tell them how important it is to remain involved in civic life. That everyone has an obligation to continue to try to solve problems and not turn their back.

I really enjoyed my years with the fellow program because it was so rewarding to watch people begin to understand that the process of problem solving in a public setting is not as easy as they think it is at the outset. And watching that transition in the year from, "I know what to do," to "Wow, this is way harder than it looks," was always rewarding. I feel like we helped people establish roots in careers where they are really doing wonderful work now.

                    Nettie Sabelhaus, Director, Senate Fellowship Program

It's a rare individual that it's not a meaningful experience for and a life-changing experience. Not always an easy experience. It's amazing how often people will have a tough period of time in their office and they get around that. They turn that corner and things end on a very positive note.

     The part that I love [about being the director of the Senate Fellowship Program] is the ability to mentor, the privilege of interacting with such an incredible group of accomplished individuals. The applicant pool that we get now is just incredible. The things that these individuals have done. What they know. Who they are. Their involvement in nonacademic kinds of activities. It's awesome. It's inspiring. I feel that I have an opportunity to play a little bit of a role at a time in their lives that's really important to them when they are making these transitions. I put a lot into my work and my commitment to the program and I just get a tremendous amount back from the fellows.

                    Dan Friedlander, Program Director, Senate Fellowship Program

Nobody gets any training in public service anymore. People can go to public policy school where they learn a lot of theories—which I'm not critical of, it's a good thing to learn—but there are so few opportunities for actual training in public policy decision-making. . . . These young people get the experience to learn before they are the ones in public office trying to learn on their feet. There's so much disconnect between the legislature and the people. [The Senate Fellowship Program] is a way of trying to bridge that disconnect.

     Sometimes you see people who come with a real interest in public policy and they find that they're just fascinated by the politics. And the other way around—they come interested in politics and get real interested in policy. Some people come and find that they love it and want to stay. Some people come and find that they just can't wait to get out of here. The politics is too much for them and they just want to go back to academia or public policy or something else. So it's good. It's not that everybody comes in and stays in but they find out.

                    Ann Bailey, Senate Fellowship Program, Faculty Advisor

Assembly Fellows

The entire time [as a California Legislative Intern] was a wonderful experience. The internship got me acquainted with the Legislature and government and was the impetus to go to law school. My knowledge of water gained while at the [Assembly Water] Committee got me started on a career in state government that lasted until 1983 as a member of the Water Resources Control Board and Director of Water Resources.

                    Ron Robie, California Legislative Intern, 1960–1961
                    Associate Justice, Court of Appeal, Third Appellate District

[After the internship,] I was recruited to become part of the "permanent professional staff" that was then being established by Speaker Jesse Unruh. I served in that capacity for over twenty years—before being recruited to become a professional lobbyist. In short, my professional career was based on the foundation provided by the intern program.

Tom Willoughby, California Legislative Intern, 1960–1961
Manager, State Governmental Relations, Pacific Gas and Electric Co., Retired

[The internship program] was of great value. You were seeing the legislative process from inside. You were in direct contact with both the legislators and the staff and the lobbying influences, the Third House, and a little bit, the media. In terms of knowing the process, it was the kind of thing you aren't going to get from textbooks and you're not going to get from just being an activist or a volunteer in political campaigns.

[The Assembly internship program] was a career decisive move on my part. Would I have ended up [in elected office] on some other path? Maybe, but this really sharpened my interest in doing it and helped prepare me for it as well.

Howard Berman, California Legislative Intern, 1965–1966
Member of Congress

My academic career has focused on "Education Politics and Policy," and my experience as a California Legislative Intern provided "flesh on the skeleton" for much of my teaching, research, and public service at the University of Wisconsin, Madison, from 1966–1999.

My experience as a Legislative Intern led to a 35-year involvement with the Wisconsin legislature and educational interest groups as a consultant, policy researcher, and a member of legislative "interim" study committees. My experience in California caused me to understand and "like" legislative politics, legislators, and staff and led to effective work with the legislative, budgetary, and rulemaking processes.

Experience in the California Legislative Internship program led me to participate actively in politics at the local and state level from managing local and state-wide campaigns to being elected to a city council and mayor (1973–1981) and appointment as the Deputy Wisconsin State Superintendent of Public Instruction (1981–1986).

B. Dean Bowles, California Legislative Intern, 1965–1966
Emeritus Professor of Educational Administration
University of Wisconsin-Madison

I was always very good as a student. This was my first real world experience in a serious job. I had to learn a lot of lessons about how to get things done with people, learn about process such as working with people, that I otherwise hadn't had an opportunity to do. . . . In the sense that it directed me to an interest in public policy and budgetary politics as a lifetime pursuit, it was very important. I hadn't had that thought previously.

Lindsay Desrochers, Assembly Intern, 1974–1975
Vice Chancellor for Administration
University of California, Merced

[After my fellowship], I immediately used my knowledge as an artist interested in change and was selected to serve on the committee to develop an arts commission for the City and County of Sacramento. I later served on the Arts Commission and it is still a major aspect of [that] community. I learned the avenue and approaches to apply community action and experience and for a short period of time I was a statewide Advocate for the Arts (registered lobbyist).

John F. King, Assembly Fellow, 1975–1976

The knowledge/experience I gained [as a fellow] was the springboard and foundation for my 25+ year career working for the Legislature.

Nancy Rose Anton, Assembly Fellow, 1977–1978
Consultant, Senate Education Committee

I liked everything about my experience. It was intellectually interesting, it was fascinating politically and I met all kinds of intelligent and activist people. I really enjoyed analyzing legislation and watching people debate policies in committee meetings. I also enjoyed the "behind the scenes" policymaking. My experience as an Assembly Fellow gave me a very positive view of government. I came as an idealist and left as one!

My best experience was managing legislation to legalize home beer brewing, a personal hobby. It was initially introduced by Mr. Gualco [Democratic Assemblyman from Sacramento], but when he decided to run for Congress (and lost to Bob Matsui), he felt he should shed any "liquor" bills. So it was picked up by Tom Bates from Berkeley. It was opposed by the California Grocers Association, but we found that many of the members had fond memories of home brewing. We had a lot of fun with the bill, and eventually, it passed and was signed into law. In subsequent sessions, the brewing laws in California were further relaxed, allowing for the growth of the small, boutique breweries.

[After the fellowship], I returned to my previous job of newspaper reporter and the experience was very useful, particularly when covering local government and politics. Since 1982, I have worked in the Legislature.

Alison Harvey, Assembly Fellow, 1977–1978
Chief of Staff to Senate President pro Tem John L. Burton

I use my knowledge of public policy in my law practice on a regular basis. I think I'm a better lawyer and a better advocate for my clients because I understand how government works. I take an independent approach towards interpreting statutes. My practice involves negotiation and problem-solving skills I began to learn as a fellow. It's a GREAT experience and I'm grateful to have had it.

Karen Nardi, Assembly Fellow, 1977–1978

[After my fellowship], I never left the legislative arena. All the jobs that I've had since then, almost twenty-five years ago, maybe more, have been legislatively, public policy related. All of them. I find the work very worthwhile and very gratifying. [The fellowship] definitely changed my entire direction.

Lilly Spitz, Assembly Fellow, 1977–1978
Chief Legal Counsel, California Planned Parenthood Education Fund

You really do get a sense of being in a fellowship class. There is really a connection that [the fellows] have. I'm thinking right now of trying to help organize a push to have a twenty-five year reunion. I would be very interested in seeing where my colleagues are. That seems to be a very common thing. It is really a formative experience. Not the least of which is people coming from all these different places and they end up together. They're each other's peers in a way that you aren't for most jobs. . . . There's a bond there that stays with people. It holds for a long time.

Ted Lascher, Assembly Fellow, 1978–1979
Chair, Department of Public Policy and Administration, Sacramento State

I have vivid memories [of the fellowship experience]. I have some of my best friends from that period of time and I stay in touch with most of the twelve fellows from my class. One of them was Mike Thompson who is now the Congressperson from Napa. . . . The fellowship experience gave me the sense that I could do anything.

Loretta Lynch, Assembly Fellow, 1983–1984
California Public Utilities Commission

[The fellowship] improves on the institution of representative government in a number of different ways. It becomes a de facto training ground for individuals who are involved or want to be involved in the legislative process, in the institution of representative government. Those who stay in the legislature are better trained and better equipped to work on issues that are important to the people of California. Those who leave and go somewhere else take with them a much better understanding of government and the process than they otherwise would have. In addition to that, it enables the institution to be able to bring people in who may not otherwise have that exposure.

[The fellowship] was a great experience. It was priceless. Had I not done that, I doubt that I would have ever run for the State Senate. Had I not done that, I doubt that I ever would have run for or served in Congress. It made a difference.

Mike Thompson, Assembly Fellow, 1983–1984
Member of Congress

There was no formal academic component to the fellowship program at that time, although I learned a tremendous amount. It was a kind of "learn by fire" approach, as we simply had to jump in and learn by doing. It was a great experience.

My best experience was working on the state budget, which included around the clock (all-nighters) work with other committee staff the last weekend before the deadline in June. It really gave me a good appreciation for the tremendous work of the budget committee staff, and how much behind the scenes negotiation and sweat it involved.

After the fellowship, I decided to go to law school. The fellowship experience was instrumental in that decision. I now work as a lobbyist and legal counsel for a trade association on insurance issues.

G. Diane Colborn, Assembly Fellow, 1984–1985
Lobbyist and Legal Counsel

I have worked most of the years since I was a Fellow as a Capitol staffer, with a couple of years off for graduate school, a year to travel, and a couple of years to lobby. The fellowship helped me, probably more than any other year, to make contacts in and around the Capitol. I am sure I learned much about the legislative process, although I believe I learned even more after my fellowship, when I spent two years working for the Assembly Rules Committee. There is nothing like a leadership office to learn the real process.

> Carrie Cornwell, Assembly Fellow, 1986–1987
> Chief Consultant, Senator Tom Torlakson

I don't use my [fellowship] background academically or politically in the work that I am paid to do, however, I do use it extensively in my volunteer work with the California YMCA Model Legislature and Court, as well as in my capacities on boards, committees, etc. where Roberts Rules do come in handy.

> Katherine Yoshii, Assembly Fellow, 1986–1987

I was already working in the Philippine Congress as Chief of Staff when I was selected for the JMU [Jesse Marvin Unruh Assembly] fellowship so I understood most of the processes and dynamics in legislative decision making. What the fellowship gave me was a comparative and international perspective that was extremely useful when I went back to the Philippines. This knowledge was useful in my work as a professor of public administration at the University of the Philippines and as a consultant to various Senators in the Philippine Senate.

> J. Prospero de Vera, Assembly Fellow, 1991–1992
> Professor of Public Administration,
> University of the Philippines Consultant, Philippine Senate

The work was a great experience overall. I'm in graduate school now and I have a context for comparison between what I'm learning and the "real" world.

> Lizelda Lopez, Assembly Fellow, 1999–2000
> Graduate Student, Harvard University, Kennedy School of Government

Executive Fellows

The [Executive Fellowship] program provided [an] entrée to State government that would not otherwise have been available to me. It offered the opportunity to participate in the Executive Branch of government and learn from an insider's perspective.

> Sue Bost, Executive Fellow, 1987–1988
> Assistant Program Budget Manager for Business Transportation, Housing,
> Trade and Technology Department of Finance

I had several mentors at work. There was my direct supervisor, who helped train me in what I needed to do. There was also the executive director of the Commission [on State Finance] staff, who acted more as my mentor. He was taking time off from being a Vice President at Goldman Sachs, and so I think he brought a different perspective from the "lifer" state worker mentality that you find so often in the executive branch.

What was different for me was that both of my mentors were people of color. As a person of color myself, I had not had that many role models who were successful minority men in a professional environment, even having come from a very diverse university. I think this really helped me get comfortable in an office. I look back on it now and think that this was really important to my confidence in the workplace now.

I really felt welcomed in Sacramento. There was an existing network of people who were used to fellows and I felt like I fit right in.

Brian M. Wong, Executive Fellow, 1992–1993
Lawyer, Pillsbury Winthrop LLP

I had already served seven months as an intern with the Office of the Chief Clerk of the Assembly and wished to continue to gain experience in state government. The Executive Fellowship provided the exposure and opportunities that I was seeking, and the ability to work in the higher levels of state government without partisan influences.

My understanding of the architecture of the executive branch has been invaluable for research and special projects. It is often difficult to navigate around the state's executive agencies; my experiences and contacts have given me important tools and resources when issues arise that cross legislative and executive spheres.

The friends and contacts developed during the program [are] probably one of the greatest benefits of the program.

Hugh Slayden, Executive Fellow, 1997–1998
Office of the Chief Clerk of the Assembly

The fellowship gave me the confidence to trust my skills. Eventually, I applied all of the professional skills I learned—budgeting, organization, communication, problem solving, and basic administrative skills—and went into partnership with a co-worker from a different job and opened a small publishing firm. We produce a weekly newspaper and a sports magazine. I did not possess the fundamental skills to succeed in this endeavor without the fellowship, and more importantly, I would not have had the courage or the confidence to take that risk prior to the fellowship.

Bill Hicks, Executive Fellow, 1998–1999
UNC Publishing

The best part about the academic component for me was that it set aside time for all of us to share what we were doing in work with our fellow classmates and begin to codify a bigger picture policy discussion. I was not as academically inclined as many of my classmates, and I remember sitting there and realizing that here was a guy with a Ph.D., a woman with a law degree and two women with master's degrees and they were going through the same "first work experience/first political work experience" as the rest of us fresh from undergrad and being relieved that they shared the same anxiety/excitement about this new adventure. Our class really became a large family/support group for that year.

[I realized] that politics often wins out over good governance. It's a lesson that if not kept in check can quickly shatter the youthful idealism that we're working towards something that is really benefiting the people of California, but it's a valuable lesson to learn, and undoubtedly, having the fellows network of political upstarts to bounce frustration off of softened the blow somewhat. It's actually a good lesson for business in the private sector too, just replace "governance" with "management."

I definitely used my fellowship experience. I'm employed by a global public relations/public affairs firm and I use the in-depth knowledge earned by trial-by-fire Sacramento/political fellowship experiences daily. I've used everything from a basic knowledge of how government here works to the ever-evolving network of experienced mentors that the fellowship program gave me to help assist clients in navigating their public affairs needs.

Brian E. Micek, Executive Fellow, 1999–2000
Hill and Knowlton, Inc.

My best experience was getting to know the people I worked with and being inspired by their enthusiasm for issues affecting children ages zero to five. My mentor, Emily Nahat, is an amazing woman that I feel incredibly lucky to have worked with.

I currently work for the Alameda County Children and Families Commission and thus use the skills and knowledge I gained as a fellow almost every day. One key lesson I learned as a fellow is the need to network and treat all people as future employers/friends/etc.

Kelly Hicks, Executive Fellow, 2000–2001
Community Grants Associate, Every Child Counts, First Five
Alameda County, San Leandro, California

Judicial Administration Fellows

Working with court administrators and judges has rooted my law degree in reality and given me a crash course in the dynamics of how courts work. I know that this experience will prove to be invaluable.

Phil Busse, Judicial Administration Fellow, 1997–1998

I entered my year as a Judicial Administration Fellow with theories of law, public policy, and the criminal justice system. I was, however, naïve to the art of judicial administration and the complexity of the decision-making process. The practical knowledge I gained over this past year [as a fellow] has deeply enriched my perspective and laid the foundation for my continued professional and personal growth.

Kyong Yi, Judicial Administration Fellow, 1997–1998

My colleagues, four exceptional fellows, provided a network of support and friendship. A diverse group, we each contributed intellectual, social and cultural perspectives to our fellowship experience and case study on AB 233 (California Trial Court Funding). This was a unique opportunity to enter a charged environment where collaborative inquiry, decision-making practices and independent thought were strongly encouraged by the Center for California Studies.

Gary Flores, Judicial Administration Fellow, 1998–1999

My year as a Judicial Fellow was a rewarding and enlightening experience. . . . I was assigned to the Community Focused Court Planning Committee where I learned organizing strategies, implementation plans and effective research skills. This experience has furthered my interest in community outreach and ways of involving the public in building effective public institutions. Working with the court gave me first hand experiences in a variety of areas from professional conduct to teamwork and leadership.

The Judicial Fellowship Program has broadened my views, ambitions and goals. I am taking so many wonderful things from this experience in the hopes of applying them to my future endeavors and making a significant impact on societal issues and public policy.

Jorja Jackson, Judicial Administration Fellow, 1998–1999
Law Student, Hastings College of Law

The fellowship gave me a tremendous opportunity to develop not only professionally, but personally as well. There are things that I learned that I would never have learned in a classroom and I experienced things that I know I would not have experienced without the fellowship. I feel very fortunate to have spent this last year participating in the fellowship and I can say without hesitation that it affected my life deeply on many different levels.

Henry Oh, Judicial Administration Fellow, 1998–1999

This is a very dynamic time for the California judicial system. Policy makers are wrestling with increasing caseloads, prison overcrowding, funding and consolidation issues. I was very fortunate to have been a Judicial Administration Fellow at the Second District Court of Appeal at such a critical period. Through the fellowship I expected to learn about administration in the courts, however my learning experience went beyond judicial administration and I gained valuable leadership, analysis and problem solving skills. . . .

Finally, and perhaps most valuable, I have developed lasting friendships with some very wonderful people at my placement. In every way, my experience in the Judicial Administration Fellowship has been a positive one.

Mohammed Wardak, Judicial Administration Fellow, 1999–2000

My year as a Judicial Administration Fellow provided me with a hands-on, inside perspective of the trial court system in California. . . . To put it simply, my year as a Judicial Administration Fellow was truly amazing. I came into the program with a desire to gain a clear understanding of the inner workings of the Court system, and I am struck by how much I have gained from the experience. It is incredibly rewarding to participate in the fellowship program and to be a part of all the changes currently underway in the courts.

Amy Loeliger, Judicial Administration Fellow, 1999–2000

My year as a Judicial Administration Fellow at the Judicial Council Office of Governmental Affairs has been a truly remarkable and educational experience. . . . My exposure to the intricacies of the legislative and budget processes broadened my understanding and appreciation for how the judicial branch functions as an integral part of our state government. I truly believe that the skills I have gained throughout the course of the fellowship will enhance my future professional endeavors.

Sanna Singer, Judicial Administration Fellow, 1999–2000

Senate Fellows

I used the [Senate Fellowship] experience to begin a career in state government. I'm extremely grateful for my start as a fellow. I don't see how I would have accomplished my goal [otherwise].

Diana Fuentes-Michel, Senate Fellow, 1979–1980

My relationship with Senator [Milton] Marks and Caroline ([his] wife) was a close working relationship—driving him back to San Francisco, staying with the family on Jordan Ave. and attending every birthday, social and bar mitzvah possible. It was a great experience that I will not ever forget.

Joshua Pane, Senate Fellow, 1980–1981

I didn't see the Senator much during my time as a Fellow. He also spent a lot of time in his home district so he wasn't always in Sacramento. My mentor was his chief aide and she was really terrific. She tried to make the fellowship both a learning process as well as one that had true value. I kept in contact with her for many years after my fellowship.

I later became the Mayor of my hometown and the Legislative experience was helpful. Today, as a department head for a city government, I still make use of some of my Legislative experience in terms of tracking and advocating positions on certain bills affecting local government.

Zane Johnston, Senate Fellow, 1980–1981
President, California Society of Municipal Finance Officers

I value the contacts I made as a Fellow. I went on from there to do a year of governmental affairs work for the California Community Colleges and a little lobbying for the deaf. I am retired now, but my last job was as the Executive Director of the Harry S. Truman Club for ten years. The Truman Club raises money for local Democratic candidates up through Congress. My fellowship experience gave me an abiding interest in California politics with a depth of understanding how the system works.

Linda Tochterman, Senate Fellow, 1984–1985
Executive Director, Harry S. Truman Club, Retired

The [Senate Fellowship] program provided me with an opportunity to gain the necessary legislative skills that I, as a Member of the Assembly, still use today. Writing analyses, press releases, and letters—and having the opportunity to staff bills—were all valuable aspects of my fellowship. I really was able to quickly get an insider's perspective on how the Legislature and law-making in general work.

Dean Florez, Senate Fellow, 1987–1988
Member of the California Senate

As a city administrator in California, I am much better able today to understand the complexities facing the State Legislature during budget crises [because of my fellowship experience]. It makes me far less able to comfortably bash the Legislature for whatever budget solutions it reaches. I also am able to remain objective about what legislative ideas have a chance at passage and which do not. I was able to use some of my contacts gained in 1988–89 to help get a very important bill (for my city, at least) passed in 2001.

Dave Kiff, Senate Fellow, 1988–1989

My fellowship experience helped me to get an opportunity to co-found Morrison and Foerster's Sacramento office in 1991 and establish the [law] firm's presence in the capital. More recently, I have become a political science professor and I teach, among other things, courses in California politics. I often draw on the knowledge and relationships I gained as a fellow.

Ken Miller, Senate Fellow, 1988–1989

The Senate Fellow Program offered me an opportunity to use my skills and experience to shape public policy in the public health and human services area. It also provided me experience with resolving policy concerns in highly political environments. But perhaps the most important aspect of my Senate fellowship was the ability to establish valuable relationships with, and learn from, experts in a wide array of subjects representing a broad range of policy and political perspectives. I feel confident that the lifelong skills I have developed through these experiences will continue to help me regardless of whatever endeavor I choose to undertake.

Betty Yee, Senate Fellow, 1988–1989
Chief Deputy Director, Department of Finance

After studying political science and interning in Washington, D.C., for Senator Pete Wilson, I thought the Senate Fellowship was a great way to experience state policymaking. Without the fellowship, I wouldn't have known how to break into state politics.

After serving as the principal consultant to the Senate Local Government Committee [following the fellowship], I left in 1998 to raise my children. In addition to parenting my children, I consult part-time on public finance issues for a policy advice organization.

April Manatt, Senate Fellow, 1990–1991

As a member of OWL (Older Women's League—an advocacy group for older women), I learned about the [Senate Fellowship] program, applied, and when accepted, was rather an anomaly. Fellows are usually in their twenties. I was sixty-five.

In my own job [on the Committee on Housing and Urban Affairs], I received many bills related to mobile homes. Often there was a dreadful conflict between the homeowners and the mobile park owners. I truly began to feel the sad situation in which the homeowners often found themselves. At a committee meeting, the lobbyist for the park owners came over and said: "You really seem affected by this. You must learn to be like me. I am a hired gun; I can argue equally well on both sides of an issue." My blood ran cold. I decided then that I was not of the fiber necessary for political activity. But, I must say, I did come away with high regard for my own senator, Mike Thompson.

Pearl Stein Selinsky, Senate Fellow, 1991–1992

My [Senate] fellowship experience was life changing. It was exactly what I wanted to do—be with like-minded individuals, from different walks of life, who were passionate about public policy.

Peter Shiao, Senate Fellow, 1991–1992
President and Executive Producer, Celestial Pictures

I developed a wonderful relationship with Senator Quentin L. Kopp, Dan Friedlander, his chief of staff, and the rest of the senator's staff. I received incredible opportunities to staff legislation for the senator in areas ranging from tax law to criminal and civil procedure to state constitutional amendments.

The experience gave me the confidence to serve in public and government service and in intensely political environments. I do not come from a political family, and indeed I am the first in my family ever to go to law school or to pursue government service as a professional career. The experience in Sacramento gave me the strength and confidence to know that, even though politics is all too often a mean and dirty business, I could learn to negotiate that treacherous world and find a meaningful career trying to promote causes I believe in.

James C. Ho, Senate Fellow, 1995–1996
Attorney Advisor U.S. Department of Justice, Office of Legal Counsel

I staffed Senator [Dede] Alpert for the Natural Resources Committee, carried (I think) eight bills, and handled the majority of the Capitol office's constituent mail responsibilities. All these assignments helped me better understand the process, the district and the work ethic necessary to succeed in this environment.

In terms of a mentor, I didn't really have one in the office per se. I really wanted to work for a female member—the opportunities for that type of mentoring in government politics are few and far between, and I wanted to take advantage of it here.

As a result of the fellowship, I decided to stay in the Capitol and continue to work as a legislative staffer. I use the experience and lessons of the fellowship every single day!

Nora Lynn, Senate Fellow, 1996–1997
Consultant, Senate Committee on Appropriations

The best experience was being able to take off running on legislative assignments, even with no experience. The people in the program were all fantastic, and we all became very good friends. Meeting other wonderful people in the Capitol was very rewarding, and I remain friends with many people I met through the program.

I now work as a practicing attorney, and I really appreciate being able to be a part of the legislative process. The legislative arena is a very unfamiliar world for many lawyers, and it's helpful to know the terminology involved with the process as well as where to find legislative history.

Kara Ueda, Senate Fellow, 1996–1997
Attorney

I was attracted to the [Senate Fellowship] program originally by the opportunity to become immediately and intimately familiar with the legislative process. The program's most influential "selling point" was that I would be given real responsibility; that I'd be taking part in the legislative process, not observing it from the sidelines. The program delivered as advertised.

I enjoyed very much the academic portion of my fellowship. It was invigorating and enlightening to discuss policy issues with such an accomplished group of colleagues. There was a true collegiality among my classmates. I also enjoyed the case study project, which provided me the opportunity to develop further my research and writing skills by becoming immersed in an interesting aspect of California public policy.

The knowledge and experience that I gained as a fellow is largely responsible for the position I hold now. I was recently promoted to a management position at the nation's leading state government relations firm, where experience as a state legislative staffer is a requirement for employment. My intimate familiarity with the legislative process has been instrumental in my success, as my ability to advise clients confidently is due directly to the skills I gained and contacts I made in Sacramento. My fellowship has been a tremendous boon to my career.

Owen M. Sweeney, Senate Fellow, 1997–1998
Stateside Associates, Arlington, Va.

Appendix 1
1955 Conference on Streamlining State Legislatures
List of Participants[1]

Name	Affiliation
Andrews, William S.	California Gas & Electric Companies
Bachtold, Harold E.	Assistant to the Speaker of the Assembly
Barclay, Thomas	Professor of Political Science, Stanford University
Beaver, Jack A.	Member of the Assembly
Bee, Carlos	Member of the Assembly
Beek, Joseph A.	Secretary of the Senate
Bone, Hugh A.	Professor of Political Science, University of Washington
Booe, Agnes	Sacramento Newsletter
Caldecott, Thomas W.	Member of the Assembly
Carpenter, Richard	League of California Cities
Carr, Francis J.	Pacific Gas & Electric Company
Chernin, Milton	School of Social Welfare and Bureau of Public Administration, University of California, Berkeley
Clarvoe, Frank A.	Santa Barbara News Press
Cobey, James A.	Member of the Senate
Coolidge, Glenn E.	Member of the Assembly
Dahl, Walter I.	Member of the Assembly
Englebert, Ernest	Professor of Political Science, University of California, Los Angeles
Farr, Fred	Member of the Senate
Griffin, Philip F.	Professor of Journalism, University of California, Berkeley
Guild, Frederic	Director of Research, Kansas Legislative Council
Harris, Joseph P.	Professor of Political Science, University of California, Berkeley
Holmer, Jean	President, California League of Women Voters
Irwin, Frank H.	California Taxpayers Association
Jones, Victor	Professor of Political Science, University of California, Berkeley
Kennedy, Vincent D.	Retailers Association of California
Kirkwood, Robert C.	State Controller

---

[1] Scott, 82-83.

Kleps, Ralph N.	California Legislative Counsel
Knorp, Albert F.	Home Builders Council of California
Kragen, Adrian A.	Professor of Law, University of California, Berkeley
Landels, Edward D.	Bankers Association of California
Leary, Mary Ellen	*San Francisco News*
Lincoln, Luther H.	Speaker of the Assembly
Lindsay, Francis C.	Member of the Assembly
Little, Walter J.	Association of Steam Railways
Maloney, Thomas A.	Member of the Assembly
Mason, Paul	State Director of Motor Vehicles
McConnell, Grant	Professor of Political Science, University of California, Berkeley
McDonough, John M.	Professor of Law, Stanford University
McHenry, Dean E.	Professor of Political Science, University of California, Los Angeles
McKay, Robert E.	California Teachers Association
Miller, Allen	Member of the Assembly
Miller, George, Jr.	Member of the Senate
Neuberger, Richard L.	Member of the United States Senate
Neuberger, Mrs. Richard L.	Member of the Oregon Assembly
Newman, Frank	Professor of Law, University of California, Berkeley
Odegard, Peter H.	Professor of Political Science, University of California, Berkeley
Post, A. Alan	California Legislative Auditor
Pryor, Robert	California Manufacturers Association
Ross, Jane	California League of Women Voters
Rumford, William Byron	Member of the Assembly
Schofield, William R.	California Forest Protective Association
Scott, Stanley	Bureau of Public Administration, University of California, Berkeley
Sherry, Arthur H.	Professor of Law, University of California, Berkeley
Spaeth, Carl	Professor of Law, Stanford University
Taylor, Paul H.	California Agricultural Council
Thomas, Don	Oakland Tribune
Vieg, John A.	Professor of Government, Pomona College
Walker, Robert A.	Professor of Political Science, Stanford University
Weinberger, Caspar W.	Member of the Assembly
Wiltsee, Herbert	Council of State Governments, Chicago

Wood, Samuel E.

Research Director, Assembly Interim Committee on Conservation, Planning and Public Works

Ylvisaker, Paul

Ford Foundation, New York

Appendix 2
Legislative Intern Program: 1957–1965
2.1. Assembly Resolution Regarding the Creation of the Legislative Intern Program[1]

RESOLUTIONS

The following resolution was offered:

By Messrs. Kelly, Samuel R. Geddes, Belotti, Bee, Lindsay, Hawkins, Bonelli, Unruh, Doyle, Lincoln, McCollister, House, Grant, Bradley, Bruce F. Allen, Dahl, O'Connell, Meyers, Miller, Ernest R. Geddes, Luckel, MacBride, Rumford, Crawford, Schrade, Brown, Frew, Winton, and Shell:

House Resolution No. 34
Relative to the legislative interns

WHEREAS, The Assembly has initiated this year a Legislative Internship Program modeled after the Congressional Intern Program in operation in Washington, D.C., since 1953; and

WHEREAS, Each year under the plan, up to 15 graduate students from five sponsoring California universities will serve with the Legislature in a variety of positions for 10 months; and

WHEREAS, The Ford Foundation has agreed to share the cost of the program with the Assembly for a period of five years; and

WHEREAS, The first eight interns selected to participate in this program are Linus J. DeWald, James Driscoll, Roderic Duncan, Richard Harvey, Carman Hews, Ruth Ross, Charles Kunsman, Jr., and William Scheuermann, Jr.; and

WHEREAS, This program by which the interns supplement their academic studies with responsible experience in the legislative progress, and the legislators and legislative committees in turn benefit from the valuable assistance rendered by the interns, has already produced an enthusiastic response and many favorable comments; now, therefore, be it.

Resolved by the Assembly of the State of California, That the members express their satisfaction with the excellent results already achieved from the program, and commend the interns for their fine work and co-operative spirit; and be it further

Resolved, That the Chief Clerk of the Assembly is directed to transmit a suitably prepared copy of this resolution to each legislative intern.

Request for Unanimous Consent

---

[1] *Assembly Journal*, March 29, 1958, 317–18.

Mr. Kelly asked for, and was granted, unanimous consent that those members so desiring be permitted to affix their signatures, as co-authors of the resolution at the desk.

Request for Unanimous Consent

Mr. Kelly asked for, and was granted, unanimous consent to take up House Resolution No. 34, at this time, without reference to committee or file.

Resolution read, and adopted unanimously.

2.2. Intern Names and Placements

1957–1958

Driscoll, James	Assembly Member H. W. Kelly; Manufacturing, Oil & Mining Industry Committee
Duncan, Roderic	Speaker Luther H. "Abe" Lincoln
Harvey, Richard	Assembly Member Allen Miller
Hunt, Carmen	Assembly Member Donald Doyle; Education Committee
Kunsman, Charles	Assembly Member Francis C. Lindsay; Conservation, Planning & Public Works
Ross, Ruth	Assembly Member Glen Coolidge, Ways & Means Committee
Scheuermann, Jr., William	Assembly Member Frank Belotti, Fish & Game Committee
Wald, Linus J.	Assembly Member Bruce Allen; Judiciary Committee

1958–1959

Anderson, Stanley	Interim Committee on Judiciary Criminal Procedure Committee
Byrne, Richard	Interim Committee on Judiciary Manufacturing, Oil and Mining Industry Committee
Hall, Stuart	Speaker Luther H. "Abe" Lincoln Assembly Desk; Water Committee
Levy, Edward	Interim Committee on Public Health Finance and Insurance Committee
Sexton, Roy	Education Committee
Smart, John	Manufacturing, Oil and Mining Industry Committee Government Organization Committee
Stevens, Jan	Interim Committee on Conservation, Planning, and Public Works
Vichules, Leo, Jr.	Revenue and Taxation Committee
Zimmerman, Robert	Rules Committee

1959–1960

Angelo, Louis	Interim Committee on Elections and Reapportionment
Coben, Melvyn	Interim Committee on Criminal Procedure
Condren, Clive	Interim Committee on Education
Conwill, Sarah	Interim Committee on Revenue and Taxation
Culver, Willis	Interim Committee on Ways and Means
Day, Richard	Interim Committee on Ways and Means

Doerr, David	Interim Committee on Government Organization
Evans, Stanley	Interim Committee on Finance and Insurance
Harper, Harold	Interim Committee on Water Office of the Speaker
Ingro, John	Interim Committee on the Judiciary – Civil
Judd, Robert	Interim Committee on Livestock and Dairies
Spear, John	Interim Committee on Manufacturing, Oil, and Mining Industry
Wiggins, James M.	Interim Committee on Governmental Efficiency and Economy

1960–1961

Bird, Rose	Government Organization Committee
Bolinger, Bruce	Elections and Reapportionment Committee
Carmack, John	Social Welfare Committee
Ellenberg, Marvin	Finance and Insurance Committee; Assembly Desk
Ellis, John	Assembly Research Center
Fisher, Lawrence	Ways and Means Committee
Gunnell, John	Constitutional Amendments Committee; Assembly Research Center
Heaphey, James	Assembly Research Center
Hill, Douglas	Manufacturing, Oil and Mining Industry Committee; Education Committee
Hoss, Richard	Assembly Research Center Finance and Insurance Committee
McGhee, Milton	Criminal Procedure Committee
Patsey, Richard	Judiciary Committee
Robie, Ronald	Water Committee
Rusco, Elmer	Elections and Reapportionment Committee
Willoughby, Thomas	Public Health Committee

1961–1962

Courtemanche, Robert	Ways and Means Committee
Flanagan, James, Jr.	Water Committee
Geyer, William	Agriculture Committee
Joe, Thomas	Social Welfare Committee
Jones, David	Judiciary Committee
Joseph, Anthony	Finance and Insurance Committee
Larson, Ronald	Education Committee
Leyval, Eugene	Constitutional Amendments Committee
Newman, Jack	Revenue and Taxation Committee
Padgett, Robert	Ways and Means Committee
Poschman, Gene	Public Health Committee

Springer, Barbara   Elections and Reapportionment Committee

1962–1963

Baer, Carl   Municipal and County Government Committee
Baker, Paul   Revenue and Taxation Committee
Binford, R. Keith   Government Organization Committee
Grafft, David   Speaker Jesse M. Unruh
Jenkins, A. Dobie   Governmental Efficiency and Economy Committee
Kaplan, Philip   Social Welfare Committee
Kauffman, Stephen   Rules Committee
Kavanagh, Dennis   Finance and Insurance Committee
Milem, John   Education Committee
Perry, Jerold   Ways and Means Committee
Sands, Michael   Criminal Procedure Committee
Segal, Morley   Elections and Reapportionment Committee
Willoughby, W. Jackson   Judiciary Committee

1963–1964

Cohan, Phyllis Louellyn   Municipal and County Government
Feinbaum, Robert   Governmental Efficiency and Economy Committee
     Public Health Committee
Garcia, Arthur   Rules Committee
Keiser, William   Criminal Procedure Committee
Oster, Gilbert   Education Committee
Silk, Thomas, Jr.   Judiciary Committee
Spellman, John   Ways and Means Committee
Wald, Michael   Rules Committee

1964–1965

Anawalt, Howard   Judiciary Committee
Blackmon, Clyde   Natural Resources, Planning and Public Works
     Committee; Criminal Procedure Committee
Blicker, David   Education Committee
Denny, Laura   Municipal and County Government Committee
Epstein, David   Water Committee
Fitzrandolph, John   Joint Constitutional Revision Commission
     Legislative Organization Committee
Juers, Edward, Jr.   Ways and Means Committee
Keene, Barry   Criminal Procedure Committee
     Natural Resources, Planning and Public Works
     Committee
Leigh, Peter   Public Health Committee
Robbins, George   Agriculture Committee

2.3. Legislative Intern Program: Demographics and Statistics

California Legislative Intern Program	1957–1958	1958–1959	1959–1960	1960–1961	1961–1962	1962–1963	1963–1964	1964–1965
Interns (Total)	8	9	13	15	12	13	9	10
Men	6	9	12	14	11	13	7	9
Women	2	0	1	1	1	0	2	1
Institutions								
Claremont	1	1	1	1	0	1	0	0
Stanford	0	1	2	0	2	2	1	1
UC Berkeley	3	4	5	10	5	8	4	6
UCLA	3	1	4	2	2	1	2	1
USC	1	2	0	2	1	0	1	2
UCSB	0	0	0	0	1	1	0	0
San Jose State	0	0	1	0	0	0	0	0
Loyola	0	0	0	0	1	0	0	0
Fields of Study								
Criminology	0	0	0	0	0	0	1	1
Economics	0	0	0	1	0	0	0	0
History	0	0	0	0	2	0	0	0
Journalism	3	1	3	2	0	1	1	0
Law	1	2	4	4	5	5	3	6
Political Science*	4	6	6	8	5	7	3	3
Sociology	0	0	0	0	0	0	1	0
Age Range	24–33	23–30	22–30	22–32	22–32	22–35	24–35	24–29

* One political science student in each of the years, 1958–1959 and 1962–1963, also held an LL.B. degree.

2.3. cont.

Degrees

Bachelor's	1	1	5	3	3	2	4	1
Master's	6	5	5	7	5	5	2	3
LL.B.	1	3	4	3	4	6	2	6
Ph.D.	0	0	0	2	0	0	0	0

2.4. Occupations of Former Interns as of July 1965[*]

Position	Subtotal	Total
Legislative Aide		20
California Assembly	18	
California Senate	1	
U.S. Congress	1	
Public Administration		11
California Educational Agencies	4	
California Attorney General	3	
California District Attorney or County Counsel	4	
Graduate and Professional Study		18
Law	4	
Social Sciences	14	
Teaching		9
College – Political Science	7	
Secondary School	2	
Private Law Practice		15
Business		5
Political Organization		3
Military Service		1
Journalism		1
Research for Labor Organization		1
Community Service		1
Unknown		3
TOTAL		88

---

[*] University of California, Berkeley. Department of Political Science, *Eighth Annual Report, California Legislative Intern Program* (Berkeley, Calif.: The Department, 1965), 5.

2.5. Legislative Interns and Assembly Staff

Year	Total Assembly Staff	Number of Former Interns on Assembly Staff	Former Interns as Percentage of Assembly Staff
1957	14	n/a	
1958	n/a	4	
1959	16 +	6	37.5
1960		13	
1961	18	16	88.8
1962	n/a	13	
1963	44	12	27.2
1964	n/a	15	
1965	64	18	35.5

2.6. Available Application Statistics for the California Assembly Fellowship Program, 1975–1985[1]

Fellowship Year[2]	1975	1976	1977	1978	1979	1980	1981
Total Number of Applications				471	252	151	196
N. California				264	127	78	107
S. California				183	111	67	77
Outside California				24	14	6	12
Asians				22		3	10
Blacks				17		6	6
Hispanics				25		11	14
Whites				407		131	166
Highest Degrees Obtained							
Bachelor's				335	182	110	
Master's				97	48	17	
Ph.D.				13	2	1	
J.D.				26	20	6	
Invited for Personal Interview				107	84	68	88
N. California				58	48	34	43
S. California				43	28	30	40
Outside California				6	8	4	5
Men				53	45	34	39
Women				54	39	34	44
Invited to Sacramento				32	28	28	34
N. California				18	15	14	16
S. California				12	10	12	16
Outside California				2	3	2	2
Men				16	16	18	17
Women				16	12	10	15
	10[1]	9[2]	15	15	12	12	12

[1] Ronald Loveridge to Members, Executive Board, California Assembly Fellowship Program, memorandum, October 8, 1976, ARCP; Statistics dated April 8, 1980 on Assembly Rules Committee letterhead; "Profile—California Assembly Fellows/1978–79," ARCP; "California Assembly Fellowship Program 1978–1979 Applications Profile," ARCP; "California Assembly Fellowship Program 1979–80 Applications Profile," ARCP; "California Assembly Fellowship Program 1980–1981 Applications Profile," ARCP; "California Assembly Fellowship Program, 1981–82 Applications Profile," ARCP. If not listed, statistics are currently not available.

[2] The year indicated is for the fall of the fellowship year. For example, 1975 is for the fellowship year 1975–1976.

Finalists						
N. California					7	
S. California					5	
Men	6	10	8	9	4	8
Women	3	5	7	3	8	4
Bachelor's	4	8	8		8	11
Master's	1	4	4		4	
Ph.d.	2	1	1		0	
J.D.	2	2	2		0	1
Asians		1	4	0	1	0
Blacks		1	1	2	1	2
Hispanics		2	1	1	2	1
Whites		11	9	8	8	9

---

[1] An eleventh fellow was added by the Rules Committee after ten fellows were chosen by the Executive Board.

[2] Fourteen fellows were selected but five declined or resigned. Two accepted Coro fellowships. One accepted a contract to do air pollution research in the South Coast Basin. One accepted a staff position with the Assembly Judiciary Committee. The fifth was too fatigued from preparing for and taking the Bar examination.

Appendix 3
The Assembly Fellows Program

3.1. Assembly Resolution Naming the Jesse M. Unruh Assembly Fellowship Program

House Resolution 20
By Speaker of the Assembly Willie Lewis Brown, Jr.
Relative to the Jesse Marvin Unruh Assembly Fellowship Program

WHEREAS, Jesse Marvin Unruh was elected Speaker of the California State Assembly on September 30, 1961, and distinguished himself in that position for nearly seven and a half years; and

WHEREAS, Jesse Marvin Unruh is considered one of the greatest Speakers of the California State Assembly; and

WHEREAS, In the course of his Speakership, Jesse Unruh established high standards of professional conduct for members of the Assembly staff as evidenced by other states adopting the California model;

WHEREAS, One aspect of the professionalization of the California State Assembly was the development of the California State Assembly Fellowship Program; and

WHEREAS, The fellowship program offers participants practical, first-hand knowledge of the Legislature through work experience and provides staff assistance for Members of the Assembly and for legislative committees; and

WHEREAS, During the last 30 years, this program has produced excellent career staff for the Legislature as well as many who have gone on to successful careers in law, education, business, community service, and elective office; and

WHEREAS, Former Speaker Jesse Marvin Unruh praised the fellowship program as "an excellent vehicle for tapping keen young minds from our outstanding system of higher education"; and

WHEREAS, The fellowship program stands as a tribute to the legacy of Jesse Marvin Unruh, former Speaker of the California State Assembly, brilliant political leader, and beloved Californian; now, therefore, be it

Resolved by the Assembly of the State of California, That in honor of former Speaker Jesse Marvin Unruh's contributions to the California State Assembly Fellowship Program, the program will hereafter be known as the "Jesse Marvin Unruh Assembly Fellowship Program"; and be it further

Resolved, That the Chief Clerk of the Assembly transmit a suitably prepared copy of this resolution to the immediate members of his family.

H.R. 20, California Assembly, 1987–1988 Regular Session, *Journal of the Assembly* (17 August 1987): 3872–73.

3.2. Assembly Fellow Names and Placements: 1965–1966 to 2005–2006

1965–1966
Berman, Howard	Agriculture Committee
Bowles, B. Dean	Education Committee
Caton, George	
Hirsch, Richard	Government Organization Committee
Howald, Walter	
Monk, Robert	
Nasatir, Michael	
Rosin, Alan	Social Welfare Committee
Shearer, Harry	
Visnich, Daniel	Assembly Member Mervyn Dymally

1966–1967
Axtell, Keith	Ways and Means Committee
Buck, Richard	Revenue and Taxation Committee
Feldman, Trent	Public Health Committee
Green, Donald	Criminal Procedure Committee
Murphy, Robert	Minority Caucus; Judiciary Committee
Robeck, Bruce	Education Committee
Waelti, John	Water Committee
Welo, Tobias	Municipal and County Government Committee

1967–1968
Azevedo, Arthur
Bowden, Kathleen
Fultz, Gordon
Hackman, Michael
Robart, Andrew
Scott, Hal
Smiland, William
Spence, John
Wartick, Gary
Weiss, Michael
Zatkin, Steve

1968–1969
Bauer, Arthur	Transportation Committee
Byrne, James	Ways and Means Committee
Calderone, Gerald	Majority Caucus
Cartabruno, Leah	

Duncan, David
Elliott, Renee   Revenue and Taxation Committee
Gill, Emily   Education Committee
Ivey, Richard

1969–1970
Garcia, Robert   Democratic Caucus
Iglehart, Richard   Criminal Justice Committee
Jones, Robert   Education Committee
Leonard, William   Assembly Member Jack Knox; Local Government
                                    Committee

Lucchese, David
Pecarich, Pamela   Revenue and Taxation Committee
Sparrow, Glen
Wilson, Lionel   Judiciary Committee

1970–1971
Abbott, Eugene   Health Committee
Ackerman, David   Ways and Means Committee
Cole, Charles   Ways and Means Committee
Friedlander, Daniel   Education Committee
Gelbart, Wendy
Graham, Andrea
Horowitz, Fred
Kaldor, Ron
O'Hara, David
Rugani, Frank   Democratic Caucus

1971–1972
Cromwell, Dean
Cummings, Jerry   Education Committee
Doubleday, David
Doyle, James
Dykes, Stephen   Revenue and Taxation Committee
Kersten, Elisabeth   Ways and Means Committee
Perry, Jim
Sanchez, Marc   Assembly Member Peter Chacon
Stockstill, Michael   Assembly Member John Burton

1972–1973
Franken, Renee
Keller, William, III
McNeece, John, III
Minor, John, III

Molmen, William
Moore, Barbara
Nimmo, Mary
O'Connor, Colleen
Rosenthal, Bruce
Thompson, Sandra

1973–1974

Baumann, Rebecca	Assembly Speaker Bob Moretti
Castelli Nauman, Julie	Local Government Committee
Chao, Cedric	Assemblymember John Burton
Cramer, Tyler	
Jensen, Peter	Assemblymember John Dunlap
Perry, Timothy	
Sparks, Maxine	
Walt, Christopher	Assemblymember Frank Lanterman

1974–1975

Aguallo, Robert, Jr.	Assembly Member Peter Chacon
Ashmun, Charlotte	
Boyd, Susan	Minority Consultants
Dahl, Michael	Minority Consultants
Desrochers, Lindsay	Assembly Member Frank Lanterman
Ferguson, Denise	Assembly Member Barry Keene
Holmes, Claybourne	Assembly Member Julian Dixon
Johnson, Susie	Assembly Member Walter Ingalls
Kadish, David	Assembly Member John Francis Foran
Matomura, Hiroshi	Assembly Member Jim Keysor

1975–1976

French, Barbara	Assembly Member Eugene Gualco
Herum, Steve	Assembly Member Gary K. Hart
King, John	Assembly Member Teresa Hughes
McConnell, Fran	Assembly Member Joseph Montoya
McKee, Steve	Assembly Member Tom Bane
Perales, David	Assembly Member Art Torres
Powell, Ellen	Assembly Member John Thurman
Rodriguez, Maria	Assembly Member Peter Chacon
Turney, Clarice	Assembly Member Jerry Lewis
Vescera, Lawrence	Assembly Member Lawrence Kapiloff
Willins, Paula	Assembly Member Barry Keene

1976–1977

Capistrano, Carolina	Assembly Member Terry Goggins
Clark, William	Assembly Member Floyd Mori
Friedman, Paul	Assembly Member Herschel Rosenthal/Assembly Member Daniel Boatwright
Hill, John	Assembly Member Charles Warren
Kitahata, Gary	Assembly Member Eugene Gualco
LaGarda, Lidia	Assembly Member Leo T. McCarthy/ Assembly Member Art Agnos
Meisel, Joan	Assembly Member Howard Berman
Meyer, Paul	Assembly Member Bill Lockyer
Robinson, Calvin	Assembly Member Lawrence Kapiloff/ Assembly Member John Vasconcellos

1977–1978

Akerson, Karen	Assembly Member Vic Fazio
Anton, Nancy	Assembly Member Bill Lockyer; Labor, Employment and Consumer Affairs
Bragdon, Richard	Assembly Member Michael Gage/Assembly Member Daniel Boatwright
Brown, Corey	Assembly Member Joseph Montoya
Brownlow, Terri	Assembly Member Herschel Rosenthal/ Assembly Member Leo T. McCarthy
Chavez, Bill	Assembly Member Richard Alatorre/ Assembly Member Daniel Boatwright
Francisco, Rupert	Assembly Member Ken Maddy
Harvey, Alison	Assembly Member Eugene Gualco; Water, Parks and Wildlife Committee
McMenamin, Paul	Assembly Member Gary K. Hart/ Assembly Member Leo T. McCarthy
Nardi, Karen	Assembly Member Victor Calvo; Resources, Land Use and Energy Committee
Pacheco, David	Assembly Member Dennis Mangers
Powell, Greg	Assembly Member Charles Imbrecht/Assembly Member Bruce Nestande
Spitz, Lilly	Assembly Member Willie C. Brown, Jr.
Tajima, Mark	Assembly Member Henry J. Mello/ Assembly Member Peter Chacon

1978–1979

Archuletta, Keith	Assembly Member Art Agnos
Boyer-Stewart, Robyn	Assembly Member Mel Levine
Castillo, Elvira	Assembly Member Henry Mello
Galliani, Frances	Assembly Member Leo McCarthy
Kane, Thomas	Assembly Member S. Floyd Mori

Krevoy, Bradley	Assembly Member Michael Roos
Lascher, Ted	Assembly Member Michael Gage
Ma, Kathryn	Assembly Member Gary Hart
Miller, Alan	Assembly Member John Knox
Pontisso, Debra	Assembly Member Lawrence Kapilof
Sarmiento, Juliette	Assembly Member Bruce Young
Taxy, Neil	Assembly Member Larry Chimbole
Tom, Jennifer	Assembly Member Herschel Rosenthal
Trembley, Tony	Assembly Member Charles Imbrecht
Wirth, Gabrielle	Assembly Member Marilyn Ryan

1979–1980

Dearth, Chris	Assembly Member Tom Bates
Goldsmith, Mark	Assembly Member Bill McVittie; Criminal Justice Committee
Johnson, Rodney	Assembly Member Richard Alatorre
Moller, Dorothy	Assembly Member Calvo; Resources, Land Use and Energy Committee
Liberman, Adi	Assembly Member Art Torres
Morehous, Dean	Assembly Member John Vasconcellos; Subcommittee on Post Secondary Education
Reyes, Maria	Assembly Member John Vasconcellos; Budget Subcommittee Number Two
Schilling, Joe	Assembly Member Dan Boatwright; Subcommittee on State Administration
Shultz, Jim	Assembly Member Gary Hart; Subcommittee on Education Reform
Wilson, Dotson	Assembly Member Teresa Hughes
Worcester, Ellen	Assembly Member Wadie Deddeh; Revenue and Taxation Committee

1980–1981

Cartwright, Suzanne	Assembly Member Bill Leonard
Ditora, David	Assembly Member Tom Bane
Faulk, Daniel	Assembly Member Marilyn Ryan
Frost, Lynda	Assembly Member Marian Bergeson
Fukushima, Harriet	Assembly Member Elihu Harris
Marr, Margaret	Assembly Member Tom Hannigan
Panush, David	Assembly Member S. Floyd Mori
Sanchez, Veronica	Assembly Member Art Torres
Speers, JoAnne	Assembly Member Doug Bosco
Tompakov, Fran	Assembly Member Jean Moorhead
Villasenor, Richard	Assembly Member Bruce Young
Williams, Charlotte	Assembly Member Gordon Duffy

1981–1982

Ajemian, Van	Assembly Member Matthew Martinez
Anderson, Alison	Assembly Member Jean Moorhead
Chavez, Cynthia	Assembly Member Art Agnos
Cislowski, Joseph	Assembly Member Richard Katz
Clark, Fred	Assembly Member Richard Lehman
Johnson, Timothy	Assembly Member Byron Sher
Platter, David	Assembly Member Carol Hallett
Quann, Warren	Assembly Member Gwen Moore
Sherwood, Peter	Assembly Member Stan Statham
Solorio, Paula	Assembly Member Gary Hart
Staman, Barbara	Assembly Member Bruce Young
Statton, John	Assembly Member Doug Bosco

1982–1983

Cape, James
De Meester, Paul
Krause, Kathy
Newman, Ann
Sprowls, Sharon
Tolbert, Tony
Uslan, Brian

1983–1984

Battson, Richard	Assembly Member Phil Isenberg
Crouter, Mary	
Lloyd, Barbara	
Herse, Laura	
Judge, Robert	
Lynch, Loretta	Assembly Member Johan Klehs
Martinez, Alma	
Schneider, Robin	
Slavkin, Mark	
Thompson, Michael	Assembly Member Teresa Hughes
Wallach, Joyce	
Wenker, Jerry	

1984–1985

Andres-Taylor, Coralyn	Assembly Member John Vasconcellos
Colborn, Diane	Assembly Member Phil Isenberg
Dearing, James	Assembly Member Johan Klehs
Dunmoyer, Dan	Assembly Member Pat Nolan
Gomez, Alexander, Jr.	Assembly Member Charles Calderon
Guanzon, Nilda	Assembly Member Gary Condit

Magnani-Knox, Sally   Assembly Member Lloyd Connelly
Martin, Dan   Assembly Member Tom Hayden
Ochoa, Maria   Assembly Member Gloria Molina
Turman, Richard   Assembly Member Robert Campbell
White, Kenneth   Assembly Member Sally Tanner
Zingale, Dan   Assembly Member Gray Davis

1985–1986

Dubay, Ann   Assembly Member Tom Hannigan
Eisenbise, Margaret   Assembly Member Elihu Harris
Essex, Susan   Assembly Member John Vasconcellos
Friedenthal, Ellen   Assembly Member Rusty Areias
Giroux, Robert   Assembly Member Dick Floyd
Hall, Velma   Assembly Member Robert Campbell
Higgins, Tom   Assembly Member Mike Roos
Hunt, Jeffrey   Assembly Member Bruce Bronzan
Morris, Leah   Assembly Member Lloyd Connelly
Russo, Anthony   Assembly Member Pat Nolan
Saucedo, Stephen   Assembly Member Bill Leonard
                             Assembly Member Frank Vicencia/
                             Intergovernmental Relations
Thompson, Sky   Assembly Member Gary Condit

1986–1987

Blue, Gloria   Assembly Member Pat Nolan
                             Assembly Member Teresa Hughes
Cornwell, Carrie   Assembly Member Tom Hannigan
                             Assembly Member Art Agnos
Cushnir, Andrew   Assembly Member Richard Katz
                             Assembly Member Richard Katz/Transportation
Klein, Charles   Assembly Member Lloyd Connelly
                             Ways and Means Committee
Maguire, Mary   Assembly Member Michael Roos
                             Assembly Member Michael Roos/Office of
                             Speaker pro Tem
Nevarez, Tony   Assembly Member Elihu Harris
                             Assembly Member Elihu Harris/Judiciary
Noel, Julie   Assembly Member Phil Isenberg
                             Assembly Member Tucker/Health
Patlan, Richard   Assembly Member Dominic Cortese
                             Assembly Member Dominic Cortese/Local
                             Government
Rios, Robert   Assembly Member Johan Klehs/Revenue and
                             Taxation

Schelen, Robert	Assembly Member Jerry Eaves
Torres, Mark	Assembly Member Gloria Molina
	Assembly Member Gary Condit/Governmental Organization
Yoshii, Katherine	Assembly Member Sam Farr; Economic Development and New Technologies

1987–1988

Cairel, Gigi Ann	Assembly Member Delaine Eastin
Evans, Cori	Assembly Member Bill Filante
Gonzales, Gilda	Assembly Member Jim Costa
Hale, Debra	Assembly Member Johan Klehs
Harris, Marianna	Assembly Member Steve Clute
Hawkins, Michael	Assembly Member Tom Hannigan
Laird, James	Assembly Member Bill Leonard
Lee, Tina	Assembly Member Tom Bates
McNitt, Robert	Assembly Member Tom Bane
Morrigan, Casey	Assembly Member Phil Isenberg
Nguyen, Dung (Zoon)	Assembly Member Robert Campbell
Sanchez, Lorraine	Assembly Member Lucille Roybal-Allard

1988–1989

Faulkner, Riel	Assembly Member Johan Klehs
Fife, Kelly	Assembly Member Phil Isenberg
Gomez, Gustavo	Assembly Member Dominic Cortese
Guess, Robin	Assembly Member Bruce Bronzan
Heppler, Kurt	Assembly Member Gerald Felando
Hosler, Michael	Assembly Member Bev Hansen
Isenberg, Jennifer	Assembly Member Tom Hayden
Jones, Devin	Assembly Member Richard Katz
MiYun, Kim	Assembly Member Robert Campbell
McCarthy, Kevin	Assembly Member Tom Bates
Mirabal, Nancy	Assembly Member Steve Clute
Nguyen, Kieu-Oanh	Assembly Ways and Means Committee
Pimentel, John	Assembly Member Pat Nolan
Privette, Martin	Assembly Member Phillip Wyman
Redway, Bettina	Assembly Member Tom Hannigan
Smith, Paul	Assembly Member Norman Waters
Tanguilig, France Reina	Assembly Member Jackie Speier
Thurmond, Howard	Assembly Member Burt Margolin

1989–1990

Bergeron, Nicole	Assembly Member Richard Katz
Bucheli, Sophia	Assembly Member Robert Campbell
Chang, Jeffrey	Assembly Member John Vasconcellos

Craig, Gary	Labor and Employment Committee
Dugas, Sonya	Higher Education Committee
Fabrizio, Vincent	Assembly Member Cathie Wright
Haver, Julie	Assembly Member Johan Klehs
Kendall, Julie	Assembly Member Gwen Moore
Lee, Carol	Ways and Means Committee
McDonald, Susan	Minority Ways and Means Committee
Roman, Jesus	Assembly Member Tom Bates
Savage, Philip	Assembly Member Paul Woodruff
Scott, Kelley	Assembly Member Tom Hannigan
Singh, Sharon	Ways and Means Committee
Stewart, Patrick	Assembly Member Teresa Hughes
Weisner, Carol	Assembly Member Delaine Eastin
White, Lorraine	Judiciary Committee
Wolff, Jason	Assembly Member Pat Nolan

1990–1991

Atteberry, Krista	Assembly Member Xavier Becerra
Dickey, Laurie	Assembly Member Marguerite Archie-Hudson
Ellis, Dennis	Assembly Member Carol Bentley
Fenton, Elizabeth	Ways and Means Committee
Galehouse, Jennifer	Assembly Member Johan Klehs
Hertert, Linda	Assembly Member Jack O'Connell
Imperato, Pamela	Water, Parks and Wildlife Committee
Liu, Brian	Assembly Member Bruce Bronzan
Martinez, Martha	Assembly Member Delaine Eastin
Migacz, Mishka	Assembly Member Barbara Lee
Murase, Miriam	Assembly Member Tom Bates; Human Services Committee
Nguyen, Nam	Assembly Member John Burton
Weber, William	Republican Caucus
White, Lori	Higher Education Committee
Williams, Anthony	Assembly Member Tom Hannigan
Wodinsky, Jenny	Ways and Means Committee
Young, John	Assembly Member Phil Isenberg
Ysunza, Angela	Transportation Committee

1991–1992

Akhenaton, Jamal	Assembly Member Marguerite Archie-Hudson; Assembly Member Teresa Hughes
Bowie, Arthur	Assembly Member John Burton
De Vera, J. Prospero	Assembly Member Johan Klehs; Revenue and Taxation Committee
Diaz, Jessica	Assembly Member Jack O'Connell

Hastings, Roy	Assembly Member B.T. Collins; Republican Caucus
Herrell, Robert	Assembly Member John Vasconcellos; Ways and Means Committee
Johns, Steven	Assembly Member Tom Hannigan
Kent, Shawn	Assembly Member Chris Chandler
Martinez, Guadalupe	Assembly Member Xavier Becerra
Ochoa, Elizabeth	Assembly Member Robert Frazee
Oh, Julie	Assembly Member Cathie Wright; Ways and Means Committee
Perez, Alicia	Assembly Member Delaine Eastin; Education Committee
Sousa, Francesca	Assembly Member Phil Isenberg; Judiciary Committee
Trommald, John	Republican Caucus
Tsang, Jeffrey	Assembly Member Richard Katz; Transportation Committee
Works, Rose	Assembly Member Tom Bates; Human Services Committee

1992–1993

Barnhart, Patrick	Assembly Member Tom Hannigan
Bronson, Jonathan	Utilities and Commerce Committee
Carter, Johnnie	Assembly Member John Burton
Chang, Andrea	Judiciary Committee
Cole, Katherine	Local Government Committee
Frazier, Rex	Assembly Member Charles Quackenbush
Huizar, Jose	Ways and Means Committee
Kelly, Shannon	Assembly Member Jan Goldsmith
Knowlton, Virginia	Revenue and Taxation Committee
Kuritz, Marc	Assembly Member Ted Weggeland
Matsuo, Tracy	Assembly Member Curt Pringle
Reeder, Mark	Assembly Member Dean Andal
Salter, James	Transportation Committee
Spencer, Sedrick	Assembly Member Robert Campbell
Stites, Catherine	Assembly Member Tom Umberg
Tanden, Neera	Education Committee
Von Haam, Peter	Water, Parks and Wildlife Committee
Vue, Pa Lai	Higher Education Committee

1993–1994

Bain, Scott	Judiciary Committee
Crenshaw, Dwayne	Assembly Member Jack O'Connell
Cromartie, Tim	Assembly Member Julie Bornstein
Dillon, Frederick	Revenue and Taxation Committee
Easterly, Eureka	Assembly Member Joe Baca

Felizatto, Daniel	Assembly Member Charles Quackenbush
Hale, Lesley	Assembly Member Barbara Friedman
Henriquez, Jose	Assembly Member Tom Hannigan
Hughes, Trudi	Assembly Member Trice Harvey
Kelly, Teri	Higher Education Committee
Lye, Linda	Ways and Means Committee
Martin, Chris	Assembly Member Jan Goldsmith
Miller, Robert	Water, Parks and Wildlife Committee
Morales, Maria	Human Services Committee
Rhee, Patty	Environmental Safety and Toxic Materials Committee
Smith, William	Assembly Member Dean Andal
Snyder, Julie	Transportation Committee
Tamondong, Cesar	Assembly Member Ray Haynes

1994–1995

Alvarez, Patricia	Assembly Member Phil Isenberg
Bert, Alicia	Assembly Member Marguerite Archie-Hudson
Chong, Sandra	Assembly Member Richard Katz
Fernandez, Soyla	Assembly Member Denise Moreno Ducheny
Garcia, Eloy	Assembly Member Joe Baca
Hough, John	Assembly Member Kerry Mazzoni
Jacobson, Myron	Assembly Member Jan Goldsmith
Krause, Mark	Assembly Member John Burton
McFadden, Brett	Assembly Member Steven Kuykendall
Morrisroe, Darby	Assembly Member Ted Weggeland
Ng, Jayna	Assembly Member Robert Campbell
Poole, Dia	Assembly Member Barbara Lee
Reid, Scott	Assembly Member Ted Aguiar
Rice, Everett	Assembly Member Bruce Thompson
Richard, Jennifer	Assembly Member Sheila Kuehl
Sarboraria, Matthew	Assembly Member Curt Pringle
Tehrani, Pouneh	Assembly Member James Rogan
Trinh, Linh	Assembly Member Tom Hannigan

1995–1996

Arakelian, Anahid	Assembly Member James Rogan
Avila, Minerva	Assembly Member Dede Alpert
De Billwiller-Kiss, Anna Maria	Assembly Member Richard Rainey
Finkler, Victoria	Assembly Member Tom Bates
Hartman, Keith	Assembly Member Ted Weggeland
Hightower, Tracy	Assembly Member Marguerite Archie-Hudson
Laffoon-Villegas, Robert	Assembly Member John Burton
Lamola, Leanna	Assembly Member Sal Cannella

Marchand, Vincent   Assembly Member Tom Hannigan
Pugno, Andrew   Assembly Member Pete Knight
Rockenstein, Mike   Assembly Member Brooks Firestone
Shipley, Patrick   Assembly Member Chuck Poochigian
Sparks, Kyri   Assembly Member Kerry Mazzoni
Stewart, Mark   Assembly Member Bill Morrow
Toma, James   Assembly Member Valerie Brown
Webster, Dale   Assembly Member Steve Baldwin
Williams, Bruce   Assembly Member George House
Young, Morgan   Assembly Member Richard Katz

1996–1997

Berger, John   Assembly Member Ted Lempert
Boor, Stacey   Assembly Member Jim Cuneen
Carson, Audra   Assembly Member Bill Campbell
Givargis, Ashur   Assembly Member Brett Granlund
Hotchkin, Michael   Assembly Member Debra Bowen
Kim, Daniel   Assembly Member Michael Sweeney
King, Nicole   Assembly Member Sheila Kuehl
Mills, Spencer   Assembly Member Jim Battin
Reslock, Eric   Assembly Member Bill Leonard
Rich, Sharon   Assembly Member Louis Caldera
Silva, Francisco   Assembly Member Denise Moreno Ducheny
Silveira, Caroline   Assembly Member Chuck Poochigian
Stivers, Mark   Assembly Member Kevin Shelley
Taomina, Cosmo   Assembly Member Lou Papan
Tapio, G. Christopher   Assembly Member Helen Thomson
Velasquez, M. abriela   Assembly Member Carole Migden
Warren, Rebekah   Assembly Member George Runner
Yoshida, Kerry   Assembly Member Keith Olberg

1997–1998

Alden, John   Assembly Member Kevin Shelley
Anastasoff, Jennifer   Assembly Member Ted Lempert
Barnes, John   Assembly Member Dion Aroner
Campbell, Tom   Assembly Member Jim Cuneen
Clifford, Thomas   Assembly Member Robert Hertzberg
Cordero, Celine   Assembly Member Martin Gallegos
Craig, Brian   Assembly Member George Runner
Gonzalez, Guillermo   Assembly Member Denise Moreno Ducheny
Green, Everett   Assembly Member Mike Honda
Guillen, Abel   Assembly Member Carole Migden
Kelly, Anthony   Assembly Member Fred Aguiar
Kniffen, Susanna   Assembly Member Tom Bordonaro
Kolpitcke, Kirstin   Assembly Member Bill Campbell

List, Susan	Assembly Member Jim Morrissey
McNeil, Carrie	Assembly Member Sheila Kuehl
Miller, Gayle	Assembly Member Tom Torlakson
Price, Catherine	Assembly Member Wally Knox
Wucetich, Jason	Assembly Member Steve Kuykendall

1998–1999

Anaya, Timothy	Assembly Member Tony Strickland
Aseltine, Bethany	Assembly Member Sheila Kuehl
Austin, Betsy	Assembly Member Susan Davis
Avila, Laura	Assembly Member Gil Cedillo
Below, Curtis	Assembly Member Herb Wesson
Byrne, Joe	Assembly Member Robert Hertzberg
Chi, Karis	Assembly Member Jim Cuneen
Chin, Cindy	Assembly Member Jim Battin
Csizmar, Eric	Assembly Member George Runner
Ermoian, Harry	Assembly Member Fred Keeley
Ford, Emilee	Assembly Member Kevin Shelley
Nakasone, Sarah	Assembly Member Lynne Leach
Ngo, Steve	Assembly Member Denise Moreno Ducheny
O'Donnell, Patrick	Assembly Member Alan Lowenthal
Rasada, Pamela	Assembly Member Virginia Strom-Martin
Rice, Tony	Assembly Member Carole Migden
Ro, Tom	Assembly Member Bill Leonard
Ryoo, Cathy	Assembly Member Dion Aroner

1999–2000

Abrajano, Marisa	Assembly Member Gil Cedillo
Agirre, Edgar	Assembly Member Hanna-Beth Jackson
Banken, Monica	Assembly Member Tom McClintock
Buttle, Jonathan	Assembly Member Roderick Wright
Callahan, Lindsay	Assembly Member Robert Hertzberg
Cato, Mohammed	Assembly Member Mike Honda
Diaz, Christopher	Assembly Member Antonio Villaraigosa
Johnson, Melinda	Assembly Member Scott Baugh
Lopez, Lizelda	Assembly Member Denise Moreno Ducheny
Martinez, Francisco, Jr.	Assembly Member Tony Cardenas
Medina, Jorge	Assembly Member Jim Cunneen
Olson, Patricia (Inga)	Assembly Member Fred Keeley
Quan, Jennifer	Assembly Member George Runner
Scutetta, Anna-Marie	Assembly Member Patricia Bates
Stites, Natalie	Assembly Member Carole Migden
Valencia, Manuel, III	Assembly Member Darrell Steinberg
VanSickle-Ward, Rachel	Assembly Member Helen Thomson

Yaquian-Illescas, Rafael   Assembly Member Sarah Reyes

2000–2001

Alli, Naiomi	Assembly Member Alan Lowenthol
Anderson, James	Assembly Member Juan Vargas
Applegarth, Michael	Assembly Member Tim Leslie
Blanco, Ricardo	Assembly Member Helen Thomson
Calero, Alexander	Assembly Member Bill Leonard
Estacio, Donna	Assembly Member Tony Cardenas
Franklin, Jennifer	Assembly Member Rod Pacheco
Huezo, Cristina	Assembly Member Gil Cedillo
Jackson, Carlos	Assembly Member Paul Koretz
Jones, Ethan	Assembly Member John Longville
Lowry, John	Assembly Member George Runner
Martinez, Erica	Assembly Member Robert Hertzberg
Rasberry, Tamara	Assembly Member Herb Wesson
Riddick, Jason	Assembly Member Patricia Bates
Sanchez, Jose Armando	Assembly Member Manny Diaz
Taylor, Preston	Assembly Member Joe Simitian
Twidwell, Shari	Assembly Member Carole Migden

2001–2002

Alejo, Luis Angel	Assembly Member Manny Diaz
Althausen, David	Assembly Member Richard Dickerson
Angel, Sarah	Assembly Member Joe Canciamilla
Boghosian, Sasha	Assemblymember Joe Canciamilla
Bryant, Jason	Assembly Member Charlene Zettel
Burch, Christopher	Assembly Member David Cogdill
Carmona, Arturo	Assembly Member Marco Firebaugh
Dominguez, Christiana	Assembly Member Herb Wesson
Gervacio, Lindsay	Assembly Member Gill Cedillo
Hu, Jimmy	Assembly Member Patricia Bates
Levy, Amanda	Assembly Member Robert Hertzberg
Martinez-Wade, Joycelyn	Assembly Member Wilma Chan
Mitchell, Jason	Assembly Member Jerome Horton
Moore, Karin	Assembly Member John Campbell
Olson, Tiffany	Assembly Member Tom Harman
Plucker, Cober	Assembly Member George Runner
Shah, Sanjay	Assembly Member Darrell Steinberg
Warren, Tamara	Assembly Member John Longville

2002–2003

Avina-Santiago, Marisol	Assembly Member Manny Diaz
Cameron, Shakari	Assembly Member Jackie Goldberg
Chang, Annie	Assembly Member Carol Liu

Christensen, Amy   Assembly Member Cindy Montanez
Esparza, Alejandro   Assembly Member Lou Correa
Honda, Penny   Assembly Member Loni Hancock
Hunt, Adam   Assembly Member Lloyd Levine
Johsz, Brian   Assembly Member Patricia Bates
Kawamoto, Ryan   Assembly Member Wilma Chan
Martinez, Juanita   Assembly Member Fabian Nunez
McDonald, Mary   Assembly Member Tim Leslie
Myers, Sara   Assembly Member John Campbell
Norman, Janus   Assembly Member Darrell Steinberg
Power, Laura   Assembly Member Sharon Runner
Ramesh, Jenna   Assembly Member Dave Cox
Read, Lindsey   Assembly Member Dario Frommer
Riley, Jason   Assembly Member Dave Cogdill
Silverman, Andrew   Assembly Member Joe Simitian

2003–2004

Adler, Dawn   Assembly Member Dario Frommer
Blackwell, Jaime   Assembly Member Russ Bogh
Calderon, Olivia   Assembly Member Jenny Oropeza
Castillo, Graciela   Assembly Member Lloyd Levine
Chan, Rosaline   Assembly Member Judy Chu
Chang, Annabel   Assembly Member Juan Vargas
Contreras, Erika   Assembly Member Marco Firebaugh
Fitts, Mike   Assembly Member Sharon Runner
Gallagher, Jamie (James)   Assembly Member Doug LaMalfa
Harris, Ayana   Assembly Member Christine Kehoe
Kolla, Sheila   Assembly Member Kevin McCarthy
Ocen, Priscilla   Assembly Member Mark Ridley-Thomas
Power, Jamison   Assembly Member Rudy Bermudez
Ramirez, Josefina   Assembly Member Jackie Goldberg
Rawson, Sean   Assembly Member John Campbell
Seiden, Daniel   Assembly Member Ray Haynes
Tashima, Robert   Assembly Member Mark Leno
Wadlé, Dane   Assembly Member Todd Spitzer

2004–2005

Bolivar, Jonathan   Assembly Member Guy Houston
Carlisle Salgueiro, Ambar   Assembly Member Wilma Chan
Charles, Qiana   Assembly Member Dario Frommer
Gonzalez, Erica   Assembly Member Hector De La Torre
Gunderson, Jessica   Assembly Member Karen Bass
Gutierrez, Daniel   Assembly Member Gene Mullin
Hoag, Andrew   Assembly Member Juan Arambula

Hu, Alice	Assembly Member Lloyd Levine
Kennedy, John	Assembly Member Kevin McCarthy
Leader, Anne	Assembly Member Lynn Daucher
Leon, Manuel	Assembly Member John Laird
Magill, Sam	Assembly Member Lois Wolk
Packham, Kyle	Assembly Member Sharon Runner
Perez, Roland	Assembly Member Van Tran
Smith, Jacqueline	Assembly Member Loni Hancock
Trigg, Adam	Assembly Member Todd Spitzer
Wood, Adam	Assembly Member Dave Cogdill
Yang, Amorette	Assembly Member Dave Jones

2005–2006

Acquah, Ama	Assembly Member David Cogdill
Archibald, Christine	Assembly Member Sally Lieber
Caligiuri, Jeffrey	Assembly Member Alan Nakanishi
Choi, Francis	Assembly Member Pedro Nava
Cox, David	Assembly Member Rick Keene
Darling, Rebecca	Assembly Member Dave Jones
Dondro, Adam	Assembly Member John Laird/Budget Committee
Fernandez, Jesus	Assembly Member Merv Dymally
Lee, Yang	Assembly Member Loni Hancock
Patterson, Joseph	Assembly Member Todd Spitzer
Ramirez, Fernando	Assembly Member Mark Ridley-Thomas
Rodriguez, Jazmin	Assembly Member Noreen Evans
Sadovnik, Shella	Assembly Member Sharon Runner
Takahama, Sarah	Assembly Member Karen Bass
Washington, Whitney	Assembly Member Hector De La Torre
Wolfe, David	Assembly Member Guy Houston
Wood, Joshua	Assembly Member Tim Leslie
Zapata, Jennet	Assembly Member Alberto Torrico

3.3. Assembly Fellowship Program:
Executive Board Members, 1972–1973 to 1987–1988

1972–1973 [1]

Anderson, Totton J.	University of Southern California,
Bell, Charles	California State University, Fullerton
Guzman, Ralph	
Jones, Victor	University of California, Berkeley,
Leiniger, Joseph	Stanford University, Law School
Loveridge, Ronald	University of California, Riverside,
McDaniel, Gerald	California State University, Sacramento,
Morland, Robert	University of Redland
Price, Charles	Chico State College
Stubblebine, W. Craig	Claremont Men's College

1976–1977 [2]

Anderson, Totton J.	University of Southern California,
Christensen, Marc	Minority Consultants Office
Hurst, Jim	Assembly Office of Research
Jones, Victor	University of California, Berkeley,
Lammers, William	University of Southern California,
Leiniger, Joseph	Stanford University, Law School
Loveridge, Ronald (chair)	University of California, Riverside,
Miles, E. Walter	California State University, San Diego,
Morland, Robert	University of Redlands,
Muir, William K.	University of California, Berkeley,
Price, Charles	Chico State College,
Snowiss, Leo M.	University of California, Los Angeles,
Stone, Barbara	California State University, Fullerton,
Stubblebine, W. Craig	Claremont Mens' College
Taugher, Frederick J.	Assembly Rules Committee, Chief Administrative Officer
Tirado, Miguel (director)	Assembly Rules Committee

1978–1979 [3]

Brandsma, Richard	Assembly Office of Research
Gould, Howard	Assembly Minority Consultants

---

[1] "Assembly Rules Resolution," [1973?], ARCP.
[2] "California Assembly Fellowship Program, Executive Board Roster, 1976–1977," enclosed with Ronald O. Loveridge to Members, Executive Board, California Assembly Fellowship Program, memorandum, October 8, 1976, ARCP.
[3] "California Assembly Fellowship Program, Executive Board Roster, 1978–1979," attached to Ronald O. Loveridge to Rick Brandsma, October 30, 1978, ARCP.

Hurst, Jim	
Lammers, William	University of Southern California,
Lee, Eugene	University of California, Berkeley,
Loveridge, Ronald (chair)	University of California, Riverside,
Miles, E. Walter	California State University, San Diego
Moffat, William R.	Stanford University,
Morland, Robert	University of Redlands
Price, Charles	Chico State College
Snowiss, Leo M.	University of California, Los Angeles
Stone, Barbara	California State University, Fullerton,
Stubblebine, W. Craig	Claremont Men's College,
Tirado, Miguel (director)	Assembly Rules Committee
Tom, Maeley	Assembly Rules Committee, Deputy Administrative Officer

1979–1980 [4]

Brandsma, Richard	Assembly Office of Research
Hardy, Leroy C.	California State University, Long Beach,
Lammers, William	University of Southern California,
Lee, Eugene	University of California, Berkeley,
Loveridge, Ronald	University of California, Riverside,
Marshall, Dale	University of California, Davis
Miles, E. Walter	San Diego State University,
Muir, William K.	University of California, Berkeley,
Price, Charles (CHAIR)	Chico State College
Snowiss, Leo M.	University of California, Los Angeles,
Stubblebine, W. Craig	Claremont Men's College
Taugher, Frederick J.	Assembly Rules Committee, Chief Administrative Officer
Tirado, Miguel	Sonoma State University
Tom, Maeley	Assembly Rules Committee, Deputy Administrative Officer

1981–1982 [5]

Brandsma, Richard	Assembly Office of Research
Hardy, Leroy C.	California State University, Long Beach,
Lammers, William	University of Southern California,
Lee, Eugene	University of California, Berkeley,
Marshall, Dale	University of California, Davis

---

[4]"California Assembly Fellowship Program, Executive Board Roster, 1979–1980," n.d., ARCP.

[5] "The California Assembly Fellowship Program [brochure for 1981–1982]," [1981?], ARCP; Chuck Price to Executive Board Members, California Assembly Fellowship Program, August 27, 1980, ARCP.

Miles, E. Walter	California State University, San Diego,
Muir, William K.	University of California, Berkeley,
Price, Charles (CHAIR)	California State University, Chico,
Snowiss, Leo M.	University of California, Los Angeles,
Stubblebine, W. Craig	Claremont Men's College
Taugher, Frederick J.	Assembly Rules Committee, Chief Administrative Officer
Tirado, Miguel	California State University, Sonoma
Tom, Maeley	Assembly Rules Committee, Deputy Administrative Officer

1985–1986 [6]

Allen, William B.	Harvey Mudd College
Bell, Charles G. (chair)	California State University, Sacramento,
Chavez, Bill	Assembly Education Committee,
Culver, John	Cal Poly State University, San Luis Obispo,
Desrochers, Lindsay	University of California, Berkeley,
Dunmoyer, Daniel	Assemblymember Patrick Nolan
Gruber, Judy	University of California, Berkeley,
Hardy, Leroy C.	California State University, Long Beach,
Harvey, Alison (ex-offico)	Assemblymember Phil Isenberg
Lammers, William	University of Southern California,
Lee, Eugene (on leave)	University of California, Berkeley,
Loveridge, Ron	University of California, Riverside,
Marshall, Dale	University of California, Davis,
Morlan, Robert	University of Redlands,
Price, Charles (director)	California State University, Chico,
Stone, Barbara	California State University, Fullerton,
Taugher, Frederick J.	Assembly Rules Committee, Chief Administrative Officer
Tom, Maeley	Assembly Rules Committee, Deputy Administrative Officer
Wilson, E. Dotson	Assembly Speaker's Office

1987–1988 [7]

| Bell, Charles G. | University of California, Davis |
| Chavez, Bill | Assembly Education Committee, Bob Connelly, Assembly Rules Committee, Chief Administrative Officer |

---

[6] "California Assembly Fellowship Program, Executive Board Roster, 1985-1986," [1985?], PPO.

[7] "Assembly Fellowship Executive Board Membership [1987-1988]," [1987?], ARCP.

Desrochers, Lindsay (chair)	University of California, Berkeley,
Dunmoyer, Daniel	Assemblymember Patrick Nolan
Gruber, Judy	University of California, Berkeley,
Harvey, Alison	Assemblymember Phil Isenberg
Lammers, William	University of Southern California,
Lee, Eugene	University of California, Berkeley,
Loveridge, Ron	University of California, Riverside,
Price, Charles	California State University, Chico,
Rutland, Patty-Jo	Assembly Rules Committee
Serna, Joe	California State University, Sacramento
Stevenson, Elliot	Minority Leader's Representative
Stone, Barbara	California State University, Fullerton,
Thompson, Michael	Assemblymember Jackie Speier
Wilson, E. Dotson	Assembly Speaker's Office

1988–1989 [8]

Bell, Charles G.	University of California, Davis
Chavez, Bill	Assembly Education Committee
Clark, Ross	Assemblymember Maxine Waters
Connelly, Bob	Assembly Rules Committee, Chief Administrative Officer
Desrochers, Lindsay (chair)	University of California, Berkeley,
Dunmoyer, Daniel	Assemblymember Patrick Nolan
Gruber, Judy	University of California, Berkeley,
Harvey, Alison	Assemblymember Phil Isenberg
Lammers, William	University of Southern California
Lee, Eugene	University of California, Berkeley,
Loveridge, Ron	University of California, Riverside,
Mazlum, Elise	Assemblymember Gerald Felando
Price, Charles	California State University, Chico,
Rutland, Patty-Jo	Assembly Rules Committee
Serna, Joe	California State University, Sacramento,
Stevenson, Elliot	Minority Ways and Means Committee
Stone, Barbara	California State University, Fullerton,
Thompson, Michael	Assemblymember Jackie Speier
Wilson, E. Dotson	Assembly Speaker's Office

---

[8] "The California Assembly Fellowship Program [brochure for 1988-1989]," [1988?], ARCP.

3.4. Assembly Fellowship Program:
Directors and Faculty Advisors, 1975–1976 to 2005–2006

Fellowship Year	Program Coordinator/Director	Faculty Advisor
1975–1978	Miguel Tirado	N/A
1979–1986	Charles Price	N/A
1986–1987	Lilly Spitz	Cristy Jensen
1987–1988	Lisa Simone (7/87-10/87) Margaret McArthur (10/87-)	Cristy Jensen
1988–1989	Margaret McArthur (-2/89) Karen Sonoda (3/89-)	Cristy Jensen
1989–1990	Karen Sonoda	Ken DeBow
1990–1991	Karen Sonoda	Ken DeBow
1991–1992	Monica Neville	Ken DeBow
1992–1993	Monica Neville	Ken DeBow
1993–1994	Monica Neville	Ken DeBow
1994–1995	Monica Neville	Ken DeBow
1995–1996	Monica Neville	Ken DeBow
1996–1997	Mimi Morris	Ken DeBow
1997–1998	Mimi Morris	Ken DeBow
1998–1999	Robbin Lewis-Coaxum	Ken DeBow
1999–2000	Robbin Lewis-Coaxum	Ken DeBow
2000–2001	Robbin Lewis-Coaxum	Michael Wadlé
2001–2002	Robbin Lewis-Coaxum	Michael Wadlé
2002–2003	Robbin Lewis-Coaxum	Michael Wadlé
2003–2004	Robbin Lewis-Coaxum	Michael Wadlé
2004–2005	Robbin Lewis-Coaxum	Michael Wadlé
2005–2006	Robbin Lewis-Coaxum	Michael Wadlé
2006–2007	Robbin Lewis-Coaxum	Michael Wadlé

Appendix 4
Executive Fellowship Program

4.1. Executive Fellow Names and Placements:
1986–1987 to 2005–2006

1986–1987
Borg, Dean	Department of Commerce/Recycling Division
Carpenter, Cindy	Department of Education/Public Affairs
Chow, Bill	Department of Finance/Program Evaluation
Flewallen, Philip	Department of Health Services/Toxics Division
Garner, Rosalind	Department of Health Services/Data and Statistics
Mendes, Mike	Department of Food and Agriculture/Agriculture Export Program
Nissen, Frank	Department of Justice/Attorney General's Office
Roberson, Kati	Department of Commerce/Office of Tourism
Shearer, Mary	Department of Commerce/Enterprise Zone
White, Belinda	Health and Welfare Agency/Program and Fiscal Affairs

1987–1988
Abdullah, Cynthia	
Amon, Ricardo	Energy Commission/Agricultural Programs Office
Canon, Mary Beth	Toxics Substances Control Division/Policy and Procedure
Castorena, Robert	Governor's Office of Criminal Justice Planning/ Legislative Analysis and Policy Division
DeLeon, Russell	Health Services/Toxics Division
Hoffman, Jeff	
Jevens, Tom	
Martinez, Marco	Department of Housing and Community Development
Sanders, Jeanne	Department of Finance/Correction General Government Unit
Swanson, Kitrena	Department of Health Services/Maternal and Child Branch
Van Velkinburg, Suzanne	Department of Finance/Health and Welfare Unit

1988–1989
Abraham, Amy	Health and Welfare Agency

Billeci, Cameron	Office of the Attorney General
Blackshaw, Peter	Governor's Office of Education
Brentwood, Mary	Department of Food and Agriculture, Export Program
Driver, Glenda	Department of Corrections
McIntyre, Rita	Department of Food and Agriculture, Export Program
Mitchell, Dana	Office of the Attorney General
Nodora, Jesus	Department of Education
Smith, Kari	California Energy Commission
Traylor, Henry	California Energy Commission

1989–1990

Austin, Mark	Department of Veteran Affairs
Barnhill, Susan	Department of Transportation/Affirmative Action and Equal Opportunity
Begay, Mike	Governor's Office of Planning and Resources
Boranian, Steve	Parole and Community Services
Carr, Nicole	Department of Transportation/Personnel, Hispanic Employment Program
Cortes, James	Department of Economic Opportunity
Grandmaison, Linda	California Energy Commission
Hom, Cindy	Health and Welfare Agency
Julian, Jason	Office of Criminal Justice Planning/Legislative Division
Landes, Rebecca	Attorney General/Criminal Division (1) Employment Development Office/Planning (2)
Tirre, Amy	California Energy Commission
Wong, Ron	Department of Social Services/GAIN Policy (1) Department of Finance/Health and Welfare Unit (2)

1990–1991

Degrood, Cindy	Energy Commission
Goldstene, Claire	State Lands Commission
Gurwitz, Brian	Health and Welfare Agency
Kelly, Alison	Air Resources Board
Kirkland, James	State Lands Commission
Loera, Ana	Department of General Services
Merrill, Katie	Office of the Attorney General
Mirvali, Abaseh	Air Resources Board
Mitchell, Matthew	State Water Resources Control Board
Padilla, Roman	Department of Finance
O'Neill, Cassandra	Medical Risk Program
Oseguera, Jose	Department of Finance

1991–1992

Biggs, Jason	Governor's Press Office
DeSorcy, Simone	California Environmental Protection Agency
Jayachandran, Priya	State Treasurer's Office
Libuser, Andy	International Affairs
Lorenzen, Georgette	Commission on State Finance
Mobley, Carol	Community Colleges, Public Affairs
Nakahata, Andy	State and Consumer Services
Okimoto, Jennifer	Health and Welfare Agency
Shoaff, John	Air Resources Board
Solomon, Lisa	California World Trade Commission
Tsai, Julius	Resources Agency
Vernetti, Amy	Fair Political Practices Commission

1992–1993

Baldwin, E. Rowland, III	Governor's Office of Public Affairs
Bartz, Michael	Air Resources Board
Bottrell, Melissa	Department of Finance
Doherty, Rachel	Office of Child Development and Education
Haigh, Caroline	Resources Agency
Low, Ronald	Governor's Press and Communications Office
Macheroni, Laura	California Environmental Protection Agency
Ortiz, Sonia	Department of Food and Agriculture
Ramirez, John	Business, Transportation and Housing Agency
Rutledge, Peter (Bo)	Health and Welfare Agency
Vella, Elizabeth	Governor's Office of Planning and Research
Wong, Brian	Commission on State Finance

1993–1994

Aguilera, Gabriel	California Trade and Commerce Agency
Becerra, Glen	Governor's Office of Communications
Chang, Andrew	Governor's Office of Planning and Research
Ducote, Bryan	California Department of Food and Agriculture
Erickson, David	Department of Fish and Game
Graeber, Sarah	Health and Welfare Agency
Hirsch, Lisa	Office of External Affairs
Miller-Henson, Melissa	Resources Agency
Pepe, William	State Treasurer's Office
Sakai, Courtney	Office of the Governor
Simon, Nathalie	Office of Child Development and Education
Watrous, B.J.	Business, Transportation and Housing Agency

1994–1995

Blanks, Bobby	Commission on Improving Life Through Service

Corzine, Ian   Business, Transportation and Housing Agency
Felton, Vernon   Resources Agency
Hazeltine, Jed   Office of the Governor
Honig, Meredith   California Department of Education, Interagency
                              Children and Youth Services Division
Lassiter, Audrey   Office of Child Development and Education
Loughner, Sharon   Office of Criminal Justice Planning
Park, Michelle   Health and Welfare Agency
Persaud, Amanda   Department of Social Services
Placencia, Michael   Office of Intergovernmental Affairs
Rapallo, David   Governor's Office of Legal Affairs
Roush, Eileen   Governor's Office of Planning and Research
Topp, David   Department of Health Services
Vanalek, David   Office of Criminal Justice Planning; Board of
                              Prison Terms
Washburn, Susannah   California Conservation Corps

1995–1996
Crabbe, Philip   Commission for Improving Life Through Service
Dryden, John   Department of Food and Agriculture
Eichwald, Eve   California Research Bureau
Gardiner, Kathleen   Department of Health Services
Gursky, Mark   Business, Transportation and Housing Agency
Osborne, Cheryl-Marie   Office of Child Development and Education
Tashjian, Greg   Department of Parks and Recreation
Winger, Nicole   Health and Welfare Agency
Dana, Pamella   Trade and Commerce Agency
Durante, Gina   California Environmental Protection Agency
Gamber, Jennifer   State Treasurer's Office
Gomez, Carlos   Department of Education/Child, Youth and Family
                              Services Branch
Lam, David   Governor's Office of Office of External Affairs
Oviedo, Frank   Youth and Adult Correctional Agency/External
                              Affairs
Toth, Rebecca   Governor's Office of Intergovernmental Affairs

1996–1997
Gallagher, Katharine   Trade and Commerce Agency
Gonzalez, Trina   Department of Food and Agriculture
Hudson, Rodney   Business, Transportation and Housing Agency
Lave, Julia   Governor's Office of Intergovernmental Affairs
Movassaghi, Maziar   Resources Agency
Nava, Cesar   Commission on Improving Life through Service
Puente, John   Department of Social Services

Russell, Eva — Governor's Office of Planning and Research
Slayden, Hugh — Youth and Adult Correctional Agency
St. John, Kelly — Department of Health Services
Tahajian, Bradley — Department of Personnel Administration
Tolle, Steven — Board of Prison Terms
Weekley, Ronald — Department of Alcohol and Drug Programs
Yee, Kimberly — Department of Education/Child Development Division

1997–1998

Anders, Charles — Department of Mental Health
Birnbaum, Ariella — Health and Welfare Agency
Boaz, Cathrin — Governor's Office of Planning and Research
Bullard, Chloe — California Research Bureau
Dunakin, Christopher — Business, Transportation and Housing
Esgate, Kaira — Commission on Improving Life Through Service
Fritzler, Traci — Department of Food and Agriculture/International Trade
Gilmer, Sarah — Secretary of State
Gossage, Bryan — Department of Information Technologies
Harlick, Diana — Department of Education
Hoekstra, Sharon — Office of Criminal Justice Planning
Kaiser, Jill — California Arts Council
Lurie, Sue — Governor's Cabinet Office
McGrath, Berlita — Department of Food and Agriculture/Executive Office
Ramirez, Enrique — Managed Care Health Task Force
Ripsteen, Tim — The Virtual University
Ruparel, Shaila — Department of Health Services
Yoo, Jaeson — Trade and Commerce Agency

1998–1999

Bakhtiary, Sasan — California Environmental Protection Agency
Barel, Pieternal — Department of Health Services
Brooks, Kelly — Health and Welfare Agency
Diedrich, Susan — Department of Social Services/Legal Unit
Fraumini, Holly — Governor's Office/Administrative Unit
Garcia, Andrea — Commission on Improving Life Through Service
Harris, Rachel — Governor's Office/Legislative Unit
Hicks, Bill, Jr. — Department of Food and Agriculture/Fairs and Expositions
Joe, Allison — California Arts Council
Kim, Myung-Ahn — Department of Personnel Administration
Mangano, Robert — State Treasurer's Office

Mangum, Sarah — Department of Food and Agriculture/Policy Development and Forecasting
Nathar, Chealsea — Commission on Improving Life Through Service
Peth, Erin — California Youth Authority
Pollak, Daniel — California Research Bureau
Siu-Mendoza, Liza — Board of Prison Terms
Warlan, Courtney — Trade and Commerce

1999-2000

Buckley, Theresa — Office of Governor Gray Davis
Chih, Julia — Governor's Office of Education
Dean, Janice — Governor's Office of Planning and Research
Froome, Laura — Department of Food and Agriculture/International Trade and Commerce; Office of Criminal Justice Planning
Gomez, Blanca — Trade and Commerce Agency
Gorham, Tonya — Health and Human Services Agency
Graves, Scott — Trade and Commerce Agency
Hicks, Jonathan — State Independent Living Council
Keyes, Joyce — Commission on Improving Life Through Service
Lee, Stella — State Treasurer's Office
Micek, Brian — Governor's Office, Innovation in Government
Peterson, Sean — Governor's Office of Foreign Affairs and Administration
Quontamatteo, Cristina — Department of Health Services
Rutherford, Lyndsy — Managed Risk Medical Insurance Board
Trinchero, Beth — Department of Justice/Attorney General's Office
Vicory, Michael — Board of Prison Terms; Trade and Commerce Agency

2000–2001

Acharya, Meghana — Office of the Secretary for Education
Alexander, April — Governor's Office of Criminal Justice Planning
Aragon, Justin — Governor's Office of Foreign Affairs
Armenta, Artemio — California Environmental Protection Agency/Border Affairs Unit
Bailey, Colin — California Environmental Protection Agency/Agency, Air and Water Programs
Boysen, Laura — Governor's Office, Policy Unit
Brown, Angela — Office of the Secretary for Education
Emerson, Anya — Department of Education/External Affairs Branch
Esselman, David — Governor's Office for Innovation in Government
Fischer, Bethany — Trade and Commerce Agency/Executive Office
Hicks, Kelly — Children and Families Commission

Lashin, Reham	Managed Risk Medical Insurance Board
Martella, Jennifer	Department of Food and Agriculture
Quintero, Amanda	Commission on Improving Life Through Service
Taylor, Carlecia	Department of Justice/Attorney General's Office
Tran, Catherine	California Trade and Commerce Agency/Division of Science, Technology and Innovation

2001–2002

Birnbaum, Sabrina	California Technology, Trade and Commerce Agency, Division of Science, Technology & Innovation
Borrelli, Melissa	California Health and Human Services Agency
Brooks, Reneé	California Technology, Trade and Commerce Agency, Executive Office
Burritt, Scott	Fair Political Practices Commission
Calderon, Merlyn	Department of Consumer Affairs, Consumer Relations Outreach Unit
Carreon, Jennie	Office of Lieutenant Governor Cruz M. Bustamante
Garbacz, Catherine	California State Library, Research Bureau
Gonsalves, Jovanna	California Children and Families Commission
Gregg, Robert	California State Treasurer
Harsh, Sarah	Department of Justice, Attorney General's Office
Heald, Jennifer	California Department of Food and Agriculture
Heitstuman, David	Governor's Office, Communications Unit
Hernandez, Elisabet	Office of the Secretary for Education
Hernandez, Gisela	California Technology, Trade and Commerce Agency, California Main Street Program
Ing, William	Governor's Office on Service and Volunterrism (Go Serv)
Perez, Yovana	California Environmental Protection Agency, Environmental Justice
Quinonez, Luis	California Community Colleges, Chancellor's Office
Smith, Crystal	California Department of Education, External Affairs Branch

2002–2003

Aquino, Juan	California Environmental Protection Agency
Bajwa, Randeep	California Public Utilities Commission
Campos, Sonia	Office of Lt. Governor Cruz M. Bustamante
Castillo, Rowena	Department of Toxic Substances Control
Diaz, Nadia	State Board of Equalization
Domek, Andrew	Fair Political Practices Commission
Hansen, Stephen	State and Consumer Services
Jasinski, Cheri	Health & Human Services Agency

Kim, Tina	Office of the Secretary for Education
Lee, Anna	Office of the Attorney General
Murillo, Brittanya	Department of Housing & Community Development
Paige, Lauren	Office of Governor Gray Davis
Rabaud, Nicole	Governor's Office of Planning & Research
Riggs, Jessica	Office of the California State Treasurer
Rose, Maegen	Department of Alcohol & Drug Programs
Sumi, David	Department of Water Resources-Statewide Planning Branch
Tanner, Melissa	California Department of Education-Government Affairs
Thomas, Steven	California Postsecondary Education Commission

2003–2004

Alvarez, David	Office of the Secretary of State-Legislative Unit
Arriola, Vanessa	Office of the Secretary of Education
Dougherty, Stephanie	Fair Political Practices Commission
Glay, Glay	Department of General Services-Office of Military Support
Goddard, Tara	Department of Housing & Community Development-Division of Housing Policy
Hezchias, Sewit	Office of the State Controller
Johnson, Jennifer	Department of Education-Legislative Unit
Koistinen, Alison	California Environmental Protection Agency
Losada, Elizabeth	California State Library-Research Bureau
Mader, Anthony	Department of Finance- Office of the Deputy Director
Reamer, Jamie	Governor's Office of Legal Affairs
Reynoso, Jacqueline	Office of the Attorney General
Rodriguez, Maricela	California Community Colleges–Chancellor's Office
Ryan, Emily	Department of Consumer Affairs-Bureau of Automotive Repair
Utrapiromsuk, Pear	Department of Finance-Education Unit
Wales, Rachel	California Children and Families Commission
Wilson, LaShonda	California Health & Human Services Agency
Wong, Evan	Office of the State Treasurer

2004–2005

Ahn, Christina	Department of Finance
Andom, Jonathan	State and Consumer Services Agency
Biering, Brian	Resources Agency, Division of Energy
Dassel, Jennifer	Department of Food and Agriculture
Doshi, Megha	Department of Health Services

Finlev, Theis   Fair Political Practices Commission
Grant, Courtney   Office of the Attorney General
Hillis, Evan   Department of Parks and Recreation
McMillan, Evan   Office of First Lady Maria Shriver
Newsom, Gretchen Kinney   Office of the Treasurer
O'Keefe, Bridget   Governor's Office of Planning and Research
Pirro, Jacqueline   Office of the Secretary for Education
Raimer, David   Governor's Office of Homeland Security
Richter, Eve-Elizabeth   Department of Education, Government Affairs
Sexton, Steve   Office of the Governor, Cabinet Office
Stene, Angela   Health and Human Services Agency
Tansey, Kate   Labor and Workforce Development Agency
Valenzuela, Candice   First 5 California Children and Families
                                     Commission

2005-2006

Brooks, Viola   Office of the Lieutenant Governor
Conn, Robert   Department of Finance
Cortez, Elvira   Office of the Secretary of Education
Espinosa, Chris   Fair Political Practices Commission
Hone, Jason   Business, Transportation & Housing Agency
Iwu, Adama   Department of Managed Health Care
Kaczmarek, Matt   Office of the Treasurer
Kline, Brandon   Governor's Office
Lamb, Rosie   Office of the Attorney General
Lawlor, Katie   Office of Homeland Security
Masera, Meghan   Office of Emergency Services
Perry, Sherrice   Department of Corrections & Rehabilitation
Platin, Manolo   Office of the Governor, Cabinet Office
Roberts, Jessica   Resources Agency
Siskind, Daniel   California Service Corps
Stoops, Kyrsten   Health & Human Services Agency
Westrup, Evan   Governor's Office of Planning & Research
Yamout, Manal   Office of the Governor

2006-2007

Banks, Sekou   First 5 California
Foster, Tamar   Department of Health Services-Director
Gill, Trish   Resources Agency
Guzman, Sulma   Labor & Workforce Development Agency
Katz, Bec   Governor's Office of Emergency Services
La Torre, Jerome   Office of Treasurer Bill Lockyer
Navarra-Lujan, Shannon   Office of the Governor
Marcellus, Katie   Dept. of Health Services, Medical Care Serv.
Mason Elder, Tess   California Service Corps

Mays, Sonia	Department of Mental Health
Mohammadi, Mona	Office of the Governor
Naple, Mike	Fair Political Practices Commission
Newton, Alyssa	Governor's Office of Homeland Security
Osmundson, Krista	Health & Human Services Agency
Roughani, Ash	Business, Transportation & Housing
Shimeles, Merob	Department of Toxic Substances Control
von Gnechten, Marty	California State Parks
Weber, Marty	Governor's Office of Planning & Research

4.2. Executive Fellowship Program:
Directors, Faculty Advisors & Liaisons, 1986–1987 to 2005–2006

Fellowship Year	Program Director	Academic Advisor	Executive Liaison
1986-1987	Richard Krolak	Richard Krolak	William Cunningham
1987-1988	Richard Krolak	Richard Krolak	Peter Mehas
1988-1989	Susan McGowan	Susan McGowan	Peter Mehas (?)
1989-1990	Susan McGowan	Susan McGowan	Peter Mehas (?)
1990-1991	Miki Vohryzek-Bolden	Miki Vohryzek-Bolden	Mary Tietz
1991-1992	Miki Vohryzek-Bolden	Miki Vohryzek-Bolden	Mary Tietz
1992-1993	Sylvia Navari	Sylvia Navari	N/A
1993-1994	Donna Hoenig-Couch	John Syer	John Pimentel
1994-1995	Donna Hoenig-Couch	John Syer	John Pimentel
1995-1996	Donna Hoenig-Couch	Peter Detwiler	John Pimentel
1996-1997	Donna Hoenig-Couch	Ted Lascher	John Pimentel/ Paul Miner (after 8/96)
1997-1998	Donna Hoenig-Couch	Ted Lascher	Paul Miner
1998-1999	Donna Hoenig-Couch	Ted Lascher	Paul Miner
1999-2000	Donna Hoenig-Couch	Ted Lascher	N/A
2000-2001	Sandra Perez	Ted Lascher	Michael Flores
2001-2002	Sandra Perez	Robert Waste	Michael Flores
2002-2003	Sandra Perez	Robert Waste	Paul Miner
2003-2004	Sandra Perez	Robert Waste	Paul Miner
2004-2005	Sandra Perez	Nancy Shulock	Paul Miner/ Donna Lucas
2005-2006	Sandra Perez	Nancy Shulock	Bonnie Reiss
2006-2007	Kolleen Ostgaard	Nancy Shulock	Bonnie Reiss

Appendix 5
Judicial Administration Fellowship Program
5.1. Judicial Administration Fellow Names and Placements: 1997–1998 to 2005–2006

1997–1998

Busse, Phillip	Administrative Office of the Courts Center for Children and the Courts
Kelso, Kari	Sacramento County Superior Court
Loarie, Groegory	Administrative Office of the Courts Council and Legal Services Division
Ravazzini, Taryn	Judicial Council Office of Governmental Affairs
Yi, Kyong	Administrative Office of the Courts

1998–1999

Cuneo, Jeff	Judicial Council Office of Governmental Affairs
Flores, Gary	Sacramento County Superior Court
Jackson, Jorja	Alameda County Superior Court
Oh, Henry	Administrative Office of the Courts Information Systems Division
Rodgers, Melissa	Administrative Office of the Courts Center for Children and the Courts

1999-2000

Jones, Jamel K.	Administrative Office of the Courts Information Systems Division
Loeliger, Amy E.	Yolo County Superior court
Singer, Sanna	Judicial Council Office of Governmental Affairs
Wardak, Mohammed A.	Court of Appeal, Second Appellate District (Los Angeles)

2000–2001

Ashmon, Melvin E.	Court of Appeal, Second Appellate District (Los Angeles)
Broxmeyer, Eric J.	Supreme Court of California
Lustig, Christopher T.	Alameda County Superior Court Planning, Research, Court Services and Public Information Bureau

O'Neil, Maureen V.	Administrative Office of the Courts Center for Children and the Courts
Oshiro, Erin E.	Los Angeles Superior Court Planning and Research
Persicone, Guido F.	Santa Clara County Superior Court
Ponce de Leon, v	Judicial Council Office of Governmental Affairs
Sandler, Eve J.	Administrative Office of the Courts Trial Court Services Division
Wallace, Shana M.	Los Angeles County Superior Court Organizational Development and Education
Woods, Pamela	Yolo County Superior Court

2001–2002

Campos, Liliana	Superior Court of California, County of Los Angles, Planning and Research Unit
Jimenez,, Sandra	Superior Court of California, County of San Francisco
Kilmer, Beau	Superior Court of California, County of San Francisco
Knowles, Allison	Administrative Office of the Courts, Center for Families, Children and the Courts
Sanders, Derrick	California Court of Appeal, Second Appellate District
Shigemitsu, Laura	Superior Court of California, County of Los Angeles, Organizational Development and Education
Underhill, Stephen	Superior Court of California, County of Orange
Vorobets, Alla	Judicial Council, Office of Government Affairs
Vue, Nancy	Superior Court of California, County of Alameda, Planning Research, Court Services and Public Information Bureau
Wolf, Marc	Supreme Court of California, Office of the Clerk

2002–2003

Andronache, Christina	Superior Court of California, County of San Francisco
Gainey, Kimberly	Superior Court of California, County of Sacramento
Hwang, Dominic	Superior Court of California, County of Yolo
Magid, Adam	Superior Court of California, County of Orange
Maynard, James	Superior Court of California, County of Alameda, Planning, Research, Court Services and Public Information Bureau

Nelson, Megan	Superior Court of California, County of Los Angeles, Planning and Research Unit
Papadakos-Morafka, Sylvia	Supreme Court of California, Office of the Clerk
Patel, Sewali	Administrative Office of the Courts, Center for Families, Children and the Courts
Sanchez, Paula	California Court of Appeal, Second Appellate District
Shehadeh, Francis	Judicial Council's Office of Governmental Affairs

2003–2004

Cacananta, Jasper	Administrative Office of the Courts, Center for Families, Children and the Courts
Freedman, Michael	California Court of Appeal, Second Appellate District
Hogan, Marguerite	Superior Court of California, County of Los Angeles, Planning and Research Unit
Khuu, Jenny	Superior Court of California, County of Orange
Kirk, Brittany	Superior Court of California, Office of the Clerk
Mendez, Alejandra	Superior Court of California, County of San Francisco
Nisperos, Dalisai	Superior Court of California, County of Stanislaus
Reed, Timothy	Superior Court of California, County of Sacramento
Staley, Armilla	Superior Court of California, County of Alameda, Planning & Research Bureau

2004–2005

Cope-Vega, Bethel	Los Angeles Superior Court
Dezseran, Louis	Yolo County Superior Court
Esmail, Ashianna	San Francisco Superior Court
Logue, Andrea	Administrative Office of the Courts, Information Systems Bureau
McIntosh, Dawn Marie	Stanislaus County Superior Court
Medina, Christina	Administrative Office of the Courts, Center for Families, Children and the Courts
Murray, James	Supreme Court of California, Office of the Clerk
Sharifi, Solmaz	Second District Court of Appeal
Tudosa, Patricia	Alameda County Superior Court, Planning and Research Bureau
Young, Shaun	Judicial Council Office of Governmental Affairs

2005–2006

Andrews, Lindsay	Superior Court of California, County of Sacramento, Sacramento
Darr, Kendall	Superior Court of California, County of Stanislaus, Modesto

Jones, Kristen	Supreme Court of California, Office of the Clerk, San Francisco
Lutrario, Rosa	Superior Court of California, County of Orange, Santa Ana
Moskowitz, Rebecca	Superior Court of California, County of Los Angeles, Planning &Research Unit, Los Angeles
Rickard, Erika	Superior Court of California, County of San Francisco, Research & Planning, San Francisco
Soriano, Rolando	Superior Court of California, County of Yolo, Woodland
Tomlins, Craig	Court of Appeal, Second Appellate District, Los Angeles

2006–2007

Carpenter, Adrian	Sacramento Superior Court
Cervantes, Agustín	Los Angeles Superior Court, Office of Community Relations
Cordova, Mariana	Yolo Superior Court
Dunn, Joshua	Court of Appeal, Second Appellate District, Los Angeles
Franklin, Carmen	Alameda Superior Court
Jung, Paul	Orange Superior Court, Planning & Research Unit
Lampert, Alexandra	San Francisco Superior Court, Research & Planning
Ludd, Charles Jr.	Judicial Council Office of Governmental Affairs
Parenteau, Michael	San Diego Superior Court
Riess, Melissa	Supreme Court of California

5.2. Judicial Administration Fellowship Program:
Directors, Faculty Advisors & Liaisons, 1996–1997 to 2005–2006

Fellowship Year	Program Director	Academic Advisor	Judicial Council Liaison
1997-1998	Donna Hoenig-Couch	Patricia Clark-Ellis	Anthony Williams
1998-1999	Donna Hoenig-Couch	Anne Cowden	Anthony Williams
1999-2000	Donna Hoenig-Couch	Michael Semler	Anthony Williams
2000-2001	Sandra Perez	Michael Semler	June Clark
2001-2002	Sandra Perez & Donna Hoenig-Couch	Scott Graves	June Clark
2002-2003	Donna Hoenig-Couch	Scott Graves	June Clark
2003-2004	Donna Hoenig-Couch	Bryan Borys	June Clark
2004-2005	Donna Hoenig-Couch	Bryan Borys	June Clark
2005-2006	Donna Hoenig-Couch	Bryan Borys	June Clark
2006-2007	Donna Hoenig-Couch	Bryan Borys	June Clark

Appendix 6
Senate Intern Program: 1973–1976
6.1. Senate Resolution Creating Senate Intern Program

Senate Resolution 46
Relative to student interns

WHEREAS, The California Senate at this time has no recognized or continuing program to encourage students to participate in state government or to learn operations and functions of the Senate; and

WHEREAS, It is a recognized aim of the Senate to encourage youth to work within the system and to accomplish changes or improvements through legitimate processes; and

WHEREAS, A permanent Senate student intern program can be set up and kept functioning for small cost compared to its potentially great benefits; and

WHEREAS, Such a program can offer members of the Senate and Senate staff members an additional means of working with and helping to gain an understanding of the mood, the ideals, and the outlook of today's youth and student groups; and

WHEREAS, Informal student intern programs now functioning in some Senate offices have shown conclusively that, when well directed, such programs can be of great benefit both to students and to the Senate offices involved; and

WHEREAS, A formal student training program can help increase youth interest in state government and help provide the dedicated staff professionals and elected officials so essential to a functioning democracy; now, therefore, be it

Resolved by the Senate of the State of California, That the Senate requests the Senate Rules Committee to initiate a Senate intern program as a pilot project, to be financed from the Senate Contingent Fund and to operate on a bipartisan basis.

S.R. 46, California Senate, 1972 Regular Session, *Journal of the Senate* (4 April 1972): 1105-110

6.2. Senate Intern Names and Placements: 1973–1974 to 1975–1976

1973–1974
FULL-TIME
Bradshaw, Robert
Collins, Johnny
Prairie, Michael
Rodriguez, Eva
Weismehl, Philip
Williams, Pamela

PART-TIME

Carter, M. Susan	Senator Nicholas Petris
Griffin, Diann	Senator Alan Robbins
Guttadauro, Guy J.	Senator George Zenovich
Kiser, Randall	Senator Ralph Dills
Lucero, Reuben G.	Senator Mervyn Dymally
McPhee, Shannon L.	Senator Joseph M. Kennick
Meyer, James L.	Senator John L. Harmer
Shahabian, John A.	Senator David Roberti
Tribby, Kenneth M.	Senator Robert Lagomarsino
West, Jr., William F.	Senator Dennis Carpenter

1974–1975
FULL-TIME

Bonfilio, Kathleen A.	Government Organization Committee
Gilbert, Sabina	Education Committee
Jarrett, II, Melvyn C.	Rules Committee
Nossoff, Joel	Natural Resources Committee
Riggall, Eric Kneave	Judiciary Committee
Ronningen, Judith A.	Local Government Committee

PART-TIME

Carrico, Julie M.	Senator James Q. Wedworth
Dahlin, David R.	Senator Ralph Dills
Dihel, Laura Ann	Senator Dennis Carpenter
Hackard, Michael A.	Senator Peter Behr
Holt, Hugh L.	Senator David Roberti
Jordan, Bill	Senator Al Alquist
Kuehne, Sandra L.	Senator John W. Holmdahl
Meyers, Barry	Senator Nicholas Petris
Robinson, Calvin S.	Senator Nate Holden
Sokol, John R.	Senator Omer Rains

Winter, Margery Hastings   Senator Jerry Smith

1975–1976
FULL-TIME
Boreman, Stephen M.   Elections and Reapportionment Committee
Cardoza, Dan L.   Education Committee
Haight, Alberta   Local Government Committee
Lorentzen, Edward M.   Natural Resources and Wildlife Committee
Myers, Teresa H.   Health and Welfare Committee
Ross, Tommy   Public Utilities, Transit and Energy Committee

PART-TIME
Anderson, Scott D.   Senator Nicholas Petris
Bernard, Debra A.   Senator John Dunlap
Coward, John H.   Senator Nate Holden
DeAmicis, Lisa M.   Senator Jerry Smith
Flores, Armando M.   Senator Alfred Alquist
Gay, Ruth M.   Senator Alan Robbins
Martin, Neil D.   Senator David Roberti
Miller, Charles C.   Senator Robert Presley
Newman, Eric R.   Senator John W. Holmdahl
Shellito, Jeffrey P.   Senator Peter Behr

Appendix 7
Senate Fellowship Program:
1976–1977 to 2005–2006
7.1. Senate Fellow Names and Placements:

1976–1977

Bryant, Mickie	Local Government Committee
Graff, Gil	Business & Professions Committee
Hardy, Steve	Governmental Organization Committee
Hermocillo, Jose	Industrial Relations Committee
Mandeles, Mark	Natural Resources and Wildlife Committee
Rice, Laura	Education Committee

1977–1978

Bryggman, Mark L.	Insurance and Financial Institutions Committee
Chow, Barbara A.	Senator John Garamendi
Costa, Katherine M.	Transportation Committee
Hall, Allison Y.	Natural Resources and Wildlife Committee
Jespersen, Jonathan S.	Senator William Campbell
Jordan, Daniel V.	Senator John Stull
Light, Tonya V.	Education Committee
Nichols, Richard M.	Senator Nicholas C. Petris
Orenstein, Mark M.	Local Government Committee
Pelton, Charles	Senator Omer Rains
Powell, Robert L.	Senator Jerry Smith
Prinvale, Jean M.	Senator Newton Russell

1978–1979

Alonzo, Diana	Senator Nicolas Petris
Barszcz, Martha	Senator John Holmdahl
Feraru, Robert	Subcommittee on Social Services and Welfare
Gressani, Ann	Energy and Public Utilities Committee
Gully, Lyndi	Local Government Committee
Kerbavaz, Joanne	Senator Omer Rains
Koppelman, Lillian	Education Committee
Nguyen, Trong	Industrial Relations Committee
Purnell, Daniel	Senator John Foran
Quiroz, Robin	Senator Newton Russell

1979–1980

Barcellos, Anthony	Senator Albert S. Rodda
Earnest, Curtis	Industrial Relations Committee

Fuentes, Diana	Senator Diane Watson
Goldberg, Carole	Senator Barry Keene
Harris, Marsha	Natural Resources and Wildlife Committee
Kittner, Alan	Health and Welfare Committee
Ledda, Derek	Senator Nicholas C. Petris
Moore, Robert	Senator Omer Rains
Riley, Marilyn	Senator Alan Sieroty
Shepherd, Bruce	Energy and Public Utilities Committee
Whan, Steve	Senator John F. Foran
Zimmer, Donald Fritz	Senator Robert Presley

1980–1981

Becerra, Xavier	Senator Albert S. Rodda
Cataldo, Chris L.	Natural Resources and Wildlife Committee
Conrad, Sherri J.	Senator Omer Rains
Curtis, James E.	Senator Diane Watson
Johnston, Zane H.	Senator Newton Russell
Ferguson, Susan C.	Health and Welfare Committee
Gruen, Adam S.	Senator Barry Keene
Jackson, Otis L.	Energy and Public Utilities Committee
Karapetian, Berdj P.	Senator Robert Presley
Kotalik, Emil J., Jr.	Senator Nicholas C. Petris
McMurray, Margaret	Senator Alan Sieroty
Pane, Joshua J.	Senator Milton Marks

1981–1982

Franklin, Leslie, Sr.	Senator Nicholas C. Petris
Kirkpatrick, Craig	Finance Committee
Kuykendall, Leslie	Senator Robert Presley
Lowrey, Karen	Energy and Public Utilities Committee
Mercer, Michelle	Senator Barry Keene
Millen, John	Senator David Roberti
Miller, John D.	Senator Diane Watson
Mitchell, Carol Ann	Senator John F. Foran
Reidy, Deborah	Senator Henry J. Mello
Seymour, Anne	Rules Committee
Stafford, Rodney	Senator Alan Robbins; Insurance and Indemnity Committee
Yelverton, Karen L.	Senator Ray E. Johnson

1982–1983

Barton, Laurel	Energy and Public Utilities Committee
Chann, Teddi	Senator Leroy Greene
Dean, Amy T.	Senator Henry J. Mello

Garcia, Rahn	Senator Robert Presley
Karpilow, Kate	Senator Barry Keene
Kloss, John	Senator Diane Watson
Lake, Todd	Senator Nicholas C. Petris
Lieberman, Matt	Senator John Garamendi
Rhoades, Judith	Judiciary Committee
Roberts, Derrell	Insurance and Indemnity Committee
Roberts, Toni	Senator David Roberti
Spitzer, Todd	Senator John Seymour

1983–1984

Bagneris, Jules	Senator Alan Robbins
Block, Norma	Senator Wadie P. Deddeh
Brandt, Alfred	Senator David Roberti
Bunn, David	Senator James W. Nielsen
Henderson, Jane	Senator James W. Nielsen
Katsuranis, Frances	Senator John F. Foran
Koltun, Adele	Senator Ray E. Johnson
Law, Samuel	Senator Alan Robbins
Thiel, Karen	Senator Leroy Greene
Wang, Art	Senator H.L. Richardson
Williams, Luke	Senator Robert Beverly
Yniguez, Juan	Senator Leroy Greene

1984–1985

Ahuja, Anita	Senator Newton Russell
Carroll-Zeller, Sandra	Senator Robert Presley
Jennings, Bruce	Senator Nicolas Petris
Raphael, Tamar	Senator John Garamendi
Sektnan, Mark	Senator John Seymour
Tochterman, Linda	Senator Art Torres
Vacca, Lynn	Senator Hirsch Rosenthal
Whiten, Joyce	Senator Barry Keene

1985–1986

Brown, Mark	Senator Milton Marks
Carter, Henry	Senator Dan McCorquodale
Flynn, Dan	Senator Gary Hart
Grant, Surlene	Senator Nicolas Petris
Hall, Maureen	Senator John Seymour
Harris, Joanne	Energy and Public Utilities Committee
Hernandez, Jose Nestor	Senator David Roberti
Katz, Barbara	National Resources and Wildlife Committee
Liberman, Ruth	Senator Diane Watson
McGregor, Scott	Minority Fiscal Consultants

Simon, David Judiciary Committee
Umemoto, Keith Budget and Fiscal Review Committee

1986–1987

Brown, Consuella Senator DianeWatson; Health and Human Services Committee
Chisholm, Marge Senator John Seymour
Council, Mickie Senator William Campbell
Donahue, Margaret Appropriations Committee
Lawrence, Jeffrey Minority Fiscal Consultants
Markuson, Richard Senator Milton Marks
Lorenzato, Stefan Senator Robert Presley; Natural Resources and Wildlife Committee
Nguyen, Lilly Energy and Public Utilities Committee
Nixen, Peter Senator Barry Keene; Budget and Fiscal Review
Peasley, Kim Senator Henry Mello
Penilla, Carlos Senator Art Torres
Romero, Jesus Senator Nicholas Petris

1987–1988

Chan, Ted Insurance Claims and Corporations Committee
Dietrich, Gary Senator Dan McCorquodale
Evans, Regina Senator Diane Watson
Florez, Dean Senator Art Torres
Gonzalez, Michael Senator Nicholas Petris
Hall, Christine Judiciary Committee
Kerbs, Tom Energy and Utilities Committee
Loomis, Debora Senator Henry Mello
Rupp, Richard Senator William Campbell
Sanchez, Dolores Budget and Fiscal Review Committee
Silberstein, Sandra Senator Robert Presley
Smith, Kara Senator John Garamendi

1988–1989

Alvarez, Robert Energy and Public Utilities Committee
Campos, Yvonne Senator Gary Hart
Flacks, Charles Senator Art Torres
Kiff, David Local Government Committee
Lites, James Budget and Fiscal Review Committee
Madison, Danielle Senator Rob Hurtt
Miller, Kenneth P. Senator Rebecca Morgan
Miller, Kimberly Senator William Campbell
Velazquez, Gilbert Senator John Garamendi
Victor, Carol Senator Robert Piesley

Wensinger, Arnold — Senator Quentin Kopp
Yee, Betty — Health and Human Services Committee

1989–1990

Alexander, Kim — Energy and Public Utilities Committee
Burdette, Don — Senator Quentin Kopp
Camacho, Elizabeth — Senator Robert Presley
Casey, Paul — Senator Gary Hart
Chu, KarYen — Subcommittee on Aging
Gonzalez, Martin — Senator Bill Leonard
Gonzalez, Michelle — Senator Art Torres
Han, Theresa — Housing and Urban Affairs Committee
Hoenig-Couch, Donna — Budget and Fiscal Review Committee
Kahn, Chris — Senator Marian Bergeson
Phabmixay, Tip — Insurance, Claims, and Corporations Committee
Richman, Paul — Senator Rebecca Morgan
Siegel, Drew — Senator Dan McCorquodale
Ward, Debra — Health and Human Services Committee

1990–1991

Butler, Shawn — Senator Mike Thompson
Exum, Ethusian — Senator Dan McCorquodale
Fisher, Robyn — Senator Alfred Alquist; Budget and Fiscal Review Committee
Garza, Elida — Senator Henry Mello; Subcommittee on Aging, Joint Committee on Arts
Hou, John — Senator Gary Hart
Levine, Beth — Senator Barry Keene
Lopez, Carrie — Senator Nicholas Petris
Manatt, April — Senator Marian Bergeson
Martinez, Gilbert — Senator Herschel Rosenthal; Energy and Public Utilities Committee
Morris, Jim — Senator Robert Presley
Paul, Richard — Senator Bill Leonard
Perez, Raul — Senator Quentin Kopp
Silverman, Steve — Senator Alan Robbins; Insurance, Claims and Corporations Committee
Siu, Joanne — Senator Diane Watson; Health and Human Services Committee
Stapf-Walters, Karen — Senator Lucy Killea
Thoburn, Brian — Senator Ken Maddy
Wong, Bill — Senator Leroy Greene; Housing and Urban Affairs Committee

1991–1992

Armentrout, Nancy	Senator Robert Presley
Clark, Pernell	Senator Diane Watson; Health and Human Services Committee
Davis, Leza	Senator Newton Russell
Dinh, Tan	Senator Rebecca Morgan
Fong, Timothy	Senate Office of Research
Ford, Bridget	Senator Henry Mello; Subcommittee on Aging
Gutierrez, Paula	Senator Lucy Killea
Hilger, Jennifer	Senator Marian Bergeson
Ho, Tuyen	Senator Quentin Kopp
Jaramillo, Joseph	Senator Gary Hart
La Faille, Thomas	Senator Mike Thompson
Martell, Antonia	Senator Bill Leonard
Numark, Clifford	Senator Herschel Rosenthal; Energy and Public Utilities Committee
Ortega, Matthew	Senator Dan McCorquodale
Selinsky, Pearl	Senator Leroy Greene/ Senator Mike Thompson; Housing and Urban Affairs Committee
Shiao, Peter	Senator Art Torres
Smith, Trent	Senator Frank Hill
Walker, Sue	Senator Bill Greene

1992–1993

Anders, Kelly	Senator David Roberti
Barankin, Nathan	Judiciary Committee
Burnham, Raymonda	Senator Pat Johnston
Dana, Janet	Senator Marian Bergeson
Dektar, Ellen	Senator Gary Hart
Edwards, Jennifer	Senator Lucy Killea
Guerrero, Guillermo	Senator Mike Thompson
Hyde, Michael	Senator Rebecca Morgan
Ibarra, Delia	Senator Tom Hayden
Kabani, Nader	Senate Office of Research
Moore, Jamillah	Senator Teresa Hughes
Navarro, Paul	Health and Human Services Committee
Parikh, Kevin	Energy and Public Utilities Committee
Robinson, Gerard	Senator Bill Leonard
Shin, Patricia	Senator Art Torres
Smith, David	Senator Quentin Kopp
Solorio, Jose	Budget and Fiscal Review Committee
Wong, Collin	Senator Robert Presley

1993–1994

Bustillos, Ernest	Senator Charles Calderon; Toxics and Public Safety Committee
Flores, Jasmin	Senator Tim Leslie
Galaviz, David	Senator Mike Thompson
Golden, Bryan	Senator Phil Wyman
Heinicke, Malcolm	Senator Tom Hayden
Hong, Jane	Senator Diane Watson; Health and Human Services Committee
Huang, Andrew	Senator Dan McCorquodale
Johnson, Rita	Senator Alfred Alquist; Budget and Fiscal Review Committee
Jones, Damon	Senator Teresa Hughes
Leonard, Mark	Senator Rob Hurtt
Matocq, Lisa	Senator Pat Johnston
Nakagawa, Yoko	Senator Lucy Killea
O'Neal, Erin	Senator Bill Lockyer; Judiciary Committee
Sigala, Jose	Senator Gary Hart
Simon, Christina	Senator Art Torres
Smith, Stacy	Senator Marian Bergeson
Toole, Patrick	Senator Quentin Kopp
Wight, Christine	Senator Bill Leonard

1994–1995

Almarez, David	Senator Ray Haynes
Antwih, Andrew	Health and Human Services Committee
Bacchi, Charles	Senator Bill Leonard
Barcellona, Miriam	Criminal Procedure Committee
Barclay, Elizabeth	Senator Quentin Kopp
Feliciano, Armand	Budget and Fiscal Review Committee
Garcia, Marcela	Senator Hilda Solis
Graham, Andrea	Senator Tom Campbell
Lim, James	Senate Office of Research
Martin, Armen	Senator Rob Hurtt
McLean, Hilary	Senator Mike Thompson
Mesick, Tara	Senator Jack O'Connell
Nguyen, Yen	Senator Richard Polanco
Olson, Gary	Senator Maurice Johannessen
Parker, Steven	Senator Insurance Committee
Rios, Richard	Senator Bill Lockyer
Rubin, Stephanie	Senator Tom Hayden

1995–1996

Aguirre-Happoldt, Ingrid	Senator Hilda Solis
Brown, Carrie	Senator Maurice Johannessen

Cazares, Mixim	Senator Jack O'Connell
Garcia, Sue	Senator Jim Costa; Agriculture and Water Resources Committee
Gibson, Rachel	Senator Pat Johnston
Herron, Melinda	Senator John Lewis
Ho, James	Senator Quentin Kopp
Ihrke, William	Senator William Craven; Local Government Committee
Lee, Adam	Senator Bill Leonard
Lopez-Rojas, Charlotte	Senator Herschel Rosenthal; Insurance Committee
Martinez, Belinda	Senator Milton Marks; Criminal Procedure Committee
Martinez, Enrique	Senator Mike Thompson; Budget and Fiscal Review Committee
Nguyen, Kevin	Senator Rob Hurtt
Price, Kevin	Senator Tom Hayden
Raglin, Dennis	Senator Lucy Killea
Schafer, John	Senator Ray Haynes
Uchishiba, Naomi	Senator Henry Mello; Subcommittee on Aging
White, Lisa	Senator Diane Watson; Health and Human Services Committee

1996–1997

Bradley, Erin	Senator Quentin Kopp
Buford, Nick-Anthony	Senator Ray Haynes
Cheung, Terrance	Senator John Burton; Judiciary Committee
Kousser, Thad	Senator Tom Hayden
Lieberman, Tanya	Senator Mike Thompson; Budget and Fiscal Review Committee
Lynn, Nora	Senator Dede Alpert
Mannen, Kate	Senator William Craven; Local Government Committee
Muhlhauser, Ted	Senator Betty Karnette
Olsen, Kristin	Senator Tim Leslie
Padilla, Ian	Senator Richard Polanco
Ranchod, Sanjay	Senator Byron Sher
Soleymani, Navid	Senator Richard Rainey
Stamps, Gina	Senator John Lewis
Torres, Juan	Senator Hilda Solis
Ueda, Kara	Senator John Vasconcellos; Criminal Procedure Committee
Verardo, Traci	Senator Jack O'Connell
Vitanza, Elisa	Senator Barbara Lee

Washington, Eddie, Jr.   Senator Diane Watson; Health and Human Services Committee

1997–1998
Armendariz, Lucie   Senator John Vasconcellos; Public Safety Committee
Chin, Lisa   Senator Dede Alpert
Christofferson, Kyla   Senator Ray Haynes
Cox, Erin   Senator Jim Costa; Agriculture and Water Committee
Elam, Bobby   Senator Adam Schiff
Grinnell, Collin   Senator William Craven; Local Government Committee
Huang, Peggy   Senator Maurice Johannessen
Hughes, Jason   Senator Tim Leslie
Kelly, Lola   Senator Diane Watson; Health and Human Services Committee
Mayer, Guillermo   Senator Hilda Solis
Moulds, Don   Senator John Burton; Judiciary Committee
Olivera, Paul   Senator Richard Polanco
Paxton, Nathan   Senator Quentin Kopp
Ramirez, Angela   Senator Betty Karnette
Sweeney, Owen   Senator John Lewis
Teng, Allen   Senator Teresa Hughes
Walseth, Megan   Senator Mike Thompson; Budget and Fiscal Review Committee
White, Chip   Senator Pete Knight

1998–1999
Ashcraft, Michael   Senator Jackie Speier
Bodner, Zachary   Senator Tom Hayden; Natural Resources and Wildlife Committee
Cabrera, Rosa   Senator John Vasconcellos; Public Safety Committee
Chee, Kerlen   Senator Martha Escutia; Health and Human Services Committee
Cortés, Rosario   Agriculture and Water Resources Committee
Eisberg, Ryan   Senator John Lewis
Geevargis, Nira   Senator Hilda Solis
Givens, Nicole   Senator Adam Schiff
Jensen, Brian   Senator Dick Monteith
Lindsey, Travis   Senator Maurice Johannessen
McShane, Steve   Senator Bruce McPherson
Pacheco, Monica   Senator Liz Figueroa
Pank, Karen   Senator Charles Poochigian
Quintero, Andre   Senator Joseph Dunn
Teresi, Tony   Senator Dede Alpert

Thomas, James	Senator Ray Haynes
Thymes, Chereesse	Budget and Fiscal Review Committee
Wilkening, Karen	Senator Richard Rainey

1999–2000

Arroyo, Gustavo	Agriculture and Water Resources Committee
Botts, Cory	Senator Charles Poochigian
Dane, Carla	Senator William J. "Pete" Knight
Garcia, Anita	Senator Richard Alarcón
Grisby, Darnell	Senator Kevin Murray
Hamilton, Joshua	Senator Richard Monteith
Jack, James	Senator Bruce McPherson
Kau, Kabrina	Senator Betty Karnette
Knox, Parissh	Budget and Fiscal Review Committee
Kohleriter, Nicole	Senator Jackie Speier
Lee, Joo Young	Senator Tom Hayden
Matosantos, Ana	Senator Martha Escutia; Health and Human Services Committee
Tagre, Pablo	Senator Hilda Solis
Tyson, Vanessa	Senator John Vasconcellos; Public Safety Committee
Vyas, Nisha	Senator Don Perata
Weston, Gary, Jr.	Senator John Lewis
Wong, Megan	Senator Deborah Ortiz
Wright, Joseph	Senator Ray Haynes

2000–2001

Artis, Janel	Senator Edward Vincent
Astorga, Arnold	Senator Tom McClintock
Avila, Jorge	Senator Wes Chesbro
Benítez, Gabriel	Senator Richard Alarcón
Bhe, Anthony	Senator Michael Machado
Boloorian, Shervin	Senator John Vasconcellos; Education Committee
Carpenter, Candace	Senator Tom Torlakson; Local Government Committee
Chavez, Scott	Senator Ray Haynes
Cunningham, Jordan	Republican Policy Consultants
Duran, David	Senator Bill Morrow
Griffith, Loren	Senator Sheila Kuehl
Lane, Mari	Senator Bruce McPherson; Public Safety Committee
Moxey, Angelina	Senator Don Perata
Nguyen, Han	Senator Charles Poochigian
Schreiber, Christian	Senator Joseph Dunn; Housing and Community Development Committee
Schulte, Tanya Vandrick	Senator Bob Margett

| Sutro, Sarah | Senator Deborah Ortiz; Health and Human Services Committee |
| Vázquez, Celinda | Senator Martha Escutia; Judiciary Committee |

2001–2002

Chaires, Nancy	Senate Wes Chesbro
Cobb, III, Curtiss	Republican Fiscal Consultants
Dickstein, Jonah	Senator Deborah Ortiz/Health and Human Services Committee
Durr, Rhea	Senator Sheila Kuehl
Escobar, Eddie	Senator Richard Alarcón
Franciskovich, Emily	Agriculture and Water Resources Committee
Ha, Bryan	Senator Jack Scott
Hillery, Cyndi	Senator Ray Hayes
Liu, Marie	Senator Betty Karnette
Mizany, Kimia	Senator Tom Torlakson/Local Government Committee
Paul, Scott	Senator William J. "Pete" Knight
Roberts, Jacqueline	Republican Policy Consultants
Rosalez, Rosalinda	Senator Gloria Romero
Rutschow, Amy	Senator Charles Poochigian
Sofen, Adam	Senator Joseph Dunn
Ward, Amy	Senator Bill Morrow
Wheeler, Matthew	Senator Rico Oller
Young, Christopher	Senator John Vasconcellos/Education Committee

2002–2003

Aguilar, Daniel	Senator Joseph Dunn/Housing & Community Development Committee
Bui, Tami Thi	Senator Tom Torlakson/Local Government Committee
DeVore, Kenneth	Senator Jim Battin
Fortin, Kristin	Senator Bill Morrow
Gamiz, Ana	Senator Gloria Romero
Hale, Jeffrey	Senator Jeff Denham
Harris, John	Senator Dean Florez
Ishikawa, Derek	Senator Byron Sher
Janof, Nicholas	Senator Bruce McPherson/Public Safety Committee
Johnston, Cristy	Senator Martha Escutia/Judiciary Committee
Leal, Nadia	Senator Gilbert Cedillo
Ma, Tam	Senator Sheila Kuehl/Natural Resources & Wildlife
Metzger, Grace	Senator Charles Poochigian
Meyer, Gabriel	Senator Wes Chesbrol, Budget and Fiscal Review Committee
Ravert, Ellen	Republican Policy Consultants

Tjernell, Soren   Senator Jackie Speier/Insurance Committee
Torres, Jesús   Senator Denise Moreno Ducheny
Westbrooks, James   Senator Edward Vincent/Government Organization

2003–2004

Aguilera, Rafael   Environmental Quality Committee
Apekian, Shant   Senator Jeffrey Denham
Bohannon, Ambi   Senator Deborah Ortiz/Health & Human Services
                                Committee
Currin, Emily   Senator Dennis Hollingsworth
Enderton, Laura   Republican Policy Consultants
Ginno, Carolyn   Senator Sam Aanestad
Guerra, Eric   Senator Gilbert Cedillo
Hardeman, Nick   Senator Richard Alarcón/Labor & Industrial
                                Relations Committee
Hotelwala, Muffaddal   Senator Tom Torlakson/Local Government
                                Committee
Lee, Anka   Senator Sheila Kuehl
Martin, Katheryn   Public Safety Committee
Morgan, Amanda   Senator Bill Morrow
Mosqueda, Terri   Senator John Vasconcellos/ Education Committee
Porter, Roman   Senator Joseph Dunn
Portillo, Luis   Senator Roy Ashburn
Smith, Mark   Senator Charles Poochigian
Willey, Alyson   Senator Thomas "Rico" Oller
Zazueta, Edgar   Senator Denise Moreno Ducheny/ Housing &
                                Community Development Committee

2004–2005

Almazán, Araceli   Senator Gilbert Cedillo
Chávez, Patricia   Senator George Runner
Christensen, Lance   Senator Tom McClintock
Chung, Tiffany   Senator Carole Migden
Duque, Beatriz   Senator John Campbell
Gonzales, Gilbert   Senator Robert Dutton
Gress, Jennifer   Senator Tom Torlakson
Harris, Kendra   Senator Gloria Romero
Jackson, Mark   Senator Bill Morrow
Malhi, Satinder   Senator Jackie Speier
Montemayor, Linda   Senator Elaine Alquist
Neville, Anne   Senator Sheila Kuehl
Onishi, Rei   Senator Joe Simitian
Razavi, Layla   Senator Joseph Dunn
Rodriguez, David   Senator Richard Alarcón

Schrap, Matthew — Senator Dave Cox
Seliverstov, Helen — Senator Charles Poochigian
Wagner, Camille — Senator Christine Kehoe

2005–2006

Ambriz, Andrea — Senator Joseph Dunn
Anderson, Rebekah — Senator Dave Cox
Bachilla, Pamela — Senator Debra Bowen
Chapman, Ahmad — Senator Elaine Alquist
Chen, Julius — Senator George Runner
Finley, Robin — Senator Charles Poochigian
Furman, Deanna — Senator Richard Alarcón
Galvan, Estéban — Senator Carole Migden
Haney, Matthew — Senator Joseph Simitian
Keeney, Jetta — Senator Tom McClintock
Miller, Nicole — Senator Gilbert Cedillo
Moreali, Matthew — Senator Abel Maldonado
Roberson, Todd — Senator Jeffrey J. Denham
Salcido, Pedro — Senator Denise Ducheney
Snowden, Jonathan — Senator Sheila Kuhel
Spencer, Jason — Senator Tom Torlakson
Wong, Christina — Senator Christine Kehoe

2006–2007

Alarcón, Lisa — Senator Alex Padilla
Assagai, Caliph — Senator Leland Yee
Baum, Gideon — Labor and Industrial Relations Committee
Burchill, Kiyomi — Senator Darrell Steinberg
Clay, Delilah — Senator Denise Moreno Ducheny
Diaz, Sonia — Senator Sheila Kuehl
Dueñas, Tomasa — Senator Jenny Oropeza
Eisenhammer, Eric — Senator Bob Dutton
Hargrove, September — Senator Elaine Alquist
Heidorn, Nicolas — Senator Mark Ridley-Thomas
Icanberry, Megan — Senator David Cogdill
Jarred, Michael — Senator Ellen Corbett
Johnson, Katherine — Senator Tom Torlakson
Kapoor, Nina — Senator Joseph Simitian/Environmental Quality Committee
Kim, Sophia (Sophie) — Local Government Committee
Radosevich, Martin — Senator Gilbert Cedillo
Rodriguez, Ana — Senator Patricia Wiggins
Santiago, Gregory — Senator Sam Aanestad

7.2. Senate Fellows Program: Directors and Faculty Advisors, 1976–1977 to 2005–2006

Fellowship Year	Program Coordinator/ Director	Academic Advisor
1976–1977	Jim McCauley	N/A
1977–1979	Derek Pogson	N/A
1979–1980	Dan Blackburn	N/A
1980–1981	Lori Snell	N/A
1981–1982	Karen Frick (9/81) Anne Seymour (10/81-6/82)	N/A
1982–1983	Janet Reiser	N/A
1983–1984	Janet Reiser Cassie	N/A
1984–1985	Nettie Sabelhaus	John Syer
1986–1987	Nettie Sabelhaus	John Syer
1987–1988	Nettie Sabelhaus	John Syer
1988–1989	Nettie Sabelhaus	John Syer
1989–1990	Nettie Sabelhaus	John Syer
1990–1991	Nettie Sabelhaus	John Syer
1991–1992	Nettie Sabelhaus	John Syer
1992–1993	Nettie Sabelhaus	John Syer
1993–1994	Nettie Sabelhaus	Jerry Briscoe and Barry Keene
1994–1995	Nettie Sabelhaus	Ann Bailey
1995–1996	Nettie Sabelhaus	Ann Bailey
1996–1997	Nettie Sabelhaus	Ann Bailey
1997–1998	Nettie Sabelhaus	Ann Bailey
1998–1999	Dan Friedlander	Ann Bailey
1999–2000	Dan Friedlander	Ann Bailey
2000–2001	Dan Friedlander	Ann Bailey (to12/00) Patrick Johnston (after 1/01)
2001–2002	Dan Friedlander	Patrick Johnston
2002–2003	Dan Friedlander	Roger Dunston
2003–2004	Dan Friedlander	Vince Latino
2004–2005	Dan Friedlander	Vince Latino
2005–2006	David Pacheco	Vince Latino
2006–2007	David Pacheco	Vince Latino

7.3. Senate Fellows Program: Selection Committee Members: 1976–1977 to 1989–1990

1976–1977
Senator George N. Zenovich, acting chairman
Senator Craig Biddle
Senator Albert S. Rodda
Baldwin, Charles
McDaniel, Gerald (California State University, Sacramento, Government Department)
Sokolow, Alvin D. (University of California, Davis)
Whiteley, Nelson

1977–1978
William Kier, acting chairman (director, Senate Office of Research)
Senator Albert S. Rodda
Carrington, Michael (administrative assistant to Senator Robert S. Stevens)
Lewis, Jonathan (administrative assistant to Senator Nicholas C. Petris)
Sokolow, Alvin D.
Testa, Robert (consultant, Natural Resources and Wildlife Committee)

1978–1979
William Kier, acting chairman
Senator John Stull
Senator Jerry Smith
Calef, Sally (associate consultant, H & W Committee)
Duerksen, Roger (administrative assistant to Senator Russell)
Huff, Jesse (coordinator, Senate Republican Caucus)
Ross, Tommy (associate consultant, PUT&E Committee)
Schmidt, Barbara (California State University, Sacramento)
Tidwell, William (San Jose State University)
Wilson, Jack (administrative assistant to Senator John Stull)
Woo, Michael (administrative assistant to Senator David Roberti)

1979–1980
William Kier, acting chairman
Carrington, Michael (administrative aide to Senator H. L. Richardson)
Duerksen, Roger (administrative assistant to Senator Russell)
Gressani, Ann (Senate fellow, Energy and Public Utilities Committee)
Johnson, Scott (administrative aide to Senator Robert Nimmo)
Lowe, Ida (administrative aide to Senator Paul Carpenter)
Megino, Gloria (associate consultant, Judiciary Committee)
Schmidt, Barbara (California State University, Sacramento)

Thornton, Arthur (consultant, Senate Office of Research)
Tidwell, William (San Jose State University)
Woo, Michael (administrative assistant to Senator David Roberti)

1980–1981
Dr. Judith Lamare, acting chair (Senate Office of Research)
Haleva, Jerry (executive assistant to Senator William Campbell)
Hausey, Willie (district representative, Senator Albert S. Rodda)
Miller, Terry (consultant, Insurance and Financial Institutions Committee)
Woo, Michael (administrative assistant to Senator David Roberti)
Zimmer, Fritz (Senate fellow, Office of Senator Robert Presley)

1981–1982
Dr. Judith Lamare, acting chair (Senate Office of Research)
Capistrano, Carolina (administrative assistant to Senator Nicholas Petris)
Feraru, Rob (majority consultant)
Imura, Georgette (administrative assistant to Senator Diane Watson)
Jackson, Otis (Senate fellow, Committee on Energy and Public Utilities)
Jesperson, Jon (minority consultant)
Johnson, Scott (administrative assistant to Senator William Craven)

1982–1983
Berg, Cliff (chief of staff, Office of Senator David Roberti)
Frick, Karen (Senate Rules Committee)
Imura, Georgette (Senate Democratic Caucus)
Johnson, Scott (administrative assistant to Senator William Craven)
Seymour, Anne (Senate fellow, Senate Rules Committee)

1983–1984
Flores, Alicia
Frick, Karen (consultant, Business and Professions Committee)
Imura, Georgette
Johnson, Scott
Lott, Jim
Lowrey, Karen

1984–1985
Bagneris, Jules (Senate fellow, Senator Alan Robbins)
Branham, Jim (chief of staff, Senator James W. Nielsen)
Frick, Karen (consultant, Business and Professions Committee)
Johnson, Scott (senior consultant, Senator William A. Craven)
Lott, Jim (chief of staff, Health and Welfare)
Miller, John (consultant, Health and Welfare)

Sabelhaus, Nettie (Senator David Roberti)
Valdez, Martha (Senate Office of Research)

1985–1986
Bartholomew, Traci (Senator Nielsen)
Burns, Tom (Senate Rules Committee, Deputy Executive Officer)
Cowden, Ann (California State University, Sacramento)
Grant, Surlene (Senate fellow)
Johnson, Scott (Senator Craven)
Lott, Jim (Health Committee)
Morales, Bob (Senator Torres)
Sabelhaus, Nettie (Senate Rules Committee)
Syer, John (California State University, Sacramento)
Torcum, Jean (California State University, Sacramento)

1986–1987
Bartholomew, Traci
Burns, Tom (Senator Campbell)
Cowden, Ann
Johnson, Scott (Senator Craven)
Lott, Jim
Morales, Bob
Romero, Jesus (fellow from Senator Nicholas Petris' Office)
Sabelhaus, Nettie
Syer, John (California State University, Sacramento)
Torcum, Jean (California State University, Sacramento)

1987–1988
Bartholomew, Traci
Burns, Tom (Senator Campbell)
Chavez, Cynthia (Senator Petris)
Davis, Jack (Senator Kopp)
Johnson, Scott (Senator Craven)
Lott, Jim
Morales, Bob
Nguyen, Lilly (Senate fellow, Energy Committee)
Sabelhaus, Nettie (Senate Rules Committee)
Syer, John (California State University, Sacramento)

1989–1990
Burns, Tom (Senator Campbell)
Baughman, Mark (Senator Doolittle)
Campos, Yvonne
Johnson, Scott (Senator Craven)

Morales, Bob
Perez, Roy (Senator Roberti)
Robinson, Carolyn (Senator Watson)
Sabelhaus, Nettie (Senate Rules Committee)
Syer, John (California State University, Sacramento)
Tom, Maeley (Senator Roberti)

Appendix 8
Capital Fellows Demographics and Statistics

8.1. Fellow Application Data 1993-1994 to 2005-2006

Year	Assembly	Executive	Judicial	Senate	Total
1993–94	300	241	n/a	529	1070
1994–95	300	280	n/a	490	1070
1995–96	250	156	n/a	391	797
1996–97	180	190	n/a	346	716
1997–98	170	125	34	322	651
1998–99	161	92	37	274	564
1999–00	235	194	40	313	782
2000–01	210	128	54	224	616
2001–02	238	146	35	252	671
2002–03	328	295	107	359	1089
2003–04	343	308	122	432	1205
2004–05	333	220	170	432	1155
2005–06	271	231	156	436	1094
Total	3,319	2,606	755	4,800	11,480

Note: Data prior to 1993–1994 unavailable.

8.2. Capital Fellows Education Background:
Percentage of Applicant Pool with Degrees from CSU, UC, California
Independents and Out of State

Year	CSU	UC	California Independent	Out of State
2001–02	31	29	n/a	n/a
2002–03	20	44	20	16
2003–04	20	44	19	17
2004–05	21	43	20	16
2005–06	21	38	25	17

Note: Data prior to 2001–02 unavailable.

8.3. Capital Fellows Program Demographics

Year	Program	African American	%	Asian Pacific	%	Latino	%	Other / DTS *	%	White	%	Women %	Men %
1998–1999	Assembly	0	0	6	33	1	6	0	0	11	61	50	50
	Senate	2	11	1	6	3	17	1	6	11	61	50	50
	Executive	0	0	4	22	1	6	0	0	13	72	72	28
	Judicial	1	20	1	20	1	20	0	0	2	40	40	60
1999–2000	Assembly	2	11	2	11	6	33	2	11	6	33	56	44
	Senate	3	17	4	22	4	22	0	0	7	39	50	50
	Executive	3	17	2	11	3	17	0	0	10	56	78	22
	Judicial	1	20	1	20	0	0	1	20	2	40	80	20
2001–2002	Assembly	2	11	2	11	4	22	2	11	8	44	44	56
	Senate	2	11	2	11	4	22	1	6	9	50	56	44
	Executive	1	6	2	11	6	33	0	0	9	50	72	28
	Judicial	1	10	2	20	2	20	0	0	5	50	60	40
2002–2003	Assembly	2	11	3	17	3	17	0	0	10	56	61	39
	Senate	2	11	3	17	5	28	0	0	8	44	44	56
	Executive	3	17	5	28	4	22	0	0	6	33	72	28
	Judicial	0	0	2	20	1	10	0	0	7	70	60	40

8.3. cont.

Year	Program	African American	%	Asian Pacific	%	Latino	%	Other / DTS *	%	White	%	Women %	Men %
2003–2004	Assembly	2	11	4	22	4	22	0	0	8	45	61	39
	Senate	1	6	2	11	6	33	1	6	8	45	45	55
	Executive	3	17	2	11	7	38	0	0	6	33	83	17
	Judicial	2	20	2	20	2	20	2	20	2	20	70	30
2004–2005	Assembly	2	11	2	11	5	28	2	11	7	39	44	56
	Senate	2	11	2	11	6	33	1	6	7	39	61	39
	Executive	1	6	2	11	0	0	7	39	8	44	67	33
	Judicial	0	0	1	10	1	10	2	20	6	60	70	30
2005–2006	Assembly	3	17	3	17	3	17	2	11	7	39	44	56
	Senate	2	11	0	0	5	28	4	22	7	39	50	50
	Executive	3	17	0	0	3	17	3	17	9	50	56	44
	Judicial	1	10	0	0	2	20	1	10	6	60	60	40

* Multi-racial, Native American, and No Response categories were combined to retain parity with previous categorization methods for the fellowship programs. Categories for the 2005–2006 fellowship applicant pool are as follows: Asian, African American, Latino, Multi-racial, Native American, White, Other, Decline to State, and No Response.

Note: Data prior to 1998–1999 unavailable.

Appendix 9

Capital Fellows Alumni Questionnaire Respondents

In March 2003, the Capital Fellows Alumni Questionnaire was mailed to all alumni of the Capital Fellows Programs for whom addresses were available. The questionnaire asked:

- What originally attracted you to the internship/fellowship program?
- Describe your placement (e.g., the kinds of assignments that you received, your relationship with your mentor).
- Describe the academic aspects of your internship/fellowship year.
- What was your best experience? Your worst experience?
- How have you used the knowledge and experience that you gained as an intern/fellow?
- Please attach a current resume and add any other information that you would like to share.

The sixty-five respondents to the questionnaire were:

California Legislative Internship Program
Bolinger, Bruce	1960–1961
Carmack, John	1960–1961
Flanagan, James, Jr.	1961–1962
Keiser, William	1963–1964
Levy, Edward	1958–1959
Patsey, Richard	1960–1961
Robie, Ronald	1960–1961
Willoughby, Tom	1960–1961

Assembly Internship/Fellowship Program
Anton, Nancy Rose	1977–1978
Banken, Monica	1999–2000
Bowles, B. Dean	1965–1966
Bryant, Jason	2001–2002
Colborn, G. Diane	1984–1985
Cornwell, Carrie	1986–1987
De Vera, J. Prospero	1991–1992
Ford, Emilee	1998–1999
Harvey, Alison	1977–1978
Hirsch, Richard	1965–1966
Kawamoto, Ryan	2002–2003
King, John	1975–1976
Lopez, Lizelda	1999–2000

McClellan, Kyri Sparks 1995–1996
Morehous, Dean 1979–1980
Murphy, Robert 1966–1967
Nardi, Karen 1977–1978
Ng, Jayna 1994–1995
Nguyen, Kieu-Oanh 1988–1989
O'Donnell, Patrick 1998–1999
Rich, Sharon 1996–1997
Rome, Victoria Finkler 1995-1996
Shah, Sanjay 2001–2002
Stivers, Mark 1996–1997
Works, Rose 1991–1992
Yoshii, Katherine 1986–1987
Young, Morgan 1995–1996

Executive Fellowship Program
Baldwin, E. Rowland, III 1992–1993
Barnhill, Susan 1989–1990
Bost, Sue Van Velkinburgh 1987–1988
Chang, Andrew 1993–1994
Garbacz, Catherine 2001–2002
Gregg, Robert 2001–2002
Hicks, Bill 1998–1999
Hicks, Kelly 2000–2001
Kaiser, Jill 1997–1998
Micek, Brian 1999–2000
Slayden, Hugh 1996–1997
Wong, Brian 1992–1993

Judicial Administration Fellowship Program
Sanna Singer 1999–2000

Senate Internship/Associates/Fellowship Program
Cobb, Curtis 2001–2002
Fuentes-Michel, Diana 1979–1980
Ho, James 1995–1996
Johnston, Zane 1980–1981
Liberman, Ruthie 1985–1986
Lynn, Nora 1996–1997
Manatt, April 1990–1991
Miller, Kenneth 1988–1989
Pane, Joshua 1980–1981
Schermer, Charlotte 1995–1996
Schreiber, Christian 2000–2001

Selinsky, Pearl	1991–1992
Simmons, Charlene Wear	1969–1970
Sweeney, Owen	1997–1998
Tochterman, Linda	1984–1985
Ueda, Kara	1996–1997
Yelverton Zamarripa, Kara	1981–1982

Bibliography

Primary Sources

Archives and Manuscripts

California. Assembly. Rules Committee. Papers. California State Archives, Sacramento, Calif.

California. Senate. Rules Committee. Papers. California State Archives, Sacramento, Calif.

California State University, Sacramento. President's Office Papers (RG 88). California State University, Sacramento, Archives and Special Collections, Sacramento, Calif.

Oral Histories: Published

Alquist, Alfred E. *Oral History Interview*. Conducted in 1987 by Gabrielle Morris, Regional Oral History Office, University of California, Berkeley, for the California State Archives, State Government Oral History Program. Sacramento, Calif. [1988].

Bane, Tom. *Oral History Interview*. Conducted in 1994 and 1995 by Steven L. Isoardi, Oral History Program, University of California, Los Angeles, for the California State Archives, State Government Oral History Program. Sacramento, Calif. [1995].

Beilenson, Anthony C. *Oral History Interview*. 2 v. Conducted in 1997 and 1998 by Susan Douglass Yates, Oral History Program, University of California, Los Angeles, for the California State Archives, State Government Oral History Program. Sacramento, Calif. [1998].

Beverly, Robert G. *Oral History Interview*. Conducted in 1997 by Donald B. Seney, California State University, Sacramento, for the California State Archives, State Government Oral History Program. Sacramento, Calif. [1997].

Britschgi, Carl A. *Oral History Interview*. Conducted in 1988 by Carole Hicke, Regional Oral History Office, University of California, Berkeley, for the California State Archives, State Government Oral History Program. Sacramento, Calif. [1988].

Bronzan, Bruce. *Oral History Interview*. Conducted in 1994 and 1995 by Germaine LaBerge, Regional Oral History Office, University of California, Berkeley, for the California State Archives, State Government Oral History Program. Sacramento, Calif. [1995].

Connelly, John Robert. *Oral History Interview*. Conducted in 2001 by Charles Wollenberg, Regional Oral History Office, University of California, Berkeley, for the California State Archives, State Government Oral History Program. Sacramento, Calif. [2001].

Harris, Joseph P. "Professor and Practitioner: Government, Election Reform, and the Votomatic." *Oral History Interview*. Conducted in 1980 by Harriet Nathan, Regional Oral History Office, Bancroft Library, University of California, Berkeley. Berkeley, Calif. [1983].

Hayes, James A. *Oral History Interview*. Conducted in 1990 by Carlos Vasquez, Oral History Program, University of California, Los Angeles, for the California State Archives, State Government Oral History Program. Sacramento, Calif. [1990].

Keene, Barry. *Oral History Interview*. Conducted in 1994 by Carole Hicke, Regional Oral History Office, University of California, Berkeley, for the California State Archives, State Government Oral History Program. Sacramento, Calif. [1994].

Lewis, Jonathan C. "Tax Reform and Fiscal Policies." *Oral History Interview*. Conducted in 1989 by Gabrielle Morris, Regional Oral History Office, University of California, Berkeley, for the California State Archives, State Government Oral History Program. Sacramento, Calif. [1989].

Margolis, Larry. *Oral History Interview*. Conducted in 1989 by Carole Hicke, Regional Oral History Office, University of California, Berkeley, for the California State Archives, State Government Oral History Program. Sacramento, Calif. [1989].

Marks, Milton. *Oral History Interview*. 2 v. Conducted in 1996 by Donald B. Seney, California State University, Sacramento, for the California State Archives, State Government Oral History Program. Sacramento, Calif. [1996].

Miller, Allen. *Oral History Interview*. Conducted in 1987 by Carlos Vasquez, Oral History Program, University of California, Los Angeles, for the California State Archives, State Government Oral History Program. Sacramento, Calif. [1987].

Nichols, Leland. *Oral History Interview*. Conducted in 1991 by Donald B. Seney, California State University, Sacramento, for the California State Archives, State Government Oral History Program. Sacramento, Calif. [1991].

Papan, Louis J. *Oral History Interview*. Conducted in 1988 by Carole Hicke, Regional Oral History Office, University of California, Berkeley, for the California State Archives, State Government Oral History Program. Sacramento, Calif. [1988].

Patsey, Richard L. "Legislative and Political Reform in California." *Oral History Interview*. Conducted in 1988 by Carole Hicke, Regional Oral History Office, University of California, Berkeley, for the California State Archives, State Government Oral History Program. Sacramento, Calif. [1988].

Quinn, T. Anthony. *Oral History Interview*. Conducted in 1991 by Donald B. Seney, California State University, Sacramento, for the California State Archives, State Government Oral History Program. Sacramento, Calif. [1991].

Rees, Thomas M. *Oral History Interview*. Conducted in 1987 by Carlos Vasquez, Oral History Program, University of California, Los Angeles, for the California State Archives, State Government Oral History Program. Sacramento, Calif. [1987].

Schott, Phillip H. "Legislative and Political Reform in California." *Oral History Interview*. Conducted in 1990 by Carole Hicke, Regional Oral History Office, University of California, Berkeley, for the California State Archives, State Government Oral History Program. Sacramento, Calif. [1990].

Thelin, Howard J. *Oral History Interview*. Conducted in 1987 by Lawrence B. de Graaf, California State University, Fullerton, for the California State Archives, State Government Oral History Program. Sacramento, Calif. [1987].

Veysey, Victor V. *Oral History Interview*. Conducted in 1988 by Enid Hart Douglass, Oral History Program, Claremont Graduate School, for the California State Archives, State Government Oral History Program. Sacramento, Calif. [1988].

Waldie, Jerome. *Oral History Interview*. Conducted in 1987 by Gabrielle Morris, Regional Oral History Office, University of California at Berkeley, for the California State Archives, State Government Oral History Program. Sacramento, Calif. [1987].

Walsh, Lawrence E. *Oral History Interview*. Conducted in 1990 by Donald B. Seney, California State University, Sacramento, for the California State Archives, State Government Oral History Program. Sacramento, Calif. [1990].

Willoughby, Thomas. *Oral History Interview*. Conducted in 1988 by Ann Lage, Regional Oral History Office, University of California, Berkeley, for the California State Archives, State Government Oral History Program. Sacramento, Calif., [1988].

Winton, Gordon H. *Oral History Interview*. Conducted in 1987 by Enid Hart Douglass, Oral History Program, Claremont Graduate School, for the California State Archives, State Government Oral History Program. Sacramento, Calif. [1987].

Oral Histories: Unpublished

All unpublished oral histories were conducted by the author. Tapes and transcripts are available at California State University, Sacramento, Library, Special Collections and University Archives.

Berman, Howard. "History of the Capital Fellows Programs." *Oral History Interview with Howard Berman*. Conducted in 2003.

Clark, June. "History of the Capital Fellows Programs." *Oral History Interview with June Clark*. Conducted in 2002.

DeBow, Ken. "History of the Capital Fellows Programs." *Oral History Interview with Ken DeBow*. Conducted in 2002.

Desrochers, Lindsay. "History of the Capital Fellows Programs." *Oral History Interview with Lindsay Desrochers*. Conducted in 2003.

Friedlander, Dan. "History of the Capital Fellows Programs." *Oral History Interview with Dan Friedlander*. Conducted in 2002.

Gerth, Donald. "History of the Capital Fellows Programs." *Oral History Interview with Donald Gerth*. Conducted in 2002.

Hodson, Timothy. "History of the Capital Fellows Programs." *Oral History Interview with Timothy A. Hodson*. Conducted in 2002.

Hoenig-Couch, Donna. "History of the Capital Fellows Programs." *Oral History Interview with Donna Hoenig-Couch.* Conducted in 2002.

Jensen, Cristy. "History of the Capital Fellows Programs." *Oral History Interview with Cristy Jensen.* Conducted in 2002.

Keene, Barry. "History of the Capital Fellows Programs." *Oral History Interview with Barry Keene.* Conducted in 2003.

Krolak, Richard. "History of the Capital Fellows Programs." *Oral History Interview with Rich Krolak.* Conducted in 2002.

Lascher, Ted. "History of the Capital Fellows Programs." *Oral History Interview with Ted Lascher.* Conducted in 2002.

Lewis-Coaxum, Robbin. "History of the Capital Fellows Programs." *Oral History Interview with Robbin Lewis-Coaxum.* Conducted in 2003.

Loveridge, Ronald. "History of the Capital Fellows Programs." *Oral History Interview with Ronald Loveridge.* Conducted in 2003.

Lustig, Jeff. "History of the Capital Fellows Programs." *Oral History Interview with Jeff Lustig.* Conducted in 2002.

McDaniel, Gerald. "History of the Capital Fellows Programs." *Oral History Interview with Gerald McDaniel.* Conducted in 2002.

Moulds, Elizabeth. "History of the Capital Fellows Programs." *Oral History Interview with Elizabeth Moulds.* Conducted in 2002.

Perez, Sandra. "History of the Capital Fellows Programs." *Oral History Interview with Sandra Perez.* Conducted in 2002.

Ross, Ruth. "History of the Capital Fellows Programs." *Oral History Interview with Ruth Ross.* Conducted in 2002.

Sabelhaus, Nettie. "History of the Capital Fellows Programs." *Oral History Interview with Nettie Sabelhaus.* Conducted in 2002.

Seymour, Anne. "History of the Capital Fellows Programs." *Oral History Interview with Anne Seynour.* Conducted in 2003.

Smart, John. "History of the Capital Fellows Programs." *Oral History Interview with John Smart.* Conducted in 2002.

Sokolow, Al. "History of the Capital Fellows Programs." *Oral History Interview with Al Sokolow.* Conducted in 2002.

Spitz, Lilly. "History of the Capital Fellows Programs." *Oral History Interview with Lilly Spitz.* Conducted in 2002.

Syer, John. "History of the Capital Fellows Programs." *Oral History Interview with John Syer.* Conducted in 2002.

Thompson, Mike. "History of the Capital Fellows Programs." *Oral History Interview with Mike Thompson.* Conducted in 2003.

Vohryzek-Bolden, Miki. "History of the Capital Fellows Programs." *Oral History Interview with Miki Vohryzek-Bolden.* Conducted in 2002.

Williams, Anthony. "History of the Capital Fellows Programs." *Oral History Interview with Anthony Williams.* Conducted in 2003.

Interviews by Author
Bailey, Ann. Telephone interview. Tape recording. Sacramento, Calif., December 3, 2002.
LeBov, Ray. Telephone interview. Sacramento, Calif., December 6, 2002.
Lee, Eugene. Telephone interview. Sacramento, Calif., September 27, 2002.
Price, Charles. Telephone interview. Sacramento, Calif., September 20, 2002.
Rosin, Alan. Interview. Tape recording. Sacramento, Calif., June 24, 2003.
Samuel, Bruce. Telephone interview. Sacramento, Calif., October 2, 2002.
Wilson, Dotson. Telephone interview. Sacramento, Calif., September 30, 2002.

Other Primary Sources
Center for California Studies. Files of the Capital Fellows Programs.
Doubleday, Jay. "The California Legislative Internship Program, 1959." TMs, Institute of Governmental Studies, Library, University of California, Berkeley.
Nichols, Lee. "The California Experience; Recruitment, Training and Promotion of State Legislative Staff, [1966]." TMs. Institute of Governmental Studies, Library, University of California, Berkeley, 1966.
Segal, Morley. "Evaluation of the California Legislative Internship Program by Former Interns, [1964?]." TMs. Institute of Governmental Studies, Library, University of California, Berkeley.

Secondary Sources

Serials
Assembly Fellowship Program Journal.
California Executive Fellows Journal.
California Legislature at Sacramento. Sacramento, Calif.: California State Printing Office.
California's Legislature. Sacramento, Calif.: California State Assembly.
Center for California Studies. *Annual Report.*
_____. Californiana; the Newsletter of the Center for California Studies.
_____. Newsletter.
Ford Foundation. *Annual Report.*
The Legislature of California. Sacramento, Calif.: California State Assembly.
University of California, Berkeley. Department of Political Science. *Annual Report, California Legislative Internship Program.*

Journal Articles
Aro, Karl and Susan Swords. "Getting and Keeping Legislative Staff." *State Legislatures* 26 (July 2000): 50–54.
Block, A. G. "The Minnies." *California Journal* 31, no. 6 (June 2000): 8–19.
_____ and Robert S. Fairbanks. "The Legislature's Staff—No. 1 Growth Industry in the Capitol." *California Journal* (June 1983): 214–19.

Boulard, Garry. "Legislative Staff Face the Future." *State Legislatures* 26 (July 2000): 46–52.

Cooper, Claire. "Impending Gann Layoffs Jolt Senate Workers." *Sacramento Bee*, 24 June 1984, sec. B.

Hammond, Susan Webb. "Recent Research on Legislative Staffs." *Legislative Studies Quarterly* 21, no. 4 (November 1996): 543–76.

Hy, Ronald John, Monte Venhaus, and Richard G. Sims. "Academics in Service to the Legislature: Legislative Utilization of College and University Faculty and Staff." *Public Administration Review* 55, no. 5 (September-October 1995): 468–74.

Jeffe, Sherry Bebitch. "For Legislative Staff, Policy Takes a Back Seat to Politics." *California Journal* (January 1987): 42–45.

Katches, Mark. "No More Museum Pieces: the California Legislature is a Whole New Place Since Term Limits Have Swept It Clean." *State Legislatures* 25 (February 1999): 24–27.

Lee, Eugene. "The California Legislative Intern Program." *American Bar Association Journal* (1958): 461–62, 283.

Lincoln, Luther H. "California's Legislative Internship Program." *State Government* (1958): 12–13, 20.

Matthews, Jon. "Physician Uses Fellowship to Try New Career: Auburn Doctor Helps Make Policy as Senate 'Associate.'" *Sacramento Bee*, February 14, 1999, A4.

Mecoy, Laura. "CSUS Comes to the Rescue of Senate Fellowship Program." *Sacramento Bee*, November 17, 1984, sec. A.

Meller, Norman. "Legislative Staff Services: Toxin, Specific, or Placebo for the Legislature's Ills." *Western Political Quarterly* 20 (June 1967): 381–89.

Pollard, Vic. "Legislative Staff; Coping with Term Limits and an Unstable Job Market." *California Journal* 25, no. 6 (1994): 15–16.

Rosenthal, Alan. "The Care and Feeding of Legislative Interns." *State Legislatures* 26 (July 2000): 43.

Scott, Steve. "Speaker 'Hugsburg'." *California Journal* 31, no. 6 (June 2000): 30–37.

Seaver, Robert. "Internships and Legislative Staffing." *State Legislatures Progress Reporter* (supplement) 2, no. 3 (December 1966): 2 p.

Unruh, Jesse. "California's Legislative Internship Program; an Appraisal After Eight Years." *State Government* 38 (Summer 1965): 154–59.

Weberg, Brian. "Change Ahead for Legislative Staffs." *State Legislatures* 19, no. 2 (February 1993): 22–23.

Weberg, Brian. "New Age Dawns for Legislative Staffs." *State Legislatures* 23, no. 1 (January 1997): 26–31.

York, Anthony. "The New Legislature: Resisting Temptation." *California Journal* 30, no. 1 (January 1999): 18–25.

Books and Other Sources

Bell, Charles G., and Charles M. Price. *California Government Today: Politics of Reform.* 4th ed. Pacific Grove, Calif.: Brooks/Cole, 1992.

BeVier, Michael J. *Politics Backstage: Inside the California Legislature.* Philadelphia: Temple University, 1979.

California Conference on State Government. California State Government: Its Task and Organization; Background Papers Prepared for the Use of Participants in the California Conference on State Government, Stanford University, September 13–16, 1956. Stanford, Calif.: California Assembly, [1956].

Cannon, Lou. *Ronnie and Jesse: A Political Odyssey.* Garden City, New York: Doubleday, 1969.

Center for California Studies. Opportunity and Responsibility: the Link between Public Universities and State Capitals; a National Conference, April 14–16, 1993 at California State University, Sacramento, Conference Proceedings. Sacramento, Calif.: California State University, Sacramento, 1993.

Citizens Conference on State Legislatures. *The Sometime Governments.* New York: Bantam, 1971.

Crouch, Winston, et al. *California Government and Politics.* 4th ed. Englewood Cliffs, N.J.: Prentice-Hall, 1967.

DeBow, Ken and John C. Syer. *Power and Politics in California.* 6th ed. New York: Longman, 2000.

Delmatier, Royce D., Clarence F. McIntosh and Earl G. Waters, eds. *The Rumble of California Politics, 1848–1970.* New York: Wiley, 1970.

Hoeber, Thomas R., and Charles M. Price, eds. *California Government and Politics Annual 85/86.* Sacramento, Calif.: California Journal Press, 1985.

Keene, Barry, ed. *California Public Management Casebook.* Berkeley, Calif.: Institute of Governmental Studies, 1999.

_____. Making Government Work: California Cases in Policy, Politics, and Public Management. Berkeley, Calif.: Institute of Governmental Studies, 2000.

Lubenow, Gerald C., and Bruce E. Cain, eds. *Governing California: Politics, Government, and Public Policy in the Golden State.* Berkeley, Calif.: Institute of Governmental Studies, 1997.

Michael, Jay, and Dan Walters. *The Third House: Lobbyists, Money, and Power in Sacramento.* Berkeley, Calif.: Berkeley Public Policy Press, 2002.

Mills, James R. *A Disorderly House; The Brown-Unruh Years in Sacramento.* Berkeley, Calif.: Heyday Books, 1987.

Monagan, Robert T. *The Disappearance of Representative Government; A California Solution.* Grass Valley, Calif.: Comstock Bonanza Press, 1990.

Muir, William K., Jr. *Legislature: California's School for Politics.* Chicago and London: University of Chicago Press, 1982.

Petracca, Mark P. *A Legislature in Transition: The California Experience with Term Limits.* Institute of Governmental Studies Working Paper 96–19. Berkeley, Calif.: Institute of Governmental Studies, 1996.

Pincetl, Stephanie S. *Transforming California: A Political History of Land Use and Development*. Baltimore & London: Johns Hopkins University Press, 1999.

Putnam, Jackson K. *Modern California Politics*. 4th ed. Sparks, Nev.: MTL, 1996.

Rawls, James J., and Walton Bean. *California: An Interpretive History*. 7th ed. Boston: McGraw-Hill, 1998.

Richardson, James. *Willie Brown: A Biography*. Berkeley, Los Angeles, London: University of California Press, 1996.

Ross, Ruth, and Barbara Stone. *California's Political Process*. New York: Random House, 1973.

Schrag, Peter. Paradise Lost: California's Experience, America's Future. New York: New Press, 1998.

Scott, Stanley. "Streamlining State Legislatures"; Report of a Conference held at the University of California, Berkeley, October 27–29, 1995. Berkeley, Calif.: University of California, Berkeley, Bureau of Public Administration, 1956.

Smith, Martin. "The Rise and Decline of the California Legislature." In *Governing California: Politics, Government, and Public Policy in the Golden State*, ed. Gerald C. Lubenow and Bruce E. Cain. Berkeley, Calif.: IGS Press, 1997.

Staniford, Edward F. *Legislative Assistance*. Legislative Problems, 1957, No. 2. Berkeley, Calif.: University of California, Bureau of Public Administration, 1957.

Walters, Dan. *The New California: Facing the 21st Century*. 2d ed. Sacramento, Calif.: California Journal Press, 1992.